Dynamics of Underdevelopment of Uttar Pradesh

Dynamics of Underdevelopment of Uttar Pradesh

Editors

Shri Prakash
H. Chaturvedi

BLOOMSBURY
LONDON • NEW DELHI • NEW YORK • SYDNEY

First Published, 2013

BLOOMSBURY PUBLISHING INDIA PVT. LTD.
London New Delhi New York Sydney

ISBN: 978-93-82563-32-7

Published by Bloomsbury Publishing India Pvt. Ltd.
VISHRUT Building, DDA Complex, Building No. 3, Pocket C-6 & 7
Vasant Kunj, New Delhi 110 070

Laser Typeset by SHINU
A-5/56, Moti Nagar, New Delhi 110 015

Printed at Anvi Composers
1 DDA Market, Block A-1B, Pachim Vihar, New Delhi 110 063

Contents

From Editors' Desk

All countries in the world have had their North and South. If Germany had its Bavaria, the USSR had Siberia. Therefore, it is not surprising that the developed states of India like Gujarat, Karnataka, Maharashtra, Tamil Nadu, Punjab, Haryana and Andhra Pradesh are surrounded by states such as M.P., U.P., Rajasthan, Bihar, Assam and Orissa, which have been lagging behind in development. The reason is that in the primary, especially agricultural dominated production structure, development revolves round natural resource endowment of the states, while nature has not bestowed its bounty equitably everywhere. In the pre-industrial economies, unequal development, and hence, sharp differentials of per capita income were accounted by nature's bounties or its miserliness. The scarcity of nature's bounties in a state/nation was further accentuated by human beings as reflected by the rapid growth of population, which put much greater pressure on natural resources than what was warranted.

In the industrial and post industrial ages, the historical imbalances of growth were further accentuated, because of the following factors at work in market economies: (i) Industries are located either near markets, or near the sources of raw materials and other natural resources. If the raw materials and intermediate inputs do not lose weight in the process of production, then such industries tend to be located near the source of supply of raw materials in order to reduce transportation costs. The steel industry is an example of this. As against this, if the raw materials lose weight, or weights of the finished product and raw materials do not differ much, then such industries are located near markets. Then, heavy investments and natural resource intensive development projects also tend to be located near resource centres. This facet accounts for the concentration of petro-chemical complexes, steel based industries and multi-purpose dams in a few regions of India (Prakash-Mohapatra, 1981).

Differentials of natural resource endowment are not the only reasons for Perroux's thesis of peripheries surrounding the centres or poles of high growth. The spirit of enterprise and risk taking propensities on the one hand, and willingness and ability to innovate, are also not equally distributed amongst every humans. Location of people may also affect such propensities to some extent, due to the socio-economic and other environmental influences. This is why we find that an average Panjabi is much more enterprising and innovative than an average U.P. or M.P. resident; or a Gujarati or Marwari is much more prone to get involved in commerce or business than an Oriya, or Assamese.

Similarly, Punjabis and North Eastern tribals are comparatively more *spend thrifts* than people from U.P. Efforts to bring down these autonomously operating factors by policy interventions during the era of planned development from 1951 to 1989–90 did create an development impulse in all the states of the country, yet the historical imbalances and advantage of early historical starts could not be totally eliminated (Prakash-Mohapatra, 1981 and Prakash, S., 1977; 2011). Consequently, these *facets and factors of growth and their spatial and temporal spread furnish the backdrop for any study dealing with regional aspects of development.*

However, the regional context of growth is important from the viewpoint of growth itself. If each constituent unit grows at the same optimum rate, there will be no regional inequalities of development. As against this, if some regions/states grow at higher and others at lower rates of growth, then not only the growth will not be inclusive, but it will also be sub-optimum. Besides, the dualism of existence of developed in the midst of backwaters of underdevelopment will also emerge in the process of regionally imbalanced growth, which will lead to inequalities of distribution of income and wealth among the people. Then, the backwardness or slow growth of states/regions will result in a high incidence of poverty. *The sufficient condition of optimum growth of the national economy is satisfied in that state, in which it is not possible to accelerate the growth of one regional unit without adversely affecting growth of some and leaving some units to lag behind.* The corollary of this is that the overall national growth will be the maximum, if each constituent region grows at the same optimum rate. If we have a matrix equation of SDP and growth of regions, say n, the reciprocal of Perron-Frobinus root of this equation will yield the equal maximal rate of growth for all regions.

Another facet of regional inequalities is that personal inequalities of income are directly associated with the regional inequalities of development. The poverty of the people and the backwardness, or lower growth of a state are inseparable. Similarly, the prosperity of the people Poverty/riches of the people and the higher stage of development of a state are directly related (Prakash-Mohapatra, 1980). This will also run counter to inclusive growth. Besides, poverty and the riches of the people are indivisible. In a democratic polity, the existence of poverty in the midst of riches and existence of backwaters of slower and low growth in the mids of exclaves of development are not compatible with rapid growth. The present book reflects this philosophy of development.

Recently, three edited books have been published focusing on the framework of regional development and underdevelopment. Two of these books deal with the development of 15 and six states respectively. Shovan Ray's edited book, titled '*Backwaters of Development—Six Deprived States of India,* Oxford, New Delhi deals mainly with the interrelationship between underdevelopment, poverty and human development. Three out of six chapters focus on growth and human development in Bihar and Rajasthan and also focuses on the interface between growth and human development, whereas one chapter analyses human development and growth in selected states in a comparative framework. Three chapters profile Jharkhand, and the trade-off between rapid economic growth and poverty mitigation in Madhya Pradesh, and interrelationship between inequality, poverty and development in Orissa. The chapter on Uttar Pradesh delves in-depth into the vicious circle of slower growth, gender and rural-urban divide, dualism among social-religious groups, and employment, poverty and slower growth. It is obvious that certain pivotal factors of both growth and poverty such as labour force participation rates, dependency ratios, proportion of marginal workers in the work force, literacy and higher development of professional and technical education, ratio of SC/STs and Muslims in the total population, have remained beyond the domain of analysis in these important and interesting studies. This gap is filled up by the present book.

The other volume, edited by Dr Amitabh Shukla titled '*Paradigms of Regional Planning and Development*, Deept and Deep, New Delhi has 14 chapters. As the title suggests, the focus is more on regional development in the framework of planning at the grass roots. Four chapters deal with regional dimensions of agricultural development, sustainability of agricultural development, intra-state/regional variation of agricultural development, and policy for sustainable regional agricultural development. Though one chapter touches the subject of agricultural productivity as the base for sustainable agricultural development, productivity does not get the attention it deserves. Another two chapters deal with policy measures for regional balance in growth through resource transfers and for reduction of regional disparities of development. Another two chapters emphasise the need for transforming natural resources for balanced but sustainable development, and the fallacies of constraints to such growth. Only one chapter deals with the comparison of human development among states. The last three chapters focus on decentralised and democratic processes of planned development at the grass roots with such aspects as micro finance and marketing. Obviously, the canvass of this book is wider in the coverage of topics and the number of states included. But this book also misses vital aspects of development in a wider framework of conceptual and theoretical domain. Besides, state finances, welfare and employment aspects of development, social dynamics of development, demographic facets and underdevelopment are overlooked which are covered in this book.

The third volume, edited by Venkitesh titled, '*Uttar Pradesh: The Road Ahead*', published by Academic Foundation, unlike the previous two volumes, focuses exclusively on U.P. This is the similarity between the present and the above book. Sixteen chapters in the book are thematically classified into four groups containing four chapters each. The first part focuses on social consensus in U.P. with reference to its polity, political predicament of U.P. and new social-political ideology which seems to have led to the emergence of consensus in the one and quarter century old religious divide between the Hindus and Muslims, caste and class conflicts, gender and regional divide, and economic fragmentation, hindering its growth. The overall thrust of these chapters is politics with reference to single party government after the lapse of considerable period which was expected to impart stability in the midst of earlier Aya and Gaya Rams and dirty horse trading among politicians and political parties.

Four chapters in second part of the book address the problems and prospects of economic development and past performance, while one chapter analyses the poor health care delivery system. One chapter deals with quality employment in U.P. Four chapters discuss political stability, governance and stability. Four chapters of the last part focus on regional disparities, politics of demand for division of the state and regionalism and restructuring of the state. Though the book is highly diverse in its coverage, it fails to offer a comparative picture of the development status of U.P. in the framework of regional analysis. Thus, the book misses a vital link. Even vital aspects of the concept, theory and measurement of development, especially regional development, are missing.

The present book overcomes quite a few gaps and limitations of all the three volumes. This book and all other three volumes in fact are complementary rather than being substitutes of each other. The purpose of this discussion is to furnish this backdrop of complimentarity of the existing stock of knowledge contained in these books, rather than to offer a detailed review of the same, and to pinpoint to the addition to the stock of knowledge, contained in the existing books, that the present book brings with it.

The book are briefly described herein with a view to highlight the differential character and approach of the book in hand which deals exclusively with the economy of U.P. Naturally, varied aspects covered by these studies relate to many facets, which have not been discussed elsewhere. Besides, most of the chapters in this book focus on U.P.'s economy in a comparative framework on the one hand, and cover a wider spectrum of demographic, social and economic factors, which directly or indirectly affect employment, poverty, growth, welfare, and intra and inter regional inequalities of development of the regions on the other. Another striking feature of these studies is that U.P.'s growth performance has been compared both with the growth of the Indian economy and the economies of six most developed states of the country. Besides, a comprehensive inter-state comparative framework has not been overlooked altogether.

The book includes contributions from some of the leading economists and emerging scholars of management science of India, who have spared their valuable time and intellectual capability to examine the development status of U.P. and dig below the surface to unearth causes and consequences of the dynamics of relative under-development of the economy of U.P. The authors who have contributed to the book present a good mix of experience, and youth on the one hand, and established and emerging scholars in academia on the other. Young scholars have brought a fresh vision, new aspirations and hope for a better future for them.

The book consists of twelve chapters authored by writers of great repute, high expertise in both research cum teaching and administrative experience, which has given them an insightful understanding of the problems of growth of the economy of U.P. The chapters deal with a wide range of topics and aspects of the slower and lower development of U.P. relative to its potential on the one hand, and relative to the growth of the Indian economy and the economies of some of the more developed states of the Indian union. Contrasting the growth of the economy of U.P. with the development performance of the Indian economy and economies of developed states not only provides a comparative framework of analysis of regional development on the one hand, and offers measured differentials to highlight the gaps that U.P. has to fill up in not so distant future, if it aspires to be equated on an equal footing with the comity of developed states of India.

The first chapter titled, '*Infrastructure Vision for U.P.*' authored by Dr M. Ramchandran, focuses on the infrastructure needs of the state for laying down the foundation of long term sustained growth of the economy of U.P. He has very neatly delineated the gaps and targets with regard to power, roads, hospitals, beds, shortage of doctors, post offices, potable water supply, provision of latrines, civil aviation, road and rail transportation, housing and urbanisation. Needless to say, all these not only fall in the category of economic and social infrastructure, but the facilities are the basis to fulfil basic minimum needs of the people which directly and indirectly affect the quality of life and condition/standards of living.

The second chapter titled '*The Challenge of Rapid Development of U.P.*' is authored by Dr Ajit K. Singh. He examines barriers and bottlenecks in the economy and social structure of U.P. and diagnoses their consequences on economic growth. The diagnosis leads him to suggest measures to remedy the situation with a view to impart greater impetus to the process of growth of the economy of U.P. in a given time domain. The study is characterised by an analytical thrust and diagnostic approach in order to identify the problems and challenges facing rapid growth of the economy of U.P.

This is followed by the chapter on '*A Comparative Analysis of Economic Growth of U.P.*'. The chapter is authored by Dr Shri Prakash, Dr Amit Sharma and Ms Anshu Goel. They focus on the current status of the economic growth of U.P. relative to that of India and six developed states. These states are Gujarat, Haryana, Punjab, Maharashtra, Karnataka, and Tamil Nadu. They have examined the inter-temporal changes in the share of U.P.'s SDP in the GNP of India, and changes in the share of U.P.'s SDP in the GNP of India relative to the corresponding shares of SDP of the developed states. They find that U.P. has lagged behind consistently most of these states. A striking feature is that even such states whose shares of SDP are relative to that of U.P. were lower in the base year 1980–81, have surpassed U.P. due to their rapid growth and U.P.'s sluggish growth in the subsequent period. Growth of per capita SDP of U.P., India and developed states has also been analysed in order to net out the population effect on income. Results of this part of the analysis lend further support to the inferences drawn from the analysis of SDP.

They have used both regression and ANOVA to supplement inferences drawn on the basis of the descriptive analysis.

The next chapter is by Dr Shri Prakash and Gautam Negi on '*Population, Workforce Profile and Economic Growth of U.P.*' The contents are both analytical and diagnostic. The authors have examined the population size and its gender structure, rural-urban divide, labour force participation rates, and proportion of main and marginal workers in the labour force as basic factors of growth. They find that the dependency ratio in U.P. is higher than that for India and developed states. Besides, the proportion of marginal workers is much higher for U.P. than for India and the developed states. They have examined the agricultural yield rates since U.P. continues to depend on agriculture much more than India. U.P.'s yield rate for all its major crops is much lower than the rates for Punjab. However, the yield rates in U.P. are higher than those for India and other developed states. U.P. also lags behind in investment, especially in manufacturing and tertiary sectors. All these factors, taken together, account for relatively lower and slower growth of U.P., than that of India and other developed states.

The next chapter is authored by Dr Amit Sharma and Ajeet Singh Rauthan; it deals with the growth of per capita SDP of 15 states of India. They find that U.P. lags behind not only India but also most of the other states of the country. They focus mainly on the differential impact of productivity and its growth of per capita SDP. They find a significant interrelationship between literacy, agricultural productivity and growth of per capita SDP of states. This part of their analysis can be considered on two different planes: it highlights the most important factor of differential growth of the regions on the one hand, and adds the regional dimension to the findings of the analysts like Strumilin of Soviet Russia, D.P. Chaudhary, and Shri Prakash-Brinda Balakrishann of India, Mola Husseini for Iran and two Greek authors for Greece. In a way, they also offer an explanation of the regional variations of agricultural yield rates of Indian states, which have been very well delineated by Patel and Bose. This chapter furnishes a broader framework of analysis of regional development with a narrow focus on the growth of per capita SDP of 15 states.

The next contribution is of Dr G.N. Patel and A.N. Bose on '*Cost Efficiencies for Principal Crops—A Comparative Study Among Indian States*. They have used DEA for deriving estimates of crop wise cost based efficiencies for different states. The least cost, or most efficient state in the production of a crop is treated as the bench mark for comparing the efficiency of different states in the production of that crop. Punjab emerges at the top in most cases, while U.P. is found to be below Punjab by a few rungs. They highlight possible areas for improvement.

Dr M. Muzzamil and Dr Tabassum Khatoon have analysed the adoption and implementation of educational reforms in the state of U.P. They have listed the steps that have been taken by the U.P. government in order to effectively implement reforms. They have very succinctly highlighted both the short and long period implications of these reforms with reference to quantitative expansion and qualitative improvement in education on the one hand, and improvement in the operational mechanisms of the system on the other.

Dr Shalini Sharma and Ms Gunjan Bhatnagar have focused on the current status of U.P. in the field of general higher education. The number of universities and colleges and enrolments are used as indicators of educational development. They use some simple tools of descriptive statistics to analyse the pattern of distribution/location of institutions of higher learning with a view to highlight the development effect of supply of facilities. They link this to the effective demand for higher education as represented by enrolments. To highlight the uneven distribution of supply and demand for higher general education in states they employ Lorenz Curves, which visually portrays the (i) overall pattern of distribution of facilities of general higher education among states, including U.P.; (ii) uneven nature of spatial distribution of demand for and supply of facilities of higher general education, and (iii) high degree of concentration of educational development in five relatively more developed states than other states and India as a whole. *They also highlight the paradox of high level of educational development and lower level of economic growth of U.P.*

In the study focusing in higher technical and professional education in U.P., Dr Shalini Sharma and Gunjan Bhatnagar highlight the uneven spatial distribution of higher technical education in U.P. itself. They show an extremely high degree of concentration of higher technical education in Western U.P. An interesting point, highlighted by the authors, is that whereas Eastern U.P. accounts for a disproportionately high share in public institutions of technical education, Western U.P. claims an even higher share in private institutions. They attribute it to uneven spatial economic growth in the two regions of U.P.

They also examine intra-regional distribution of institutions of higher technical education in Western U.P. itself. The authors associate these features of technical educational development with economic growth in general and industrial and agricultural development in particular on the one hand, and development of science education at the intermediate/senior secondary level on the other.

Dr M.L. Pandit has focused attention on the role of enterprise and entrepreneurs in the growth of economies across the globe. He highlights the basic resource advantage of U.P. in terms of skills and experience of its lower order work force. He suggests that the state should focus on evolution of innovations that revolve around local talent. His approach is a bottoms up approach in order to fulfil the task of inclusive growth on the one hand, and harness local human assets on the other.

Nimisha Singh and Ajeet Singh Rauthan focus on employment generation schemes for the rural poor of U.P. These schemes have been devised to realise the twin objectives of welfare of the weaker sections of society in U.P. on the one hand, and to bring growth processes nearer to inclusiveness on the other. The infrastructural activities to generate assets through provision of employment opportunities are at the centre stage of analysis. They have also analysed the impact of the implementation of the schemes on the beneficiaries. They have attempted to go into the causative factors underlying particular outcomes, and have used regression and ANOVA as the tools of data analysis.

Ms Pooja Mishra, Ms Jaya Gupta and George analyse the FDI inflows in U.P. with reference to pull factors that operate in different states of India. They focus on power, infrastructure, policy thrust and business environment. They find that U.P. has lagged behind the rest of the country in attracting and hosting FDI in the post globalisation era of the Indian economy. They highlight the fact that FDI has played an important role in the acceleration of the growth of the economies of the developed states of India. They have used the descriptive approach to data analysis.

The chapter authored by P.K. Bhargava has dealt with the emerging trend in states' finances with special reference to Uttar Pradesh. He has taken a comprehensive view of the states' finances in so far as he deals both with public revenue and public expenditure. The frame work is analytical and the method is descriptive with rigorous analysis of data. His findings may be classified into two parts: (i) broad and generic inferences drawn, and (ii) detailed case wise analysis of data.

We put the book in the domain of readers. An attempt has been made to minimize the use of approach based mathematical modeling with a view to make the book reader friendly. It is hoped that the readers will find the book useful for understanding the problems and challenges of development and reduction of poverty in the state of Uttar Pradesh. Policy makers, researchers, teachers and students may find it useful for their specific purposes.

The editors owe a great deal to the authors, especially senior authors like Dr Ramachandran, Dr A.K. Singh, Dr Muzamil, Dr M.L. Pandit, who despite their busy schedules and short time provided for supplying their respective contributions, maintained a tight time schedule. A special word of thanks is due to Prof. Bharagava, who obliged the editors by finishing his contribution within a short time span of one week. Besides, if the young and budding scholars had not responded positively to the request of the editors, the book would not have covered some of the vital areas of research interest and factors of growth. All of them richly deserve special thanks. We avoid the desire to name them personally as all of them are members of the BIMTECH family and fraternity, which also includes Dr M.L. Pandit. We are also extremely thankful to Mr Ajit Singh Rauthan, who has been of yeoman help in more than one area of editorial work.

Without the unstinted support and cooperation of all these persons it would have not been possible for the book to see the light of the day with such rich contributions.

Editors

Shri Prakash

H. Chaturvedi

June, 2012
Greater Noida

Note 1: References have not been given here since most of these find mention in one or the chapter of the book.

Section–I

Theoretical Paradigms and Fiscal and Social Infrastructure as the Base for Regional Growth

CHAPTER 1

Introduction

Regional Development in the Historical, Political and Theoretical Perspective

Shri Prakash and H. Chaturvedi

General Background of Regional Analysis

The concepts of group/organisation and ruler/leader of the communities, clan/caste and class have been evolving with the evolution of civilisation, and with the social, political and economic development across the globe. People have been coming together to forge links and inter-personal relations on the basis of geographical continuity of places of residence, homogeneity of language, culture, traditions/customs, religion, race, and even political ideology. Village *gantantars* existed in large numbers in India before Samudra Gupta, the second Emperor of the Gupta Dynasty, who conquered, eliminated and assimilated all of these into the Gupta Empire. This was the first empire in Ancient India, though several small kings and kingdoms, whose jurisdiction did not go beyond a few kilometers, existed in many parts of the Indian Peninsula. These kings did not expand their kingdom by conquering the *gantantars*, which surrounded their kingdoms. A small area under the *gantantars* and small kings' rule used to be, more or less, homogenous in social and economic space. This did not pose any challenge of inequality among regions and their diversity, and hence, the problem of regionalism. But the concept of king and kingdom had already emerged in India. Europe followed India much later, while the concepts of democracy and democratic rule emerged in Europe much later than in India as is evident from the existence of *gantantars*, which were democratically governed by elected representatives, rather than being autocratically ruled by kings.

The establishment of sprawling empires like the Gupta, Maurya, Mughal, Roman and British empires emerged much later. The kingdoms and empires led to the emergence of the concepts of a new genre of political organisation, system of institutionalisation, and patterns of the rule of common law throughout the length and breadth of the kingdom/empire. The emergence of empires also brought in their trail striking diversity among the constituent regions with regard to nationality, race, communities, language, culture, traditions and religion, etc. These differences were further reinforced by the observed differences in poverty and riches of the people of the different constituent parts and segments of the population, which this laid the foundation of the concept of regional inequalities of development. Striking differences in the lavish and conspicuous luxurious styles of living of the kings and emperors and their courtiers on the one hand, and the living conditions of the commoners, who were struggling to make both ends meet on the other, led to the formulation of the concept of inequality in the distribution of wealth and income, and regional inequalities of development.

The concepts of king/emperor, kingdom/empire, nababs/subedar, landlord/jagirdar emerged gradually from decentralisation of administration in kingdoms/empires sprawling over hugely vast tracts of geographical areas and large population segments, which differed, much more than being similar in various aspects. This necessitated the devolution of administrative power and decentralisation of decision making with a view to delivering the desired goods with efficiency and to keep the populace/subjects contented. The concept of region slowly and gradually came into vogue on the basis of similarities of the people, places, and the felt needs of the people in a scenario of diversity and differentiation. Subsequently, the concepts of nations and nationality emerged which still prevails across the globe.

Emergence of Regional Analysis and Regional Science

Many modern day nations are generally much bigger and more diverse than many of the erstwhile kingdoms and fiefdoms. Naturally, most of the nation states are conglomerates or agglomerates of geographical regions, different communities whose religion, language, culture and customs, beliefs, and in some cases, even racial traits are radically different from each other. Even economic and living conditions diverge sharply, which offer dualism and contrast like the existence of poverty and poor in the midst of prosperity and rich, developed and less developed, or undeveloped regions/ areas, shanties and *jhuggi-jhoparpatis* in the midst of palatial buildings, all of which overshadow the similarities of even geographical proximity and homogeneity of resources. These diversities are further accentuated by regional diversities of social, and physical and environmental facets, including natural resources, population size, gender, social composition and age structure, and above all, ability and skill endowment of human resources. All these factors, taken together, directly or indirectly, affect economic growth and social development of the regions. The regional diversities are reflected in social development and economic growth of the regions and their people. These differentials not only account for the prevalence of inequalities of growth of per capita SDP and poverty, or prosperity of the people at a given point in time, but the process of development and growth propelled by market forces tends to perpetuate and sharpen the same over time. Regional inequalities of development have attracted lot of research efforts of scientists of different disciplines.

Geographical locations and administrative convenience, and plausibility of being controlled by the centre, homogeneity in certain respects needed for planning as a unit and some other factors are used to distinguish regions into different categories. Modern day concepts of regions follow one of the following criteria as principles for classification of regions: (i) Feasibility of administering with a certain minimum level of efficiency (agricultural revenue and supply of raw materials to a well defined command area); (ii) Homogeneity of resource base and inter and intra-regional linkages of commodity, services and factors markets; (iii) Ethnicity, culture, language, religion and geographical proximity or remoteness; (iv) Political ethos; and (v) Units identified as planning entities (Mishra, R.P., 1974). In independent India, the first reorganisation of states was done on the principle of language of the majority of the people living in the geographical area of the state, though it has not been possible to achieve homogeneity on the basis of language in any state due to inter-region migration in the past and also presently. Then, the complaint of negligence of economic interests and denial of development benefits to specific areas and people of states such as Punjab, Bihar, U.P. and Madhya Pradesh led to the division of these states into Punjab and Haryana, Jharkhand and Bihar, Uttarakhand and U.P., Chhattisgarh and M.P. on the one hand, and division of Assam into Meghalaya, Mizoram, Assam and Nagaland have led to the recognition of the principle of plausibility of efficient administration and delivery of benefits of development on an equitable basis among all the geographical parts, and their people have also emerged in practice.

The early attempts of analysts to formalise and systematise regional analysis led to the formulation of the concept, or construct of region and the enunciation of the principle(s) to furnish guidelines for regional analysis. In the early stages, contiguity, proximity and a certain minimum level of homogeneity within and heterogeneity between the regions, geographical spread of the area, and its physical features such as rivers, mountains, valleys and plains, social traits such as culture, language, custom, social organisation, and economic features as the levels of development and resources base came to be used for classification delimitation of political and administrative boundaries of the regions. For example, the concept of Deccan Suba came into vogue during the Mughal period; this referred to all the regions south of the Vindhayas. Besides this geopgraphical divide, the other reason for this classification in official circles was the distance from Delhi/Agra, the erstwhile capital towns of the Mughals and the proclivity of *Subedars* to often emerge as rival centres of power vis-à-vis the king, Several revolts also occurred due to this propensity of the designated rulers of the south. Such principles were later modified by the British to classify geographical administrative and political units as provinces. This was replaced by the concept of states in independent India.

Modern Regional Analysis

Perroux, a French economist, was probably the first to have propounded the concepts of 'rapidly growing centre/pole and sluggishly expanding but lagging periphery of the centre, which accounts for the existence and the perpetuation of regional inequalities of income and wealth. Periphery was linked with the pole/centre by commercial and economic inter-dependency. Periphery generally supplies the inputs of raw materials and other primary products to the market and industries in the pole/centre, while the centre/pole sells value-added finished products to the periphery, and attracts human and financial resources of the periphery towards itself. The tendency of financial and human resources to move out of the periphery into centre often denudes the periphery of its human and financial resources base, which further constrains its growth and perpetuates the development inequalities.

Widening of Conceptual Envelop

Geographers put the concept and theory of regional development on a higher plane to make it revolve round the theory of differential regional development, due largely to differentials of natural resources and environmental factors. Analysts of other disciplines, including economists, joined the galaxy of geographers. This led to the emergence of regional science as a distinct branch of analysis. Economists like Isard and Karen Polenske of the U.S. Oosterhaven of the Netherlands, among others, contributed significantly to the literature on regional analysis. Leontief, Strout, Watanbe, then integrated the concepts and theory of regional analysis into sectoral analysis in programming and input output frameworks, while Hirschman and Singer integrated both sector and region taxonomy into the theory of regional and/or unbalanced growth. Ranjit Dhar (1967) was probably the first economist to have taken up the analysis of the Indian economy in a regional framework with detailed sector classifications of five regional/zonal economies of India for 1953–54. Ambika Ghosh and P.N. Mathur of India, among many others, enriched the literature of regional science; they developed models of regional development in the input output and linear programming frameworks whereas the Strout-Leontief Gravity Model and its extension and modification by P.N. Mathur to international trade among the blocks of developed and developing countries of the world, are important landmarks in the development of regional analysis and its applications to a wide range of problems of development of national economies, trade among regions and nations, location of industries like cement and steel. Dr Deepa Saran subsequently used the Leontief-Strout model as modified by Mathur to analyse India's foreign trade with the developed countries of the world. The Mathur model was further modified by Prakash-Mohanty to examine inter-regional migration within India, and estimated the contribution of migrants to economic development of the recipient economies of the migrants. V.G. Bhatia, Narian Das, S.R. Hashim extended the applications of regional analysis to the transport sector of the Indian economy. Mounis Raza, Sheel Chand Nuna, Ashok Mathur, Shri Prakash and D.K. Shrivastava extended the application of the regional framework of analysis to educational development and location of educational institutions with a view to the mapping of the locations of educational facilities among various states of India. Prakash-Shrivastava used the concepts of centre and periphery for the determination of the locations of educational institutions on the basis of minimisation of transportation cost/distance. This led to the formulation of the concept of planning of educational complexes, especially school complexes around some nodal senior secondary schools in states like Sikkim and Madhya Pradesh. Such diversification and multifaceted development of regional science, culminated in the formation of the International and Indian Regional Science Associations. Both the associations regularly publish their *Journals of Regional Science* and hold conferences periodically.

Diverse seminal contributions of regional analysts notwithstanding, modeling of regional growth in a comprehensive framework has not progressed much so far. This is well substantiated by the fact that, at the regional level, the analysis of the effects of regionalisation of growth within countries have been more limited and problematic (Partridge and Rickman, 1998, 2010; Holland, 2010). Naturally, the studies of these effects have also been limited. A likely reason for the lack of comprehensive regional studies (examples include Dixon et al., 2007; Hoffmann et al., 2006; Seuing and Waters, 2010) is that the necessary regional data in a suitable form are often not available. Moreover, a number of unresolved behavioural issues remain, including the extent of interregional factor mobility, and the uniqueness of regional goods. As a result, the levels of uncertainty and the magnitude of errors in regional models may be higher than those in national-level models (Turner, Karen, Ha, Soo Juang, Hewings, Geoffrey, J.D., Mcgrgor, Peter and Swales, Kim, 2012), Tinbergen used the concept of region to classify industries as local, regional, national and international. S.P. Kashyap and Rohit Desai linked the success of industrial estates of Gujarat to the spread of market for their products over district, state, nation, world.

Widening Concept of Economic Growth and Development

The concepts of development and economic growth have also come in critical evaluation by a host of analysts. Irma Adleman and C.T. Morris (1967) were among the earliest economists to reject the narrow concept of economic growth being reflected by per capita income, and the stage and state of development of the economy by GDP. They postulated that economic development as against economic growth is located on a much wider canvass of conventional economic factors and institutional set up on the one hand, and status of social and political factors, health, education, training, and such conditions as sanitation, water supply, etc., around which revolves the quality of life, are pivotal factors of economic development and social transformation on the other.

Human Development and Economic Growth

C.N. Vakil and P.R. Brahamananda (1956) preceded Irma Adleman and C.T. Morris (1967) in broadening the concept of development; they propounded the basic goods model of growth for the Indian economy in 1953. T.W. Schultz (1966), a Nobel Laureate, also greatly emphasised the role of investment in education and human capital in the overall stock of capital of the U.S. and growth of its economy over a period of more than half a century. These leads have been followed by analysts and researchers all over the globe since then. The concept of human capital was transformed into the concept of human resources, from which emerged the concept of human development and its measurement by an index.

However, education and health are not the only factors of social development and economic growth. Natural resource endowment of the regions, literacy rates, which represent an average accomplishment of all the people of the country as a whole, labour force participation rate, or dependence ratio, proportion of marginal workers in the total work force, population size and demographic structure, proportion of poor in the population, culture, customs and religious or social taboos, presence and its spread over space and people, or absence of scientific temper among the people, proportion of deprived sections of the people in the population, operate both as the cause and consequence of social development and economic growth. Incidentally, a large segment of the poor live in the twenty first century with mindsets of the fifteenth and sixteenth centuries, though a lot water has flown down the Ganges since then. Therefore, the degrees of diversity of these variables among the regions and the people are reflected in the levels and stages of economic growth of the regions and the poverty/prosperity of the people.

Sharp differentials in economic growth among the regions not only affect the living conditions of the people, but these also result in the presence of social and economic dualisms of different types and levels. These dualisms often lead to political schisms, social unrest and demand for division, or even separation from the dominant units of the country or states, within the country. We have witnessed the partition of the Indian peninsula into the supposedly Hindu India and Muslim Pakistan. Subsequently, Pakistan itself was partitioned into Pakistan and Bangladesh. Division of Sudan into two countries and disintegration of the USSR into several independent countries are of recent origin. East and West Germany's unification is an exception. Thus, socio-politico, linguistic and economic schisms and dualistic social, political and economic structures are neither conducive to growth, nor are these facilitators of eradication of poverty. This is the overall back-drop of analysis of regional growth and inequalities of distribution of income, and wealth among the regions, and their people. But all these factors are only generic in nature. The thrust of their causative and consequential aspects need a bit more of detailed evaluation of the specific facets of all such factors. Differentials of all such factors and variables make it difficult to conceptually visualise and discover the existence of any two regions in reality, which are perfectly homogenous in social development and economic growth. It is even more difficult to perceive the existence of numerous groups, which are totally homogenous (Prakash-Mohapatra, 1980, pp. 94–95). It is also probably because of this that the homogeneity criterion for the region as a unit of analysis that similarity, rather than sameness is emphasised (Boudeville, J.R.). Besides, the assessment of states'/regions' real dynamics of development, or underdevelopment on the basis of hugely broad and highly aggregative indices of development, comprising almost all variables/parameters of development may not capture the real dynamics of development and underdevelopment of the states/regions, because no region/state is uniformly developed in all fields. In addition to this, indices are highly sensitive to the system of weighting and parameters/variables included in the indices. This facet is associated with the intra-regional inequalities of development within the states (Prakash, S. Nair, C. Radhakrishnan, 1978, Prakash, S. Rajan, P., 1977).

Strategy of Planning and Growth

Strategy, thrust and approach to planning and development may also play a dominant role in the generation and perpetuation or mitigation of poverty and regional inequalities of development. Scarcity of resources in an emerging market economy, and differentials in productivity of investment in different sectors and regions, in which the sectors are primarily concentrated, make the already developed states/regions and sub-regions within regions magnetic poles, towards which most of the new investments and investors, both national and foreign gravitate towards; this leads to the generation of inequalities in the existing and newly emerging areas of development. In this respect, there seems to be no basic difference between planned and market oriented economies, except that in planned economies, such consequences emerge from the implementation of policy and strategy of development, while market forces lead to the emergence of such trends. Even during the planning era, marked differences in the socio-economic infrastructure, human and financial resources endowments made policy makers and planners prefer more developed regions/states for heavy investment projects. Besides, upgrading the existing infrastructure also got precedence and priority, over the creation of basic infrastructure in less developed states. For example, narrow and meter gauge railway lines were converted into broad gauge, rather than making provision for new rail routes in areas and regions having no rail connection. Doubling of railway lines, dieselisation and electrification of the existing rail routes became the priority for planned development. Steam engines and old wagons were replaced by new generation diesel and electric locomotives/engines, and the increase in number of bogies in already plying trains also became a high priority area. Replacement of old into new modernised railway stations was the natural accompaniment of all such changes. More trains were introduced on existing routes. Existing *kachcha* roads were converted into *pucca* roads and all weather roads, and old roads were repaired periodically and widened to cope with more and more buses and trucks that plied on them. The old fleet of buses and trucks were replaced by bigger and more comfortable buses and trucks. Machinery and equipment of existing industries was replaced by new modern and better machinery and equipment, and in some cases, even before the lifespan of the older machines was over. Electricity and piped water supply was improved in the already electrified towns and cities. Existing airports were modernised and more flights introduced, Dakotas were replaced by Boeing and air-bus aircraft, and new flights were introduced. In banking, insurance, health care services, educational institutions, and creation of smaller and newer districts, divisions and sub-divisions with administrative paraphernalia were created to impart impetus to the process of urbanisation, and introduction of a greater degree of decentralisation. These planned changes led to the accentuation of existing economic and developmental inequalities in several cases. Consequently, metropolitan areas and cities and towns, rural and urban areas, and more and less developed states, still present a striking contrast (Prakash-Mohapatra, 1980 and Prakash-Mohanty, 2005). Such differentials led to an ever increasing number of people, especially poor, unemployed, or seasonally employed, or employed in low wage trades, migrating from the rural to urban areas, from small towns and cities to metropolitan areas, and from less to more developed regions. The educated unemployed, as against this, tended to migrate from more educationally developed states like Kerala, Tamil Nadu, West Bengal, and U.P. to less developed areas/states like M.P., Haryana, Punjab, Rajasthan, and North-East in search of white collar jobs in the 1950s and 60s. Large scale migration from rural to urban areas transformed rural into urban poverty. Similarly, large scale rapid development of education ahead of the population and economy, transformed the unemployment of the uneducated into unemployment of the educated, and unemployment of less into unemployment of more educated. So far as India is concerned, the relatively high scarcity of resources in the early stages of planned development and differences in the productivity of investments in different regions and sectors within the regions led to the extension of selective approach from heavy and basic goods industries to other sectors of the economy. For example, multi-purpose dams like the Bhakra-Nangal, integrated steel plants, heavy electrical\equipment and heavy machinery industries gravitated towards the resource rich, such as perennial rivers and minerals, especially iron ore, coke, coal, zinc, mica regions/states of the country. Then, duplication of railway lines, broadening of the existing road network, air and rail services, etc., all got preference over creation of new infrastructure in regions their were relatively lagging. Those regions, which were already developed, got precedence in investments, which further accentuated the existing regional inequalities of development, and greater concentration of poor and incidence of poverty in the relatively less developed states. Recent reports have indicated that the largest concentration of the poor is currently in U.P., Bihar and Chhattisgarh states, which were already straddled with a large number of poor in their respective populations. This is despite the fact that there has been a slight tilt towards inclusiveness in growth, and relatively more rapid development of the economies of Bihar and U.P., than other states.

An important aspect of the analysis of regional inequalities of development and incidence of poverty among the regions and their people does not lead one anywhere, unless these empirical realities are examined within the framework of the existing theory of regional growth, or new theoretical paradigms are evolved, which may become the base of formulation of implementable policy. The thrust of the theoretical paradigms should be the explanation of the costs and benefits of the regional inequalities, or development to the economy, and their impact on the people while the policy may strive to contain and ultimately reduce the existing inequalities of development (Prakash-Mohapatra, 1980 and Kendall, M.G).

If a region is un/less developed relative to other states/regions, then relatively more developed states/regions tend to grow more rapidly than the un/less developed states/regions of the country. This trend has also been observed at the international level. According to Gunnar Myrdal (1958), the forces of market make both the development and underdevelopment process cumulative. Poverty and backwardness constitute a vicious circle, which tends to become wider and larger in the process of development, because of the ever widening gulf between the developed and less developed, resulting from an inequitable growth process. It is because human and material resources and capital are induced to move out of the un or less developed to more developed states/regions. Even the credit created by banks on the basis of deposits mobilised within the less developed states is invested in the more developed states.

During British rule, Dadabhai Naoroji formulated the Drain Theory to explain the underdevelopment of the Indian economy. In view of this, Prakash hypothesised that Dadabhai Naoroji was the '*Founder of the Theory of Underdevelopment*'. P.N. Mathur (1986, 1991) transformed Naoroji's model into an input output framework, which he used to explain the underdevelopment of countries of the third world, and highlighted that the facet of underdevelopment is explained by the in-built mechanisms of the international economic order. The current phase of globalisation has, however, brought about a definite change, in so far as capital and technology have started moving out of the developed to the developing countries of the world. Countries such as China, India, Brazil, which have derived a greater degree of benefits from these changes, have been developing much more rapidly than before, and even more rapidly than the developed countries of the world. This is postulated to bridge the economic gap between some of the developed countries and these rapidly growing economies at the international level.

Then, there is another paradoxical facet of development and underdevelopment of nations and states/regions within nations. Some nations and/or states within them, which are characterised by paucity of human capital and natural resources, are highly developed. As against this, nations and states within them, which are richly endowed with natural resources and size and the structure of population, which is the base of human resource development, do not develop to levels which reflects their resource endowment. These nations/regions make one exclaim like Dante, "*Born to ascend on the wings, why do ye fall at such a little wind*" (Ray, Shovan, 2010). Amartya Sen explains this phenomenon in terms of human development, 'The concept of human development draws on the magnificence of human potentiality amidst the widespread experience of narrowly circumscribed lives. Lack of schooling, meagre health care, inadequate economic opportunities, violation of political liberties, denial of civil liberties, and other hostile winds can totally frustrate human beings despite their potential to 'ascend on the wings' (quoted from Ray). Sen apparently explains this facet of underdevelopment with reference to human development relative to their potential. But, one may also consider economic underdevelopment in the midst of the adequacy of human and material resources, relative to the development of similar entities with lower human and/or material resources. Kerala, Mizoram, Nagaland and Meghalaya have achieved much greater human development than Punjab and Gujarat, but they are at a much lower stage of economic growth than Gujarat or Punjab. Similarly, some oil producing countries have high per capita income with low human development endowment. So, one may also wonder why such nations, or their states like Shelley's *Skylark* do not '*Soar higher and higher into the sky like the other birds of similar ilk*'. There is more to economic growth than human development alone. The approach to development in this book is defined by this statement. This approach differs from that of Sen.

A Critique of the Human Development Measurement

No doubt that the modern approach links economic growth to human development, but the concept of human development used in its measurement focuses on an extremely narrow canvass of three facets of human welfare promoting activities: per capita income, education, literacy, and health. Life expectancy or longevity is associated with the infant mortality rate and the like. Educational development is measured by enrolments in basic education and literacy. Obviously, the index of human development measured on the basis of such parameters/variables misses more than what it captures (Prakash, S., 2005). For example, literacy and basic education are at the lowest level of the pyramid. Modern growth processes are driven mainly by productivity, which depends on technology and human capital, rather than human resources. Human capital refers only to such human resources as are deployed for productive work (Prakash, S., 2000). Besides, productivity depends more on human capital endowed with higher general, professional and technical education, than literacy or basic education alone. Alternatively, productivity may be related to the mean number of completed years of education (S. Prakash and Balakrishnan, 2008 and Sharma, Amit, 2012). Then, training, both in-house and outside in-service training, formal and non-formal, on the job learning and experience are important sources of acquisition of competency. The number of hospitals and nursing homes, primary health centres per unit of geographical area and/or population covered and the number of doctors, paramedical personnel, beds, equipment, and accessibility of these facilities to the people, play an important role in the delivery of health care services. Besides, most of the studies treat the human development index as the determinant of growth of GDP, or per capita income in the regression model, or correlation analysis. It is not possible to identify the causative variables leading to the effect on the dependent variables in the correlation/ regression analysis. In correlation analysis, both X and Y variables are on an equal footing (Jean Bowman, 1964). This is totally wrong. Children, who are currently enrolled in basic education, and are an important component of the human development index, are not a part of the current work force, and therefore, they do not contribute to current GDP, or per capita income, unless they earn while they also learn (Prakash, S., 1977). This is generally not the case. It is often forgotten by researchers and policy makers that human development is conditioned and governed by income, besides the above social and political factors. For example, incidence of poverty and deprivation of the poor from economic assets, is much more among the scheduled castes and scheduled tribes. Different districts of Madhya Pradesh account for the differential incidence of poverty according to the proportion of scheduled costes and scheduled tribes in total population (Chaurasia, 2010). Similarly, the political factors of nurturing poverty among the people, who constitute the vote banks of political parties in India, is a widely recognised fact. Urban slums and members of the Muslim community and SC and STs are generally treated as vote banks. The gender divide also accounts for such a state of stagnancy of economic and educational status of girls and SC/STs. Child workers also mostly come from these segments of population (Prakash, 1992–93; Prakash-Chaubey, 1992; Prakash and Dutta, 1996). Often, analysts and researchers have confused the dividing line between the concept of human resources and human capital, as well as the distinction between the causal and effectual relations between education and growth of income. Besides these factors, the following will further clarify the distinction between human resources and human capital: "If education makes a person more efficient in commodity production, then this is clearly an enhancement of human capital. This can add to the value of production in the economy and also to the income of the person who has been educated. But even with the same level of income, a person may benefit from education in reading, communicating, arguing, in being able to choose in a more informed way, in being taken more seriously, by others, and so on. The benefits of education thus exceed its role as human capital in commodity production' (Sen, A., 2003). It may, however, be added that the economic roles and functions of education far exceed its role as human capital in commodity production (Prakash, Shri, 1976). Besides, the socio-political functions of education are also more than those listed by Sen in the earlier quotation (Harbison and Myer, 1967).

The following may clarify the distinction between the causal role of education and income in their mutual relations. It may be stated that the current investment in education depends on current income, past savings, and at times, current use of future savings, if education is financed by borrowings. As against this, current educational attainments of human capital, accumulated from past investments in education, promote growth of current and future income. Thus, education and income are sequentially, rather than concurrently related (Prakash, 1977). Then, enrolment of children in schools is financed from current income, rather than income being generated by them (Komarov, 1964).

Paradoxes of Theoretical Paradigms and Empirical Realities

Many paradoxes cloud the theoretical paradigms and empirical reality in literature on economic growth. Less developed nations and regions within them, which are well endowed with natural, material and human resources, may be dubbed as 'rich nations/states inhabited by the poor'. Another paradox is offered by oil rich countries, which have a few developed pockets/regions surrounded by backwaters of under-development. Besides, inequalities of income and wealth distribution, and educational and social development further complicates the scenario in these countries. Then there is the paradox of economically less developed states, which are very richly endowed with high human development in general, and human resources in particular. Kerala, Mizoram, Nagaland, and Meghlaya are testimony to this thesis. As against this, there are rich countries/regions with poor human resource development. Oil rich member countries of OPEC corroborate this thesis (S. Prakash, et al. 1994). Another paradox is, that even though some countries and states within them grow much more rapidly than the developed nations and regions within them, yet they continue to be less developed and home to the largest proportion of the poor and illiterate people. India, China and South Africa currently illustrate this facet at the international level. At the national level, we find that even though Uttar Pradesh, Bihar and Chhattisgarh have been growing much more rapidly than the developed states, and Bihar has grown even more rapidly than India in recent times, yet they continue to be among the laggards in the development race. Besides, these three states account for the largest number of the poor of India, and their share in the total number of poor in India is also high according to the new poverty line cut off used by the Planning Commission. It is a different matter that the new poverty line used by the Planning Commission in estimating the incidence of poverty is quite questionable. But the scenario of the poor and poverty will not be altered in U.P. and Bihar, even if the old criterion of the poverty line is used in the estimation. Incidence of poverty in India has declined by 7.3 percentage points to 29.8 per cent in 2009–10 from 37.2 per cent in 2004–05. Poverty has declined by 1.4 percentage points per annum during the period of the survey as compared to 0.8 percentage points from 1993 to 2003. The acceleration in the decline of poverty has been too slow, to significantly affect the incidence of poverty. Five states of North East India and Uttar Pradesh, are the only states where the number of poor has increased during the same period. Poverty has increased in Nagaland by 12.1 percentage points, in Manipur by 9.2 and Assam by 3.2 and Meghalaya by 1.0 percentage points. It may be noted that these tribal dominated states of North East India, used to be much more egalitarian than the rest of India during the era of planned development. Another important facet emerging from these data is that all states ruled by Non-UPA political parties, except Maharashtra, have done better than the states ruled by UPA governments (*Hindustan Times*, 2012). The case of Uttar Pradesh, Bihar and Chhattisgarh is even more contrasting. Incidence of poverty in relative terms has declined in these states from 2004–05 to 2009–10. But the decline has been at an extremely slow pace, which has resulted in an increase in the absolute number of poor. Bihar and U.P. together account for 128 million poor people, who are one-third of the total number of poor of India, and one tenth of the total number of poor in the world (*The Time of India*, March, 20, 2012). India had 360 million poor in 2012 (*Hindustan Times*, March 20, 2012). These paradoxes constitute a wide spectrum of the riddles of regional development and income, and social inequalities, associated both with development and underdevelopment. Besides all the above, the dominance of the economic structure by primary production in general and agriculture in particular, and the slow pace of diversification of the economic structure due to the slow growth of tertiary and secondary production accounts for the relatively slower growth of the economies of such laggard states as Odissa (Ramvir Singh, Padmja Mishra and Madhumita Ray, 2010).

The earlier discussion, though brief, furnishes the backdrop for the analysis of the relatively slow growth of Uttar Pradesh, when the Indian economy has been developing much more rapidly with the rest of the world, except China. In fact, India is the second fastest growing country of the world. This provides the context for a comparative analysis in a comprehensive framework.

References

Adleman, Irma and Morris, C.T. (1967). *Society, Politics, and Economic Development, A Quantitative Approach,* John Hopkins University Press, Baltimore.

Bhusan, Satya, Prakash, Shri, Gupta, Abha and Buragohain, Tarujyoti (1994). *Literacy and Economic Development—A Study of 114 Countries, 26 States and 452 Districts of India*, Project Report, Ministry of Human Resources and NIEPA, New Delhi.

Bilgic, A., King, S., Lusby, A. and Schreiner, D.F. (2002). Estimation of U.S. Regional Commodity Trade Elasticities of Substitution, *The Journal of Regional Analysis and Policy,* 32, 79–98.

Boudeville, J.R. (1966). *Problems of Regional Economic Planning*, Edinburgh, Edinburgh University Press.

Bowmam, Jean (1964). *Readings in the Economics of Education*, Unesco, Paris.

Chaurasia, Alok Ranjan (2010). A Tale of Poverty versus Growth in Madhya Pradesh, in Ray, Shovan (Editor). *Backwaters of Underdevelopment: Six Deprived States of India,* OUP Press, New Delhi.

Dhar, Ranjit (1967). The Study of Inter-regional and Inter-sectoral Relations of the Indian Economy, 1953–54, in P.N. Mathur and R.N. Bhardwaj (Editors). *Economic Analysis in Input Output Framework*, Vol. I, Input Output Research Association, Pune.

Dixon, P.B., Rimmer, M.T. and Tsigas, M.E. (2007). Regionalising Results from a Detailed CGE Model: Macro, Industry and State Effects in the U.S. of Removing Major Tariffs and Quotas. *Papers in Regional Science,* 86, 31–55.

Haddad, E.A. and Hewings, G.J.D. (2005). Market Imperfections in a Spatial Economy: Some Experimental Results. *The Quarterly Review of Economics and Finance,* 45, 476–496.

Harbison and Myer (1964). Education and Employment in Newly Developing Economies, *Comparative Education Review,* Vol. VIII, No. 1, June.

Hoffman, S. and Robinson, Subramanian, S. (2006). The Role of Defense Cuts in the California Recession Computable General Equilibrium Models and Interstate Factor Mobility. *Journal of Regional Science,* 36, 571–595.

Holland, D. (2010). What Happens when Exports Expand: Some Ideas for Closure of Regional Computable General Equilibrium Models. *Annals of Regional Science,* 45, 439–451.

Kendall, M.G. (1963). *Multivariate Statistical Analysis,* Basil Blackbel, London.

Komarov, V.E. (1964). The Relationship between Economic Development and the Development of Education, in Jean Bowman (Editor). *Readings in Economics of Education,* UNESCO, Paris.

Mahtur, P.N. (1986). *Gandhi and Schism in Indian Polity,* North Eastern Hill University Press, Shillong.

Mahtur, P.N. (1991). *Why Developing Countries Fail to Develop*? Macmillan, London.

Myrdal, Gunnar (1958). *Economic Theory and Underdeveloped Regions,* Vora Publishing House, Bombay.

Partridge, M.D. and D.S. Rickman (1998). Regional Computable General Equilibrium Modeling: A Survey and Critical Appraisal. *International Regional Science Review,* 21, 205–248.

Partridge, M.D. and Rickman, D.S. (2010). Computable General Equilibrium (CGE) Modeling for Regional Economic Development Analysis. *Regional Studies,* 44, 1311–1328.

Planning Commission, Government of India, *First Five Year Plan,* New Delhi.

Planning Commission, Government of India, *Fourth Five Year Plan, Some Points for Consideration,* New Delhi.

Planning Commission, Government of India, *Second Five Year Plan,* New Delhi.

Planning Commission, Government of India, *Third Five Year Plan,* New Delhi.

Prakash S. and Chaubey, P.K. (1992). Universalisation of Elementary Education—A Simple General Equilibrium Type Policy Model, *Manpower Journal,* Vol. 28, No. 4, Jan–March.

Prakash, S. and Dutta R. (1994). Human Resource Allocation and Employment—Education Trade-Off, *Macro Models 1994,* University of Lodz, Poland.

Prakash, Shri (1976). Input Output Models of Education with Empirical Application to Indian Economy, in P.N. Mathur (Editor). *Economic Analysis in Input Output Framework,* Vol. III, Input Output Research Association, Pune.

Prakash, Shri (1977). *Educational System of India: An Econometric Study,* Concept Publishing Co., New Delhi.

Prakash, Shri (1977). Regional Inequalities and Economic Development with Special reference to Infrastructural Facilities in India, *Indian Journal of Regional Science,* Vol. IX, No. 2.

Prakash, Shri (1993). *Problems of Education of Children of Bombay and Delhi Slums*, UNESO sponsored Project Report, NIEPA, New Delhi.

Prakash, Shri (2000). Utilisation of Human Resources—Concepts and Empirical Illustrations, *Business Perspectives,* Vol. 2, No. 2.

Prakash, Shri (2005). Human Development Index in Input Output Framework, XVth International Conference of International Input Output Association on Input Output Analysis—Theory and Applications, *IIOA's Website.*

Prakash, Shri and Balakrsihanan, Brinda (2008). *Bulletin of Political Economy,* Vol. III, No. 2, Athens.

Prakash, Shri and Dutta, Ranita (1996). Input Output Modeling of Trade-off between Employment and Education by the Children of Indian Slums, *Macro Modeling of Economies in Transition,* Vol. X, University of Lodge, Poland.

Prakash, Shri and Mohapatra, A.C. (1980). Economic Developoment in the State of Madhya Pradesh, *Third World Planning Review,* Vol. 2, No. 1, Liverpool University Press.

Prakash, Shri and Nair, Radhakrihsnan, C. (1978). Economic Development and Regional Inequalities with special reference to Madhya Pradesh, *Productivity,* Special Issue.

Prakash, Shri and Rajan, P. (1978). Economic Development and Structural Changes in Madhya Pradesh, *The Indian Journal of Economics,* Vol. LX. No. I.

Prakash, Shri, Gupta, Abha and Buragohain, Tarujyoti (1993). Literacy and Economic Development, *Journal of Educational Planning and Administration*, Special Issue on International Development of Education, No. 4, NIEPA, New Delhi.

Ray, Shovan (2010). *Backwaters of Development: Six Deprived States of India,* Oxford University Press, New Delhi.

Schultz, T.W. (1966). *Economic Value of Education,* Columbia University Press.

Sen, Amartya (2003). *Foreword, in Fukuda Parr,* Sakiko and A.K. Shiv Kumar (Editors). *Readings in Human Development,* Oxford University Press, New Delhi.

Seung, C.K. and Waters, E.C. (2010). Evaluating Supply-Side and Demand-Side Shocks for Fisheries: A Computable General Equilibrium (CGE) Model for Alaska. *Economic System Research,* 22, 87–109.

Sharma, Amit (2012). Rising Educational Qualifications and Growth of Indian Economy, Forthcoming in Rajiv Gandhi Indian Institute of Management's Quarterly *Journal of Management Science,* Shillong.

Singh, Ramvir, Mishra, Padmja and Ray, Madhumita (2010). Inequality, Poverty, and Development in Orissa, in Ray, Shovan (Editor). *Backwaters of Development: Six Deprived States of India,* Oxford University Press, New Delhi.

Turner, Karen. Ha, Soo Juang. Hewings, Geoffrey, J.D., Mcgrgor, Peter and Swales, Kim (2012). Econometric Estimation of Armington Import Elasticities for a Regional CGE Model of the Illinois Economy, *Economic Systems Research,* Vol. 24, No. 1, March, 2012.

Vakil, C.N. and Brahamananda, P.R. (1956). *Planning for an Expanding Economy: Accumulation, Employment and Technical Progress in Underdeveloped Countries,* Vora & Company, Bombay.

CHAPTER 2

Infrastructure Vision for Uttar Pradesh

M. Ramachandran

Dr V.K.R.V. Rao an eminent economist, had pointed decades ago out that the link between infrastructure and economic development is not a once and for all affair. We, as a country, are still planning for higher and higher levels of investment in infrastructure, and in the process, looking for new methods of raising finances for the same. During the eleventh five year plan period, the projected total infrastructure investment of ₹ 20 lakh plus crore has been planned, and this is to go up to ₹ 40 lakh crore, so that we can reach an investment level of 9.95 per cent of GDP by the end of the 12th plan. It is well known, in our case, that on the one hand, when we have what we call worldclass airports at least in select cities, at the same time, we also have poor connectivity of a sizeable number of villages on the outer, and therefore poverty continues to pose a big question mark, slums keep increasing in our urban areas, and there are various other such contradictions which exist, despite claims of a rapidly growing economy. This is the national picture. Thus, we have to look at state specific situations in terms of economic indicators, as to where does each state stand. What is the infrastructure index for a state? Sector wise, what is the situation, and are consistent and focussed efforts being made to bring about steady improvements wherever the state is lagging behind. If there is a structured way of doing this, and accordingly, initiatives support larger investment in infrastructure, then the state is also bound to move in step with the national scheme of steady improvement.

Uttar Pradesh is a large state and plays an important role in national politics. What is the economic status of the state, since the state which has contributed good number of Prime Ministers to the country? If we are talking about dividing the state into smaller new states, one basic reason for the same, seems to be the lack of development, and specifically, regional imbalances. It would be worthwhile looking at the state level, and region wise figures, relating to the basics of infrastructure such as the road network, connectivity, rural electrification, hours of supply of electricity, air and rail connectivity, telecom penetration, water supply, both in terms of access, and supply in both urban, and rural areas, and so on. While on the one hand, the base to start with should look good enough, if the claims of development made correct, and year wise therefore consistent improvements must also be brought about on the outer. There is a multitude of central schemes which facilitate this process, and the state also takes major initiatives to implement various infrastructure schemes. What is the result of all this? Has the state been able to fully utilise funds earmarked under the various schemes, and has it made a difference over a period of years? If so, what now remains to be prioritised and taken up with a missionary zeal, so that living conditions are better, economic activity all through the state is vibrant, and of a higher level, and if one could have either an infrastructure index, or a happiness index (like Bhutan has), will the state figure as one among the top states.

While detailed data will prove all this, there can be no two opinions as to the fact that a whole lot remains to be done to take the infrastructure level of U.P. to a satisfying, higher level. It is important to have a vision for the state, along with the means to realise that vision which has to be constantly reviewed, guided and monitored. If central and state funds are not sufficient for achieving a set annual rate of growth, there must be transparent initiatives for inviting investment including in the form of Public Private Partnerships (PPP), because even the central government recognises that during the forthcoming twelfth five year plan, something like 50 per cent of infrastructure investment will have to come from the private sector. Everyone knows that this will not just happen unless the policy scenario, investment conditions, incentives to invest governance system and above all, people's participation do not undergo a substantial change. In fact, this is the time to have empowered mechanisms with transparency as their hallmark, and clear accountability as a fundamental parameter, with the policy maker's role getting focussed on timely and transparent decisionmaking, so that the required speed in implementation is there, and the results are clearly visible. It is unfortunate, that in our complex governance system, this does not really come about, and in the process, people suffer. Our state systems fail to keep pace with the national performance levels in many sectors, and what we do not realise is the huge costs that we are incurring because of the lost opportunities and delays in decision making, as well as in implementation. Besides, faulty implementation, the root cause of several maladies, is to be eliminated.

An infrastructure vision for the state must essentially consist of a wide picture, indicating where we stand today in each of the sectors, what is it that we want to achieve, the time frame for achieving the goals, the resource availability, as well as the requirements, the comparative prioritisation of targets and how the interlinkages would be addressed. This would basically cover key sectors like roads, railways, airports, inland water transport, city and rural transport, power, irrigation, water supply and sanitation, telecom and IT. If we take the example of roads, after taking note of the national highway network, the status regarding four laning, state highways, district roads and other roads which connect the whole state, 100 per cent all weather roads to connect all villages linked to the remaining road network could be a target to be considered. One figure states that something like 33 per cent of habitations in the state are inaccessible by all weather roads. This means nearly four crore people in the state do not have proper road connectivity. How long will they have to wait to realise the dream of good road connectivity with the rest of the state? Just constructing roads is not enough, they have to be maintained properly over a period of time. Then public transport services have to be provided so that the two basics of movement of products and social infrastructure requirements are satisfactorily and continuously met. All these involve policy support, incentives for investment, facilitation in terms of land and so on. Inter nodal linkages of transport have to be properly structured and worked out, and this is where proper coordination with other central entities like the railways, inland water transport, etc., come in. In a vision statement, while various segments can be taken care of at the state level itself, when it comes to areas like the railways, airports, telecom, power generation, highways, and inland water transport, there is a higher level of coordination involved with the central entities, and this would become a critical task in the entire process of infrastructure management.

If we take the case of civil aviation, a futuristic air connectivity network will have to be thought of in terms of potential requirements, and promotion of higher levels of economic activity. While planning for expanding the existing airport facilities, providing for better access and connectivity, initiating action for new airports, and accordingly, earmarking land, inviting private participation and lining up for both air side and city side developments, would all be part of the exercise. The strategy would involve planning for more tourist inflows to prominent tourist/cultural centres, providing improved accommodation and incentives for such an initiative, better road maintenance and a whole lot of logistics improvement. It has to be kept in mind that while all this investment takes place, employment opportunities go up, they open up new avenues of self-employment, and expansion in specialised education opportunities and in the process, over all improved balanced development of the very region where all this takes place. But all this can happen only when the planning is sound, the intentions are clear, the process is transparent and people, the ultimate beneficiaries, are fully and actively involved. While compulsory acquisition of land is a painful proposition today, where the ultimate benefits of a project are clearly visible to the people of the area, they should be more than willing to participate in the process of land pooling/sharing, whereby they also derive the advantages of a major infrastructure development work undertaken.

It would be worthwhile looking at some available development indicators for the state to have a general appreciation of the tasks remaining, be it the physical, or social infrastructure areas.

CAGR of total income for 2002–07	5.3 per cent
No. of hospitals per lakh population	3
No. of beds per lakh population	39
Percentage shortage of doctors at PHCs	45.8
Length of surfaced roads per lakh population	99.2 km
No. of post offices per lakh population	10.5
Per capita power consumption	191 kWh against 366 kWh all India

Seventy-one per cent of U.P.'s population (85 in rural and 19 in urban) have no access to latrines of any type.

In 2002–03, 35.5 per cent of the state's population had access to electricity.

In 1999–2000 it was 39 per cent.

Hand pumps increased in importance as the most common drinking water supply source, with about three quarters of the population in 2002–03 reporting this as their main water source.

These figures give some indication of the fact that much more remains to be done, and the question is of having a strategy, and having the wherewithal to implement it in a time bound manner. Hence, the importance of a vision, and moving along a sound path of development, backed by a programme of action cannot be minimised.

An Urban Vision

For a long time, we all went by the statement that India lives in its villages, and so the focus and emphasis of development was on rural India. But now, this approach is changing, since there is an increasing realisation that it is the cities and towns, which contribute most to GDP, tax revenues and employment generation. Urbanisation has gone hand in hand with economic growth the world over, and our experience in India shows that the states that have had the fastest economic growth have also had the highest rates of urbanisation. States like Gujarat, Tamil Nadu, Maharashtra, Karnataka are examples. Also, we have to keep in mind that we are aiming at an impressive GDP growth rate of 9 per cent per annum which means the demand for more efficient and meaningful infrastructure is going to be strong. Though the 61st Round of NSS report shows that a large number of villages still lack meaningful physical or social infrastructure, the aggressive demand for a better and improved infrastructural framework will be driven by expanding urban population of the country.

Out of U.P.'s total population of 16.6 crore as per the 2001 census, 20.78 per cent was urban, living in 704 cities and towns of various sizes. It was estimated by the committee on slum statistics, that one-fourth of this population lives in slums. National figures show that one-fourth of the country's total urban population lives below the poverty line. As far as housing shortages are concerned, it was estimated at around 24.7 million units nationally and 99 per cent of this shortage pertains to economically weaker sections and low income groups. These figures could apply to U.P. also. If we look at the population characteristics of the state population, 54 cities had one lakh or more population, another 264 towns were in the 10,000 to 20,000 population category, and 186 were in the 20,000 to 50,000 population category. The latter category towns, are the ones which are growing fast, and extend into the adjoining peri urban areas, thereby creating an urban mess, particularly in the surrounding areas with no focus on planned development, and urban services becoming pathetic. In the notified urban areas, 54 per cent of the population had access to tap water, 32 per cent had water closet latrines within premises, 80 per cent were using electricity for lighting and only 26 per cent households were having connectivity to closed drainage for waste water outlets.

As per the 2011 census, U.P.'s population has risen to 19.9 crore. There are now 915 cities and towns of which as many as 267 are census towns, meaning that each one of them has a population of 5,000 or more, but they still figure as a village body. Though U.P. continues to be the state with the highest rural population of 15.5 crore with another 4.4 crore people living in urban areas which represents 11.8 per cent of the total urban population of the country, and it ranks second after Maharashtra in terms of top urban states of the country. Of the 28 million plus population cities in the country, seven are located in the state of U.P. Growing urban settlements have their own importance in the scheme of rapid development of any state, or country. Their efficiency largely depends on how well they are planned and developed, and how efficiently they are managed. Of the 100 fastest growing cities in the world, 26 are located in India, and five of these are in U.P. The Mckinsey report on *India's Urban Awakening* points out that India in 2030, will have 13 cities with more than four million people, and Kanpur will be one among them.

Cities and towns lack many of the essentials today. Basic services are not satisfactory, slums keep increasing, the number of people living below poverty line keeps going up, economic efficiencies are not visible, and the whole system of governance is weak. What we need basically is all the relevant basic data for the 900 odd cities, so that a proper appreciation of the problems of a city is possible. Everyone does not have access to drinking water, garbage lies all over cities, sewer coverage is low, urban transport is in a mess, integration of land use and transport planning does not take place, there is no apex system at the city level to coordinate and guide overall transport efforts, slums keep expanding because there is no focussed housing effort at the city end, spatial planning is almost missing, and there is no conscious effort to coordinate a city's development with that of the peri urban areas which later get merged with the defined city, in the form of a larger city, as has happened in the case of Bangalore, Hyderabad and Chennai becoming greater cities.

Uttar Pradesh has taken advantage of the first phase of the JNNURM (2005 to 2012) by taking up a good number of projects in the mission cities as well as certain number of smaller towns. Some headway has been made as far as reforms implementation is concerned. The state on its own has also taken up programmes to improve the urban landscape. What is required to be done now, is to think in terms of a structured urban strategy, taking into account region wise/city wise directions for development, priorities regarding infrastructure development, and possible financing options. Such efforts will identify which are the areas the state would like to develop as centres of economic activity, be it industrial/manufacturing/tourism/IT based/education centric, etc. The vision would specifically address key concerns, like how universal access to water and sanitation is to be achieved in a steady manner, how the objective of affordable housing is to be implemented, how the state plans to ensure quality and affordable public transport, how the densification requirements would be taken up and implemented, how slums rehabilitation would be an ongoing steady process and so on. Along with this vision exercise, steps need to be initiated to achieve overall balanced development of cities, to enable the cities to take advantage of the next phase of the JNNURM which would include:

- decide on a cadre structure for various levels of municipalities and see that the personnel are positioned and their capacity building is addressed in all earnestness
- update city development plans already made, and prepare new ones for the cities to be taken up under the next phase of the urban mission
- have a close look at policies which will have to play a catalytic role as far as promoting their growth are concerned
- facilitative, detailed PPP policy would be one of the key requirements especially in the context of the projected Twelfth plan requirement of half of the infrastructure investment expected to come from the private sector
- have UMTAs in position as envisaged in the national urban transport policy
- draw up an action plan in line with the national urban sanitation policy—it may be recalled that when the sanitation rating of Indian cities was undertaken in 2010, only Noida and Kanpur figured among the top 25 cities
- draw up an implementation plan for energy conservation, green buildings, etc., as envisaged in the sustainable habitat mission approach
- effectively strengthen the third level of governance by empowering the local bodies by transferring funds, functions and functionaries to the ULB system
- actively follow up on the service level benchmark agenda for each city
- proactively implement the recommendations of the 13th Finance Commission and strengthen the state finance commission system
- strategise how inclusive growth can take place, and work out how this is to be put into action, and
- go in for massive e governance arrangements for all cities and towns.

Cities and towns will have to have a much more improved governance system whereby service delivery improves substantially, e-governance becomes the rule of the day rather than the exception and active citizen involvement is facilitated by providing them access to all that is happening in their cities. Timely implementation of projects and programmes will be a major requirement, which necessitates proper exposure of local body functionaries to modern project management techniques, private participation will have to be so encouraged that the poor are not adversely affected, but the investment requirements are supported. City residents will have to get used to paying for the services they get, so that sustainability of infrastructure built is possible. Since the value of land appreciates significantly when infrastructure improves, instead of the developer usurping all the upsides of this positive development, the city should be able to capitalise on this, and deploy the additional resources for better o and m and improvement in service delivery.

CHAPTER 3

Productivity, Literacy and Per Capita State Domestic Product of Indian States

Amit Sharma and Ajeet Singh Rauthan

Introduction: Dependency Ratio and Growth

High dependency ratio pulls down State Domestic Products (SDP) and per capita SDP, unless the high dependency ratio is compensated by high productivity of the work force. As against this, low dependency ratio at a given productivity level boosts SDP, as well as per capita SDP. The relation between output and dependency ratio is therefore inverse. The dependency ratio depends on the labour force's participation rates and actual employment. The labour force participation ratio, in turn, depends on the proportion of 15–60 year olds in the total population, and opportunities for employment. Rising expected age and relative shortages of high level human resources, have opened new vistas of employment/re-employment for the 60+ population also. The shortage of highly qualified manpower and rapid expansion of job opportunities for higher and technical manpower, have resulted in a scarcity of manpower for all occupations, including teachers in institutions of higher and technical education. The UGC has raised the retirement age to 65 years and AICTE has raised it to 70 years, in order to cope with such shortages. At the other end of the spectrum, we find below 15 year old child workers and a rising proportion of women in the work force; which is an indicator of rising job opportunities in low level blue occupations. The productivity of child workers and women in blue collar jobs is low, and hence, their earnings are also low. A high proportion of children and illiterate/semi-illiterate women workers results in low wages and low productivity employment. It is these aspects of the work force and dependency ratio which influence SDP/per capita SDP greatly. Therefore, the dependency ratio has been tried as an independent factor of growth. High labour force participation rates makes the dependency ratio low, while low labour force participation rates make it high. Provided that job opportunities are available, otherwise it will lead to rising unemployment. Thus, labour force participation rates and dependency ratio are also inversely related to each other.

Social Divide

Most of the SC/ST people are illiterate, and generally employed as manual workers at low wages, and their productivity is therefore naturally also low. Besides, a large proportion of SC/ST are engaged in agriculture and agri-related activities in rural areas; another area is the low wage self-employment in urban regions. Therefore, a high proportion of SC/ST in the population may also hamper the rapid growth of the economy. Therefore, the relation between the population of SC/ST and SDP/per capita SDP is also postulated to be inverse. All these are conjectural statements, and hence, are treated as hypotheses to be tested empirically. The thrust of the argument is to highlight the degree of deprivation which SC/ST face, which precludes them from becoming eligible for high wage/earning occupations. It connotes social, economic and educational deprivation.

Education and Human Development

The role of investment in education as the base for human development and human capital accumulation has been emphasised since long. It has a pivotal role in human capital development that led C.N. Vakil and P.R. Brahmanand (1956) to advocate investment in nutrition, food, water, literacy, clothing, education and health in the Indian economy. This has come to be known as the *Basic Goods Model.* Schultz (1966) has also established that human capital accumulation has played a crucial role in the growth of the U.S. economy. Indian economists like P.R. Panchamukhi, V.N. Kothari, H.N. Pandit, Shri Prakash and several others have also emphasised the role of investment in education. Prakash-Balakrishnan (2009) and Amit Sharma (2011) have established the crucial role of productivity of the human capital in the development of the Indian economy. Ali Mollahusseini (2006) in a comparative study inferred that the Iranian economy could develop rapidly, if like India, South Korea, Singapore and Malaysia it made growth revolve around productivity. It may be noted that productivity is greatly affected by technology. But, change in technology depends on investment in machines, plant and equipment which embody advanced technology. But, the operationalisation and derivation of optimum output from a given technology is a function of human capital. If technology is constant, then productivity gains accrue from the competency of human capital. If technology changes in the process of growth, then the separation of the contribution of human capital, independent of technology, and contribution of technology, independent of human capital is a complex and intricate task (Amit Sharma, 2012 and Prakash-Balakrishnan, 2009).

As literacy is a crude indicator of educational development, Amit Sharma has used completed years of education as a determinant of productivity. Besides, Buragohain, Tarujyoti and Gupta, Abha, Prakash, S. (1993), in an extensive study of the inter-relation between literacy and economic development, and underdevelopment of 114 countries, including India, and 26 states and 452 districts of India showed that high literacy rates propel economic development, and low literacy rates are among the important factors of underdevelopment of countries and regions within them. Besides, they also empirically showed that (i) literacy rate increases in geometrical progression, and the common ratio ranges from 1.42 for districts/states to 1.53 for nations; and (ii) the male literacy rate doubles in 21 years and the female literacy rate doubles in 14 years. Their study covers a period of more than a century (Bhusan–Prakash et al., 1993). Prakash–Balakrishnan established a strong relationship between literacy and productivity, Amit Sharma highlighted the crucial role of education in the growth of productivity, which has been the main driver of economic growth of the Indian economy, especially since 1990–91. Productivity gains as stimulantes to growth have been substantially raised for Indian economy since 2001 to 2012 through accelerated substitution of graduate and above for below graduate manpower (Amit Sharma, forthcoming). It may be noted that literacy is at the bottom of the educational pyramid. Hence, it is only a crude indicator of educational development. It is this theoretical-empirical paradigm that prompted us to consider literacy as an important determinant of SDP/per capita SDP of Indian states. This study uses literacy as a proxy for education. It is in view of the above that work force participation rate, dependency ratio and literacy rate are considered major determinants of per capita SDP of Indian states in this study.

Empirical Results

Results of empirical analysis are reported sequentially.

Literacy and Productivity

We have examined the relationship between productivity and literacy (see appendix). The regression function fits the data well, and its coefficients are statistically significant. The regression function shows that an increase of one unit in literacy leads to an increase of ₹ 1827.24 in productivity. Our result is stronger than that obtained by Strumilin for Soviet agriculture, who inferred that an increase of one year in literacy raises productivity by 36 per cent. But, our result is comparable to that of D.P. Chaudhary (1979) for Panjab agriculture (Prakash, S., 1977). Chaudhary estimated the magnitude of interrelations between education and innovations on the one hand, and education and agricultural development on the other. He also examined the role of education for innovations in agriculture.

This result highlights the fact that productivity is relatively higher in such states which have attained higher literacy rates. As against this, states like U.P., Bihar, Rajasthan, M.P. and Orissa, which have relatively low literacy rates, suffer from the malady of low productivity, and low and slow growth of SDP.

Literacy and Per Capita SDP

The relationship between per capita SDP of Indian states and their literacy rates is also positive and statistically significant. It shows that literacy plays an important role in the growth of per capita SDP. An increase of one per cent in literacy rate raises per capita SDP by ₹ 641.41.

A direct implication of the result is that states having low per capita SDP ought to focus, among other factors, on raising literacy rates. These two results, taken together, show that the impact of literacy on per capita SDP is much lower than that on the growth of SDP.

SC/ST Population and Per Capita SDP

We have also examined the relation between per capita SDP with the population of SC/ST as a proportion of the total population. The result shows that the relation between the proportion of SC/STs and per capita SDP is not only negative, but it is statistically significant also. It means that a greater proportion of people of these castes lowers the per capita SDP. It may be noted that caste *per se* is not an important factor by itself. The result is impacted because it indicates the negative effect of the social backwardness, economic deprivation and denial of opportunities of education to people of these castes. Incidentally, the spread of literacy becomes the base for the subsequent development of education. Besides, the less developed states should focus on eradication of illiteracy. G&L policy intervention to get rid of social backwardness and economic underdevelopment.

All states, irrespective of their stages of development, should focus on the educational uplift of the SC/ST population. This will not only move the economy towards rapid growth, but it will also meet the needs of inclusive growth, equity and justice.

Dependency Ratio and Per Capita SDP

As discussed earlier, the dependency ratio is expected to negatively impact the growth of SDP/per capita SDP.

The results obtained by the regression model show that the dependency ratio and per capita SDP are not significantly related. This may probably be because of the relatively low differences between dependency ratios among states. Thus, there is no empirical evidence to support the thesis that the dependency ratio inversely affects growth of SDP/per capita SDP.

Table 1

S. No.	*State/UT*	*Population*	*SC/ST Total Population*	*Work Force Participation Rate*	*Literacy Rate*	*Per Captia SDP*	*Dependency*
1.	Andhra Pradesh	7,62,10,007	22.78	45.79	60.38	16373.00	54.21
2.	Arunachal Pradesh	10,97,968	64.78	43.98	53.68	14587.00	56.02
3.	Assam	2,66,55,528	19.26	35.78	62.95	10198.00	64.22
4.	Bihar	8,29,98,509	16.63	33.70	46.40	5108.00	66.30
6.	Goa	13,47,668	1.81	38.80	81.90	45105.00	61.20
7.	Gujarat	5,06,71,017	21.85	41.95	68.73	19228.00	58.05
8.	Haryana	2,11,44,564	19.35	39.62	67.11	23742.00	60.38
9.	Himachal Pradesh	60,77,900	28.74	49.24	76.39	18920.00	50.76
10.	Jammu & Kashmir	1,01,43,700	18.49	37.01	54.80	12399.00	62.99
12.	Karnataka	5,28,50,562	22.75	44.53	66.49	18041.00	55.47
13.	Kerala	3,18,41,374	10.95	32.30	90.98	19463.00	67.70
14.	Madhya Pradesh	6,03,48,023	35.44	42.74	63.18	10803.00	57.26
15.	Maharashtra	9,68,78,627	19.05	42.50	76.50	23726.00	57.50
16.	Manipur	22,93,896	36.97	43.62	70.43	12823.00	56.38
17.	Meghalaya	23,18,822	86.42	41.84	62.52	13114.00	58.16
18.	Orissa	3,68,04,660	38.66	38.79	62.93	8547.00	61.21
19.	Punjab	2,43,58,999	28.85	37.47	69.30	25048.00	62.53
20.	Rajasthan	5,65,07,188	29.72	42.06	59.78	11986.00	57.94
21.	Sikkim	5,40,851	25.62	48.64	68.22	15550.00	51.36
22.	Tamil Nadu	6,24,05,679	20.04	44.67	73.43	19889.00	55.33
23.	Tripura	31,99,203	48.42	36.25	72.97	14348.00	63.75
24.	Uttar Pradesh	16,61,97,921	21.21	32.48	54.52	9721.00	67.52
25.	West Bengal	8,01,76,197	28.52	36.77	68.32	16072.00	63.23
26.	Delhi	1,38,50,507	16.92	32.82	81.02	38864.00	67.18
27.	Pondicherry	9,74,345	16.19	35.17	81.26	31358.00	64.83

Table 2

S. No.	State/UT	Total Workers	Total SDP	Productivity	Literacy Rate	Estimated Productivity
1.	Andhra Pradesh	34896562.21	1247786444611.00	35756.72	60.38	33048.06
2.	Arunachal Pradesh	482886.33	16016059216.00	33167.35	53.68	20814.68
3.	Assam	9537347.92	271833074544.00	28501.96	62.95	37744.07
4.	Bihar	27970497.53	423956383972.00	15157.27	46.40	7512.36
6.	Goa	522895.18	60786565140.00	116250.00	81.90	72370.28
7.	Gujarat	21256491.63	974302314876.00	45835.52	68.73	48314.66
8.	Haryana	8377476.26	502014238488.00	59924.28	67.11	45354.52
9.	Himachal Pradesh	2992757.96	114993868000.00	38424.05	76.39	62302.18
10.	Jammu & Kashmir	3754183.37	125771736300.00	33501.76	54.80	22861.19
12.	Karnataka	23534355.26	953476989042.00	40514.26	66.49	44212.50
13.	Kerala	10284763.80	619728662162.00	60256.97	90.98	88970.77
14.	Madhya Pradesh	25792745.03	651939692469.00	25276.09	63.18	38164.33
15.	Maharashtra	41173416.48	2298542304202.00	55825.88	76.50	62512.32
16.	Manipur	1000597.44	29414628408.00	29397.07	70.43	51420.96
17.	Meghalaya	970195.12	30409031708.00	31343.21	62.52	36967.49
18.	Orissa	14276527.61	314569429020.00	22034.03	62.93	37716.66
19.	Punjab	9127316.93	610144206952.00	66848.15	69.30	49347.05
20.	Rajasthan	23766923.27	677295155368.00	28497.38	59.78	31951.71
21.	Sikkim	263069.93	8410233050.00	31969.57	68.22	47382.76
22.	Tamil Nadu	27876616.81	1241186549631.00	44524.29	73.43	56893.55
23.	Tripura	1159711.09	45902164644.00	39580.69	72.97	56053.02
24.	Uttar Pradesh	53981084.74	1615609990041.00	29929.19	54.52	22349.56
25.	West Bengal	29480787.64	1288591838184.00	43709.55	68.32	47556.35
26.	Delhi	4545736.40	538286104048.00	118415.60	81.02	70771.45
27.	Pondicherry	342677.14	30553510510.00	89161.22	81.26	71209.98

Productivity and Per Capita SDP

Productivity and growth are strongly hypothesised to be significantly directly related. The results derived from the regression model show that, as expected, per capita SDP is significantly related positively with productivity. Corresponding to an increase of ₹ 100 in productivity, per capita SDP increases by ₹ 34. Thus, 33 per cent growth of per capita SDP is accounted for by productivity.

As literacy is also shown to contribute to growth, we have regressed the total SDP on productivity and literacy, but the regression coefficients are not significant. Literacy and productivity are mutually related very significantly, leading to multi co-linearity, which is supposed to have made the regression coefficient not significant. This is already obvious from the regression of productivity on literacy.

An increase of ₹ 1 in productivity raises per capita SDP by ₹ 0.34. Thus, an increase of ₹ 100 in productivity will raise per capita SDP by ₹ 34. Thus, 34 per cent of overall growth of per capita SDP is accounted for by the increase in productivity.

Conclusions

Productivity is the main driver of growth of the Indian economy, and the economies of its states. But, productivity itself depends on literacy in general, and education in particular. Besides, denial of and deprivation of education to SC/STs is counter-productive. The policy instruments have to be sharpened to transform class to mass education of the SC/STs in India and its states.

References

Bhusan, S. Prakash, S., Gupta, Abha and Buragohain, Tarujyoti (1993). *Literacy and Development with Special Reference to Countries of Third World*, Report of UNESCO Sponsored Project, NIEPA, New Delhi.

C.N. Vakil and P.R. Brahmanand (1956). *Planning for an Expanding Economy: Accumulation, Employment and Technical Progress in Underdeveloped Countries,* Vora and Co., Bombay.

Chaudhary, D.P. (1979). *Education, Innovations and Agricultural Development,* Croom Helm, London.

Kothari, V.N. (1971). Educated Unemployment in India, *Artha Vikas,* Vol. VII, pp. 172–82.

Mollahosseini, Ali and Amjadi, Hossein (2006). Stress and Its Impact on Performance of Staff: A Case Study of Iranian Copper Industry, *Business Perspective*, Vol. 8, No. 1, January–June.

Panchamukhi, P.R. (1969). Economic Analysis and Planning of Education Industry. In Pandit, H.N. (Editor). *Measurement of Cost, Productivity and Efficiency of Education,* N.C.E.R.T., New Delhi.

Prakash, S. (1977). *Educational System: An Econometric Study,* Concept Publishing Company, New Delhi.

Prakash, S., Buragohain, Tarujyoti and Gupta, Abha (1993). Literacy and Development: An Analysis of 114 Countries, 26 States and 452 Districts of India, *Journal of Education Planning and Administration*, Special Issue on Literacy and Educational Development in Developing Countries, NIEPA, New Delhi.

Praksah, S. and Balakrsihnan, Brinda (2008). Input Output Modelling of Labour Productivity and its Human Capital and Technology Components in Indian Economy, *Bulletin of Political Economy*, Vol. 2, No. 2, December.

Schultz, T.W. (1966). *Economic Value of Education,* Columbia University Press.

Appendix

Sharma, Amit (2011). Upgradation of Educational Qualifications of Selected Occupations: A Study of Higher Scientific and Technical Occupations since 1981 in the Indian Economy, Ph.D. Thesis, University of Mysore, Mysore, submitted through BIMTECH.

Strumilin – Quoted from Prakash, S. (1977). Educational System—An Econometric Study, Concept Publishing Co., New Delhi.

Literacy and Productivity

$$Y = -77271.6 + 1827.241X$$
$$t = (-2.937)\ (4.7576)$$

Y = Productivity, X = Literacy

Literacy and Per Capita SDP

$$Y = -25264.79 + 641.409X$$
$$t = (-2.783)\ (4.841)$$

Y = Per Capita SDP, X = Literacy

SC/ST Population and Per Capita SDP

$$Y = 24302.867 + -218.1217X$$
$$t = (7.3491)\ (-2.1637)$$

Y = Per Capita SDP, X = SC/ST

Dependency Ratio and Per Capita SDP

$$Y = 5474.615 + 211.889X$$
$$t = (0.2327)\ (0.5427)$$

Y = Per Capita SDP, X = Dependency

Productivity and Per Capita SDP

$$Y = 2405.188 + 0.3393X$$
$$t = (2.797)\ (21.059)$$

Y = Per Capita SDP, X = Productivity

Section–II

Economic Growth of Uttar Pradesh

CHAPTER 4

The Challenge of Rapid Development of Uttar Pradesh[1]

A.K. Singh

The Downward Slide

Uttar Pradesh has played an important role in the polity and economy of the country since pre-independence days. It has been known for its prosperous and hard working peasantry and as a major producer of food-grains and horticultural crops. It also had a large number of modern and traditional industries. Numerous sugar mills dotted the rural areas throughout the state. Kanpur was a major textile centre of the country. The state was known for its good educational institutions. Students from all over the country flocked to the universities of Allahabad, Lucknow, Aligarh and Benaras. U.P. was almost at par with the national economy, in terms of per capita income, at the time of independence. It was regarded as one of the best administered states of the country. The state played a major part in the freedom struggle. The state has produced a large number of political leaders, administrators, academicians and artists of national and international stature.

Uttar Pradesh remained a major force in the polity of the nation even after independence. With eighty MPs representing the state in Parliament, it could swing the political fortunes of the country. Almost all the Prime Ministers of India, till 1990, came from Uttar Pradesh with the exception of the short tenures of Gulzari Lal Nanda as interim Prime Minister and Morarji Desai. With the breakdown of the supremacy of the Congress Party, and increasing political fracture of the state polity, U.P. lost its political eminence after 1990.

Even more dramatic than its political downfall, was the economic decline of the state, which came to be labeled as a 'Bimaru', that is a sick state along with its neighbouring states of Bihar, Madhya Pradesh and Rajasthan. Today, the very mention of the name of Uttar Pradesh, conjures up images of a backward and stagnant state, which is pulling down the rapid growth of the country. Except for a brief spell during the eighties, the growth rate of the economy has remained distinctly behind the national growth rate, while its population has continued to grow unabatedly above the national average. The result has been that the per capita income of the state, which was nearly at par with the national per capita income in 1951, has come down to almost half of the national per capita income presently and the gap is increasing.

Overview of UP's Economy

Uttar Pradesh presents all the features which characterise an underdeveloped economy. All the indicators of economic and social development of U.P. present a rather dismal and depressing picture: low per capita income, slow economic growth, high birth rates, widespread poverty, high IMR and MMR, low literacy especially among females, poor health outcomes, high incidence of child and women nutritional deficiency. U.P. is among the bottom four states of India in all these indicators (Table 1). The low levels of economic development and low status of human development in the state are mutually reinforcing phenomena (Singh et al., 2005).

Table 1: Select Human Development Indicators for U.P. and Other States

States	*IMR*	*Life Expectancy*	*Literacy Rate*		*Sex Ratio*	*Per Capita NSDP (₹)*	*% Persons Below Poverty Line*
			Total	*Female*	*0 to 6 Yrs*		
	2005	*2003*	*2001*	*2001*	*2001*	*2003–04*	*2004–05*
Andhra Pradesh	57	63.7	61.11	51.17	978	21372	15.8
Assam	68	58.0	64.28	56.03	932	12821	19.7
Bihar	61	61.0	47.53	33.57	921	7319	41.4
Gujarat	54	63.5	69.97	58.6	921	26672	16.8
Haryana	60	65.4	68.59	56.31	861	29504	14.0
Karnataka	50	64.6	67.04	57.45	964	21238	25.0
Kerala	14	73.6	90.92	87.86	1,058	13722	15.0
Madhya Pradesh	76	57.1	64.11	50.28	920	14784	38.3
Maharashtra	36	66.4	77.27	67.51	922	13732	30.8
Orissa	75	58.7	63.61	50.97	972	12645	46.4
Punjab	44	68.6	69.95	63.55	874	28607	8.4
Rajasthan	68	61.3	61.03	44.34	922	15738	22.1
Tamil Nadu	37	65.4	73.47	64.55	986	23358	22.5
Uttar Pradesh	73	59.3	57.36	42.98	898	11534	32.8
Rank of U.P.	(13)	(12)	(14)	(14)	(13)	(14)	(12)
West Bengal	38	64.1	69.22	60.22	934	20548	24.7
India	58	62.7	65.38	54.16	933	20936	27.5

Source: Government of India, *Economic Survey, 2008,* Ministry of Finance, New Delhi and Census of India 2001.

Within the overall depressing scenario of development of the state, one comes across sharp divides in the level of development of different social groups, between men and women and among different regions of the state (UPHDR, 2003). A brief mention of the same would not be out of order here.

Inequality among Social Groups

Uttar Pradesh is marked by sharp economic and social inequalities among different social and religious groups. Numerically, the largest group consists of backward castes, who lack in educational attainment, though some of them have acquired economic and political clout in recent years. Around one-fifth of the people of the state belong to the socially and economically depressed scheduled castes. Muslims, constituting around one-sixth of the state population, also suffer from low income levels and low literacy. Thus, a very sizeable part of the state population belongs to the deprived groups, which tends to depress the overall human development indicators of the state.

The marked inequalities in socio-economic conditions of different social groups have deep historical roots and are reflective of the continued dominance of the upper castes in the economic, social and political domain. The ruling elite, which till recently comprised of upper castes, did not show the required commitment for the economic and social uplift of the backward and *dalit* communities. This was also the reason for the poor implementation of land reforms and other programmes for the uplift of the weaker sections introduced in various plans.

Gender Inequality

Uttar Pradesh presents an extreme case of gender inequality. It is lagging behind most of the other states in terms of indicators of women development. The gap is particularly high in case of indicators like female literacy, work participation rate and life expectancy. On the other hand, the fertility rates in U.P. are much above the national average. Sex ratio in the state is low and has been declining. Infant and child mortality rates among girls are higher, as compared to the boys. Female life expectancy is lower than male life expectancy; this is unlike the situation in most parts of the world. The prevailing socio-cultural milieu in the state discriminates against women. The role of women's agency is particularly weak in U.P., which has implications not only for the well being of women, but also for economic development and social progress of society as a whole (Dreze and Gazdar, 1996, p. 56).

Rural and Urban Divide

Uttar Pradesh's economy is characterised by low levels of urbanisation and significant rural-urban disparities in levels of income, infrastructure and social development. Nearly 80 per cent of the state's population still lives in rural areas. In many districts, particularly in the Eastern region, less than 10 per cent of the population is urban. The pace of urbanisation has also been rather slow. Literacy levels in the rural areas are extremely low, and the medical facilities are extremely poor. This is reflected in the differences in the Human Development Index (HDI) levels in the rural and urban areas.

Regional Disparities

Being a large state, U.P. is characterised by significant variations in the levels of economic and social development among regions and districts. The western region of the state is relatively more developed economically, as compared to other regions. However, in social indicators, the situation even in this region is far from satisfactory (Singh, 2001). The eastern region and Bundelkhand are officially recognised as backward regions, and are given special attention in development plans. All the four economic regions also show considerable intra-regional variations at the district level. The sharp distinctions in levels of development among the regions of U.P. have sometimes led to the demand for division of the state into three or four smaller states. This has now been taken up officially by the state government. There is a growing feeling among the people that, in its present form, U.P. is politically and administratively an unmanageable state, and needs to be trifurcated for faster development of all the parts of the present state.

Slow Structural Shifts

The pace of structural shift in the state has been rather slow. Two-thirds of the work force in U.P. is engaged in agriculture. However, the share of the agricultural sector in state income is only one-third. Consequently, agricultural incomes are low. Moreover, the state is not able to share the gains arising from the rapid growth of services and the manufacturing sector, due to its economic structure being oriented towards the rural areas and agriculture, which are now the prime movers of growth. The excessive demographic pressure on land, leading to smaller and decreasing sizes of holdings, combined with the slow growth of non-agricultural employment, causes high incidence of rural poverty.

Growth Performance

During the first twenty five years of economic planning, U.P.'s economic growth was extremely low at around 2 to 2.5 per cent per annum, which was hardly above the population growth of the state, and even lower than the Hindu rate of growth of around 3.5 per cent experienced by the Indian economy. Growth rates in U.P. picked up from the Fifth Plan period and caught up with the national growth rate in the Sixth and the Seventh plan periods (Table 2). The growth rate was largely agriculture led growth in the wake of the green revolution (Singh, 2000). Industries also showed high growth in this period. However, since the beginning of the nineties the growth rate in U.P. decelerated markedly, and remained hardly around 3 per cent per annum. However, there seems to be some revival of growth rates in the present decade. During the Tenth Five Year Plan (2002–2007) U.P. registered a growth rate of 5.2 per cent per annum. The growth momentum has continued in the Eleventh Five Year Plan.

Table 2: Compound Annual Growth Rate of Total and Per Capita Income in U.P. and India Since 1951

Period	*CAGR of Total Income (%)*		*CAGR of Per Capita Income (%)*	
	Uttar Pradesh	*India*	*Uttar Pradesh*	*India*
1951–56	2.0	3.6	0.5	1.7
1956–61	1.9	4.0	0.3	1.9
1961–66	1.6	2.2	–0.2	0.0
1966–69	0.3	4.0	–1.5	1.8
1969–74	2.3	3.3	0.4	1.1
1974–79	5.7	5.3	3.3	2.9
1981–85	3.9	4.9	1.5	2.7
1985–90	5.7	5.8	3.3	3.6
1990–92	3.1	2.5	1.1	0.4
1992–97	3.2	6.8	1.4	4.9
1997–02	3.1	5.3	1.0	3.3
2002–07	5.2	7.8	3.2	6.1

Source: Plan Documents, Government of Uttar Pradesh.

Low Plan Investment

The slow growth of U.P.'s economy, and the fluctuations observed in the growth rate can be explained largely by low and fluctuating levels of investment in the state. Being a poor state with low tax-SDP ratio, the state revenues did not generate enough surpluses for investment from its own sources. No major public sector project was started in U.P. either in the state sector, or the central sector, during the first two decades of planning. The flow of resources from the centre through the mechanism of Finance Commissions, as well as that of the Planning Commission remained relatively low in U.P. in per capita terms. Some improvement in the flow of financial resources from the centre took place during the seventies and the eighties, but it was not adequate to overcome the neglect of the past.

Till the mid seventies, plan investment in U.P. remained below four per cent of Net State Domestic Product (NSDP) (Table 3). There was visible improvement in the

Table 3: Plan Expenditure in U.P. Under Five Year Plans

Period	*Plan Expenditure (₹ crores)*	*Plan Expenditure as Per cent of NSDP*
Five Year Plans		
1951–56	153	2.05
1956–61	233	2.66
1961–66	561	4.53
1966–69	455	3.86
1969–74	1166	4.69
1974–79	2909	7.01
1979–85	7356	7.62
1985–90	11949	7.44
1990–92	7772	7.28
1992–97	21683	4.73
1997–02	28386	3.84
Annual Plans		
1997–98	5033	3.66
1998–99	5648	3.67
1999–00	5843	3.53
2000–01	5897	3.40
2001–02	5965	3.16
2002–03	6702	3.30
2003–04	7242	3.33
2004–05	10205	4.53
2005–06 (RE)	17331	6.82
2006–07 (BE)	22106	8.20

Source: Plan Documents, Government of Uttar Pradesh.

Note: Percentages from 1997–98 are in terms of GSDP.

ratio of plan investment during the Fifth, Sixth and the Seventh Plans, which is also reflected in the relatively faster economic growth the state experienced during this period. However, the state was caught in the grip of an ever deepening fiscal crisis from the late eighties (Singh, 2007). The levels of revenue deficit, and gross fiscal deficit remained high till recently. The mounting revenue expenditure of the state government left little resources for capital expenditure. Thus, we find that the ratio of plan expenditure to NSDP dipped significantly in the nineties, and capital expenditure of the government came down to around 5–6 per cent of its total expenditure. The decline in public investment was reflected in the deceleration of the growth rate of the state economy. The recent pick up of the state economy is also due to the increased plan expenditure.

Poor Investment Climate

Besides the low public investment, the state government failed to create a favourable investment climate, which could attract private investment on a large scale to boost the state economy. All available information suggests that investment activity in U.P. is quite low. U.P.'s share in the total proposed investment through IEMs in the country between August 1991 and November 2007 was a meager 5.32 per cent. Moreover, only about one-third of proposed investments have actually been realised. Moreover, nearly four-fifths of all investments was made in only 3–4 western districts bordering Delhi.

Other indicators of investment flows also reveal a rather bleak picture. For instance, U.P.'s share in bank loans in the country was a paltry 3.30 per cent in 2006. Same was the picture with respect to U.P.'s share in loans from term lending institutions like the IDBI, ICICI and REC. These figures are a clear pointer to the fact that U.P. is not a favoured destination for investment.

Constraints on Development

The poor economic performance has been despite the fact that U.P. is endowed with vast natural and human resources. The state is endowed with one of the most fertile land tracts in the world with plentiful surface and underground water resources, plentiful rainfall and a good climate suitable for agricultural activities. It has large livestock resources. It also has a vast stock of cheap and unskilled labour as well as skilled and educated manpower. The state has been providing political leaders, bureaucrats and technocrats, who have been manning and running the best institutions in the country. In short, U.P. is a state with great potential, which alas remains largely unexploited.

The question then is, what is constraining investment and economic development of the state. Though much can be said and written on this, here we would like to highlight only a few critical factors constraining the rapid development of the state.

(a) *Poor Infrastructure*

A major handicap for U.P. is the low levels of infrastructure development, which itself is due to its economic structure, oriented towards the rural areas and agriculture due to the past failures of public policy. In terms of the composite index of infrastructural development prepared for the Twelfth Finance Commission, U.P. stood at the 15th rank among the major states (Mohanty, 2004). Power is the most critical bottleneck the state is currently facing. There has been practically no addition to the generation capacity in the state since 1990, while demand has been increasing. The distribution network is obsolete and overloaded, resulting in frequent breakdowns. All major cities and towns of the state face power cuts of 4 to 6 hours daily. The T and D losses are extremely high at around 40 per cent, with widespread and open power thefts. Consequently, the state power utilities are incurring huge financial losses and have no resources to invest in power generation and improvement of the distribution network.

The road density is also much lower in the state, as compared to the developed states. The maintenance of roads is poor adding to the cost and time for transportation. A major shortcoming is the poor linkages with the rural areas, with nearly 40 per cent villages not connected to all weather roads. Poor village connectivity is a major factor for the weak linkages between the urban and rural areas.

U.P. is deficient in rural infrastructure in terms of banking, warehousing, cold storages, roads, etc. The public irrigation system is in a bad shape, unable to recover even the operational costs. The area irrigated by canals and public tubewells has been shrinking. The cooperative credit structure in the state has almost collapsed.

The major cities of the state are suffering from problems of poor urban infrastructure. Urban services like power and water supply are in poor shape and under pressure, due to continuous in-migration from rural areas. Problems of congestion and pollution are acute. Few cities can boast of an attractive infrastructure to attract investment. The financial position of the urban bodies is poor, causing under investment in urban infrastructure.

The social infrastructure in U.P. is also inadequately developed and suffers from poor quality and limited access. The quality of public services in the field of health and education is far from satisfactory.

(b) *Poor Policy Regime*

The policy framework in the state is not fully conducive for promoting investment and economic growth. Rigidities in land, labour and product markets constraints investment and restricts economic activity. There are restrictions on conversion of agricultural land to non-agricultural land. The non-SCs are prohibited from purchasing land owned by SCs. Land leasing is banned by law, though in practice oral leases prevail.

The state government has been reluctant to bring about changes in the Agricultural Produce and Marketing Act. This prohibits entry of other agencies in the agricultural produce markets. A number of other acts put restrictions on procurement, processing and marketing of agricultural produce. All these regulations have been retarding the growth of the agro-processing industry in the state, in which U.P. has a considerable comparative advantage.

The burden of regulatory mechanisms and restrictive labour laws discourages new investment while raising the operating costs of the existing units (Basu, 2006). A large numbers of clearances have to be obtained for starting a new business. Many of the clearances need to be renewed at regular intervals. Obtaining clearances is time consuming and cumbersome, and creates avenues for rent seeking. Industrial units have to comply with a large number of labour laws, which adds to their compliance costs and proves bothersome, especially for the small scale units (Singh et al., 2004). Similarly, restrictions on contract labour poses a problem for the entrepreneurs to adjust to changing demand conditions in the market.

Over the past decade or so, the state government has come out with policy declarations on all major sectors of the economy including power, irrigation, transport, tourism, industry, agriculture, etc. These policy declarations are well intentioned and well prepared documents. However, a large gap remains between policy declarations and its follow up, causing dismay and frustration in the minds of the stakeholders. Lack of stability in policy sends conflicting signals to the investors.

(c) *Governance Issues*

There has been a marked decline in the quality of governance over the years (World Bank, 2002; UPHDR, 2003). Various surveys put U.P. at the bottom of the states, in terms of law and order, while it ranks at the top in terms of the corruption index. A survey of entrepreneurs put the poor law and order situation and corruption along with poor infrastructure as the main bottlenecks for industrial growth. The perception about corruption and law and order, impede the flow of investment into the state (Basu, 2006).

The political instability in the state has, among other things, led to a decline in the quality of governance. One dimension of this decline is the growing nexus between the political masters and some sections of the bureaucracy. The threat of frequent transfers and suspensions has demoralized the bureaucracy, and undermined its initiatives in taking policy decisions in an objective and impartial manner. Short tenures have adversely affected the efficiency of the civil servants.

The process of economic reforms in the state is slow and halting. The continuation of controls and regulations, coupled with a lack of transparency, leaves scope for rent seeking by the decision makers.

While government expenditure has increased by leaps and bounds, its impact on the outcomes is minimal. The systems of monitoring and controls have weakened, with the result that there are widespread leakages in various government programs, as several evaluation studies and reports of the CAG have revealed.

U.P. is suffering from the virus of institutional decay. The institutions, which once enjoyed repute as well performing organizations, have in most cases, become dysfunctional and sick. The quality of public services like education and health has declined, due to factors like lack of funds, vacant positions, absenteeism among employees, and poor supervision.

The process of decentralization in the state has been slow and halting, even though the local bodies are in place and three rounds of elections for the local bodies have been held since the 73rd and the 74th Constitutional Amendment Acts in 1994. Some progress in financial devolution has taken place, but the progress, with respect to the transfer of functions and functionaries to the local bodies, has been rather unsatisfactory. Very few functions have been transferred to the Panchayti Raj Institutions (PRIs). The primary education and primary health care system have not been brought under the control of the PRIs, nor a separate cadre of local bodies has been created. The urban local bodies remain under the effective control of the state government. Efforts towards empowerment and capacity building of the local bodies have remained weak and halting. The PRIs are functioning basically as agencies of the government, to implement schemes and programmes devised from above, rather than acting as genuine institutions of local self government, as envisaged in the Constitution. They have yet to be genuinely empowered.

(d) *Absence of Development Oriented Leadership*

The quality of top leadership has been a critical factor in all the states, which have shown dynamism and faster growth. Uttar Pradesh has suffered for lack of a development oriented and dynamic leadership, with a few notable exceptions. There have been few leaders with a vision for development, and a firm commitment to the same.

During the first four decades after independence, when the Congress party was in power, the state leadership remained dwarfed by the national leadership. During the last two decades, the state has been passing through a process of political and social churning, resulting in communal strife, social tensions and political instability. Political mobilisation has also been along caste and communal lines, rather than on economic and social issues, leading to the emergence of parties like the BJP, SP and BSP (Sudha Pai, 2007). These political changes go little beyond the politics of identity, and are yet to show any visible impact on the actual socio-economic conditions of the weaker sections (Mehrotra, 2006). Power for the sake of power has become the prime objective of the politicians and political parties. Under these circumstances, development has taken a back seat.

As Dreze and Gazdar (2005) have noted in their perceptive article on education in Uttar Pradesh:

> Human deprivation and social inequality did not figure as important political concerns at all. In this regard, political developments in Uttar Pradesh differed markedly from, say, West Bengal, where class organizations have been important early on, and also from Maharashtra and the south Indian states, where 'low-caste' organizations have played an important role in shaping political life.

Finally, the weak role of the civil society in the state, may be stressed as an important cause of the low growth of U.P. The intelligentsia in the state, drawn mainly from the upper castes, has not shown the kind of concerns for social and developmental issues, which was expected from them. They have little sympathy for the teeming millions of the downtrodden, illiterate and poor masses, belonging to the backward and scheduled castes. Academia in the state have also not raised the issue of social problems and lack of development in the state in a forceful manner. NGOs and the civil society movements have been relatively weak in the state, though there have been some positive developments in this direction in recent years.

The Way Forward

Uttar Pradesh is faced with the daunting challenge of speeding up its development to keep pace with the high rate of growth of the rest of the economy, and to deal with the problems of poverty, illiteracy and poor health of the people. Development has, therefore, to be put on the central agenda of the government, political parties, intelligentsia and civil society at large. The recently released report of the Planning

Commission on the *Roadmap for Rapid Economic Development of U.P.* (Planning Commission, 2008) has come out with detailed suggestions for the measures required to speed up economic development of the state. The outer would like to underline a few suggestions in this regard.

Investment has to be substantially augmented to push up the rate of growth of the state economy. While the need of public investment in the economic and social infrastructure is clearly there, the bulk of investment has to come from the private sector. Hence, the first priority of the state should be to create a suitable investment climate, and the bottlenecks faced by the industry have to be removed.

Removal of the infrastructure gap deserves the highest priority. The most critical requirement at present is improvement in the power situation, without which one cannot expect high industrial and agricultural growth. Improvement of the road network, and better connectivity of villages are needed to exploit the growth potential of the state, particularly of rural areas. The initiatives that the state government has taken to promote investment in infrastructure through public private participation are a welcome step.

Equally important, is to step up an attractive and conducive policy environment to attract investment in the state. The distortionary economic policies, affecting working of the land, labour and product market, have to be set right to make the industry become competitive. The process of economic reforms and deregulation has to be speeded up. Procedures have to be streamlined and simplified and the regulatory burden eased. The system of automatic and time bound clearances through web enabled systems has to be put in place, as some other states have done. Discretionary controls have to be minimised, to reduce opportunities for rent seeking.

Wide ranging governance reforms have to be undertaken with a view to improving the law and order situation, to minimise corruption, improve the functioning of government organisations. Transparency, accountability and responsiveness of the administration are the hallmarks of good governance. Management of critical infrastructure like power, roads and irrigation has to be professionalised. Excessive state control of organisations has to be eased, and operational autonomy has to be provided to the organisations within set parameters by the state, so that they are able to take decisions based on economic, rather than political considerations. The quality of delivery of public services has to be improved, to the cutting edge levels. The issues of shortage of staff and their training have to be addressed on a priority basis.

The process of decentralisation has to be speeded up, by empowering the local bodies and transferring functions earmarked for them in the Constitution, along with the funds and functionaries to enable them to discharge their constitutional responsibility. Measures for capacity building of the local bodies has to be carried out in right earnest. Only an empowered decentralised polity would be able to bring the administration closer to the people, improve the functioning of the grass roots level institutions, and make them responsive to peoples' needs.

The point to be stressed is that the issue of development has to go beyond the narrow objectives of faster economic growth. The development agenda in U.P. has to face the challenges of human development, and the existing caste and communal and gender divides. The poor status of human development in the state is an important constraint in rapid economic development. One cannot conceive of an economically developed U.P., if a large segment of its population remains illiterate, malnourished and economically deprived. Healthy and educated people are a prerequisite of rapid economic development of an economy, as much as higher incomes are needed to improve the levels of human development of the people. The experience of southern states, notably Kerala and Tamil Nadu holds important lessons in this regard.

The reforms agenda discussed earlier is indeed a tall order and would require a visionary leadership and determined efforts. The leadership and the people of the state have to rise to take up this challenge, if U.P. has to come out of its present political, social and economic morass, rather than continue to be labelled as an eternally sick state, which is pulling down the country's progress. It would be futile to hope that the expected changes would come on there own from the present political set up. Civil society has to exert strong pressures to nudge the system to do what is expected from it. Academia has a special responsibility in this regard. Let us hope that it comes forward to take up the challenge which history has put on its shoulders.

Note

1. This Chapter is based on the revised and updated version of the special lecture that the author delivered during the Convocation Week of Lucknow University, Lucknow.

References

________ (2001). Uttar Pradesh Development Report 2000, New Royal Book Co., Lucknow.

________ (2007). "The Economy of Uttar Pradesh since the 1990s: Economic Stagnation and Fiscal Crisis," in Pai, Sudha (ed.) (2007), *Political Process in Uttar Pradesh: Identity, Economic Reforms and Governance,* Pearson Longmans, New Delhi.

Basu, Priya (2006). *Unleashing the Industrial Growth Potential of Uttar Pradesh,* World Bank, New Delhi.

Department of Planning, Government of U.P. (2007). Uttar Pradesh Human Development Report 2003, Lucknow.

Dreze, Jean and Haris, Gazdar (1996). "Uttar Pradesh: The Burden of Inertia", in Dreze, Jean and Amartya Sen (1996), *Indian Development: Selected Regional Perspectives,* Oxford University Press, New Delhi, 1996.

Mehrotra, Santosh (2006). "Well Being and Caste in U.P.", *Economic and Political Weekly,* Vol. 41, No. 40, Oct. 7–Oct. 13.

Mohanty (2004). State Infrastructure Index, Report Prepared for Twelfth Finance Commission, New Delhi.

Pai, Sudha (ed.) (2007). *Political Process in Uttar Pradesh: Identity, Economic Reforms and Governance,* Pearson Longmans, New Delhi.

Planning Commission (2008). Report of the Study Group for Preparation of Roadmap for Rapid Development of Uttar Pradesh, New Delhi.

Singh, Ajit Kumar (2000). "Uttar Pradesh Economy under the Plans: Low Growth and Structural Stagnation", *Man and Development,* June, Chandigarh.

Singh, Ajit Kumar, Joshi, A. and Mehta, G.S. (2004). Report on Survey of Micro and Small Enterprises in Uttar Pradesh, India, Giri Institute of Development Studies, Lucknow (Mimeo).

Singh, Ajit Kumar, Mohd. Muzammil and Sanatan Nayak (2005). Economic Growth and Human Development Linkages in Uttar Pradesh, Working Paper No. 190, Giri Institute of Development Studies, Lucknow.

World Bank (2002). *Poverty in India: The Challenge of Uttar Pradesh, Poverty Reduction and Economic Management Sector Unit,* World Bank, Washington D.C.

CHAPTER 5

A Comparative Study of the Economic Growth of U.P. during 1985–86 to 2009–10

Shri Prakash, Amit Sharma and Anshu Goel

Era of Rapid Growth and Regional Inequalities of Development

The post Second World War era is characterised by unprecedented technological developments, rapid economic growth, rapid rise in standards of living in almost all the countries of the world, and international economic integration, resulting in extremely high inter-dependencies among national economies. The world economy has developed much more rapidly during this period than ever before. All the countries of the world, irrespective of their political systems and economic or organisational structures have developed more rapidly than before, during the post Second World War period, though the growth rates have varied between the countries and the years. *These changes have, however, failed to bridge the gap between the per capita incomes and living standards of the developed and developing economies of the world. Despite rapid growth of national economies, the world economy is still characterised by highly marked economic inequalities and the trend towards divergences rather than convergences of the rates of growth of income and consumption across the globe remain in operation.* In this respect, *the current state of world economy is not much different from what Gunnar Myrdal highlighted in the early 1950s. Economic growth and development continue to be spotty in time, and uneven in space.*

These above features of growth are not confined to the international scenario alone. Temporal and geographical s*pread of growth of the national economies continues to be marked by the same traits of* spottiness in time, and unevenness over space. High growth years are invariably, followed by low or no growth years, while a few regions/states grow faster than even the national economy, and the rest of the regions/states are left to bring up the rear, or laggard segments of the national economies. The Indian economy, and economies of its states, are no exception to this situation. These results are surprising, in view of the concerted efforts of international agencies of the UN and national governments' attempts to continuously propel national growth on the one hand, and endeavour to spread the momentum of growth over the regions, by regionalising the growth process on the other. In India, state planning boards were established as early as in 1970–71. The machinery to concurrently monitor and evaluate the progress of ongoing plan projects and programmes was also created both at the national and regional levels. Subsequently, further attempts to move the process of growth to the grass roots, resulted in empowering the District Collector to nurture the development process at the district level, while Panchayats were empowered to sustain the growth process in the villages.

Though agencies of the United Nations such as the IMF, World Bank, UNIDO, UNICEF, UNESCO, FAO, WHO in collaboration with national governments, have been paying special attention for the mitigation of poverty, investment in health, education, nutrition, sanitation, potable water supply, and food, yet the problems of illiteracy, high birth and high infant mortality rates, malnutrition, filthy living conditions, verging almost on subhuman living, have persisted across the globe. India and several of its states, including U.P., have their own share of such problems.

It may be noted that the development of the region/state, and the prosperity of the people are directly related; but the poverty of the people, and development of their state are inversely related. Conversely, underdevelopment of the state, and the poverty of the people, are directly related (Prakash-Mohapatra, 1980). This holds true for U.P. also.

The question of development of laggardly states and poverty of people living in such states remain among the basic concerns of analysts and policy makers. The question as to why does U.P. continue to record low growth of SDP/per capita SDP, and accounts for the largest share of illiterates and the poor of the country, has acquired greater importance than ever before. The fact that India has achieved the status of the second fastest growing nation of the world, and states such as Punjab, Haryana, Karnataka, Gujarat, Maharashtra, and Tamil Nadu, which were much less developed than U.P. in pre-independence era, makes continued low economic growth of U.P. a painful realization, not only for the people of U.P. but for the country as a whole. *The question becomes even more edgy, if we consider the fact that on the eve of independence, and at the time of reorganization of states, U.P. was among the most developed states of the country.*

Research Questions

The following research questions have been examined in this study. Is U.P. the only state which lags behind in the development race? The answer is a definite no. The following are other important questions: 'Is U.P. the poorest and the least developed state of India?, A related question is, where does U.P. stand in the comity of Indian states in development? Answers to these questions will be more relevant in the historical context of the development of the Indian economy and its states with special reference to U.P. A look at the historical background may be helpful in identifying the factors of underdevelopment of U.P., and analysing their influence on growth.

Development of U.P. in the Historical Context

Currently, U.P. has the third largest number of universities, and ranks first in the number of colleges. U.P. also has the largest number of enrolments in institutions of higher education. However, U.P. also accounts for one sixth of the total population of India. Thus, both population size and size of higher education, indexed by the number of institutions and enrolments, the twin source of human resource formation, abound in U.P. Still, U.P. ranks at almost the bottom of the pyramid in the human development index, and is among the most illiterate states of India. This is paradoxical. On the eve of independence and advent of the planning era in 1951, per capita income of U.P. was almost on par with the per capita income of India. But per capita SDP of U.P. was only one fifth that of India in 1985–86, and in 2002, it fell further down to one sixth of per capita income of India. However, its income further fell down to one tenth of income of India in 2010. The decrease in relative per capita income of U.P. is accounted for by the more rapid growth of population relative to India, and slower and lower growth of the economy of the U.P. than that of the Indian economy. It is but natural that U.P. is counted among BIMARU states of India. It was not so in the past.

Agra was the capital of Mughal India, while Varanasi, Lucknow and Rampur have also been regional capitals. Aligarh and Meerut were traditional places for producing iron based goods, like locks, knives, scissors, sport goods, and Kanpur and Agra have been famous for leather goods while Jalesar was known for moulding and Moradabad for brass based utensils. Lucknow specialised in chittan work and Varanasi in zari and saris. Kannauj was famous for itra-fulel (perfumes). Bareilly has been known for wood and cane products. Besides, the state has pilgrimage centers like Varanasi, Allahabad, Haridwar (now in Uttarakhand), while Garmukteshwar, Anoopshahr, Brijghat are also small centres of pilgrimage. These places still attract a lot of tourists (pilgrims). Agra continues to be an international tourist center. All these factors gave a huge advantage in development with the early historical start. U.P. (West) has also been the cradle of the green revolution, along with Punjab and Haryana. U.P. also led the country in land reforms, as far as abolition of the *Zamindari* (landlordism) system and the movement to consolidate holdings is concerned. U.P. is well endowed with natural resources, especially irrigation water, since U.P. is located in the Yamuna-Ganges plains. Nearly one fourth area of the state is covered by the Ganges canal. It has also other big rivers running through its length and breadth. Still, the per hectare yield of crops is lower than that of Punjab.

Several religious and social reform movements also emanated from U.P. If Kabir and Tulsidas were the embodiment of enlightened leadership in religious reforms, Dayanand Sarswati waged the battle against caste based social divisions, religions orthodoxy, and rigid Hindu *Karmkand* or rituals. The Arya Samaj movement encompassed reforms of all rituals and ceremonies from birth to death and performance of marriage ceremonies. The Arya Samaj movement also helped in the renaissance of modern education by establishing a wide spread network of DAV schools and colleges. Arya Samaj mandirs/ temples even today stand for social reforms. Even today, U.P. has a large number of followers of Arya-Samaj (Aryan society).

Not only this, U.P. also led the country in individual initiatives and enterprise in higher education. Establishment of BHU and AMU as lighthouses of modern university education, and Jat, Rajput, Jain, Vaishya, Hindu and Muslim colleges and schools across the length and breadth of U.P. in the pre-independence era heralded the spread of modern western education. Education embodied the battle against social ills, blind faith and rigid customs by spreading the message of rational thought and broad perspectives. Education even otherwise is treated as an agent of social and economic change (Prakash, S., 1977). But, the majority of the people are paradoxically still trapped in old customs, fads and blind faith.

Despite being among one of the cradles of the green revolution, per hectare crop yields of U.P. are much lower than that of Punjab. As two thirds of the workforce is engaged in agriculture, which accounts for about one third of the State Domestic Product (SDP) of U.P., productivity of per unit human capital is even lower than the yield rate per hectare. The reason is that the average size of holdings in U.P. is much lower than that of Punjab. Most of the farm holdings are small, and even marginal, which do not yield sufficient income to the farmers for investment. Besides, unlike Punjab and Rajasthan, which derived huge benefits from public investment in multi-purpose the Bhakra-Nangal dam and Indra Gandhi canal and Bihar/Jharkhand, M.P./Chhattisgarh, and Orissa, which received huge public investment per capita in large public enterprises like steel plants at Bhilai, the heavy electricals plant, Ranchi, steel plant at Rourkela, etc. It has the largest share of M.P.s in the Loksabha, and has provided many prime ministers to the country. But, both the national and state leadership, have failed the state, in so far as economic development is concerned.

U.P. has, however, lagged behind not only India, but also most other states in development, in spite of comparative resource advantages. *The slow development or relative under-development of U.P. is naturally baffling. A straight forward answer to U.P.'s relative backwardness is inefficient and underutilization of available resources. Low and slow development of U.P. may also be associated with the lack of political will and good governance. Though, U.P. boasts of highly competent civil servants and lively political leadership, yet they fail to deliver development as the end product.*

This study is a modest attempt to delineate the current growth status of U.P. in relation to India, and its seven most developed states.

Empirical Analysis

Analysis of empirical evidence follows a logical sequence.

U.P.'s Changing Percentage Share in the Indian GNP (Current Prices)

The level and growth of income of the national and regional economies is considered to be a very robust and broad index of economic growth, though per capita income is a relatively more reliable indicator of growth. In view of this, we have considered both gross and per capita income/SDP of U.P. and its growth relative to the growth of GNP and Per Capita GNP of India. *The focus on SDP/GNP is not to deny the fact that U.P. continues to lag behind other states in social and economic infrastructure such as consumption of energy per capita, industrialization, intra-state network of roads, especially rural roads, FDI/FII, health, education, high birth and high infant mortality rates, high incidence of poverty and illiteracy, and discrimination against women.* Part of this paradox of high levels development of higher education, and high backward bending mindset of the people and illiteracy, may probably be explained by the disproportionately large share of SC/STs and minorities in the total population, who happen to account for a dominant share among the poor, and low levels of health and nutrition, and illiterates in the state. Religious orthodoxy and bias against the *dalits* seem to be pulling the state down the development ladder. Widespread modern basic education and inculcation of rational thought hold the keys to this riddle. Special policy focus is needed to facilitate access of SC/STs and minorities to modern education.

The following table illustrative on some of the facets of development of U.P relative to that of India (Table 1).

Table 1: Year-wise Share of SDP of U.P. in GNP of India (Percentage)

Year	*1980–81*	*1982–83*	*1983–84*	*1984–85*	*1985–86*	*1986–87*	*1987–88*	*1988–89*
% share of SDP in GNP of India	2.18	N.A.	N.A.	2.77	3.05	3.23	3.50	3.77
Year	1989–90	1990–91	1991–92	1992–93	1993–94	1994–95	1995–96	1996–97
% share of SDP in GNP of India	4.03	4.54	5.20	5.37	5.87	0.47	6.72	7.51
Year	1997–98	1998–99	1999–00	2000–01	2001–02	2002–03	2003–04	2004–05
% share of SDP in GNP of India	7.70	7.99	8.14	8.18	8.03	8.42	8.46	6.96
Year	2004–05	2005–06	2006–07	2007–2008	2008–09	2009–10		
% share of SDP in GNP of India	6.96	7.50	7.68	7.81	8.70	9.59		

The percentage share of SDP (State Domestic Product) of U.P. in GNP (Gross National Product) of India has consistently increased from 1980–81 to 2003–04. The share of U.P.'s SDP in the GNP of India increased from 2.18 per cent in 1980–81 to 8.46 per cent of GNP in 2003–04, a 3.9 fold increase, or an increase of 6.32 percentage points from the base year during a period of 24 years. This amounts to a measly 0.263 percentage points increase per annum. However, it implies that the SDP of U.P. has increased a bit more rapidly than the GNP of India till 2003–04. It also means that the process of catching up has been in operation during this period, though the pace of bridging the gap has been extremely low and slow.

This trend was, however, reversed in 2004–05, when the share of U.P.'s SDP in GNP declined from 8.46 per cent in 2003–04 to 6.06 per cent in 2004–05. It is a decline of 1.5 percentage points in one single year. This decline neutralized the earlier gains to some extent. This may partly be explained by the fact that the Indian economy grew very rapidly from 2003–04 to 2007–08, but before that the Indian economy was growing at a slower pace. The growth of the Indian economy was adversely affected in 2008–09 by the world economic slowdown.

U.P.'s SDP share started rising again in 2005–06, and the trend continued right up to 2009–10, when the share of U.P.'s SDP in GNP rose to 9.59 per cent. Thus, U.P. raised its SDP's share in GNP by 0.239 percentage points per annum, since the base year. But U.P.'s share in GNP increased by 0.376 percentage points per annum during the last seven years, of *rapid growth of the Indian economy notwithstanding*. Thus, U.P. has raised the pace of its growth during this period substantially.

But, has the growth rate been increased significantly? One factor ANOVA is used to evaluate the significance of the inter-temporal changes in the growth rate of SDP of U.P. The results are as follows.

Table 2: One Factor ANOVA of Growth of SDP of U.P.

Source of Variations	*SS*	*Df*	*MS*	*F*	*P-value*	*F crit*
Between Groups	139.66	26	5.3714	65535	#NUM!	#NUM!
Within Groups	0	0	65535			
Total	139.66	26				

The results of the table show that the inter-temporal changes in the SDP of U.P. are highly significant statistically. So the rates of growth of SDP are significantly different from zero statistically. But, the significance of the difference of year on year U.P.'s share in GNP indicates an instable nature of growth and inter-temporal fluctuations.

Growth of Share of SDP of U.P. in the GNP

An interesting question is, whether the pace of growth of SDP of U.P. has been in sync with the pace of growth of GNP of India, and the pace of growth of SDP of the developed states of India. The answer is furnished by the analysis that follows.

Share of Developed States' SDP in Comparison to Share of SDP of U.P. in the Indian GNP

It will be interesting to compare the changes in the share of SDP of U.P. with the shares in the GNP of the relatively more developed states than U.P., during the same period.

U.P. accounts for one sixth of India's population, but accounts for slightly less than one tenth of India's GNP. It implies that the growth of SDP and per capita SDP in U.P. has been lower and slower than that of India. However, 2007–08 was the year in which the worldwide economic slow-down occurred and the growth of the Indian economy also slowed down substantially during the period of the economic crisis, though the impact on the growth of the Indian economy was delayed and much lower than that experienced by the developed economies (Prakash, Shri and Panigrahi, Ritisnigdha, 2010). It may be noted that the opening up of the Indian economy has led to a greater integration of the Indian into the world economy. This is evident from the fact that foreign trade now accounts for 53 per cent GNP of India. During the planning era, foreign trade accounted for hardly 2 per cent of India's GNP. U.P. is, however, not so much integrated into the world economy as the Indian economy. This may also be a factor for U.P.'s slower growth, compared to the developed states. The current European financial crisis has also affected the growth of the Indian economy. *It may be noted that such states as U.P., which are not integrated in the world economy, remain immune to international crises, whereas states like Gujarat, Tamil Nadu, Karnataka and others, which are more exposed to international influences, are directly affected by the buoyancy or sluggishness of the international economy.*

Table 3: Share of Developed States' SDP in GNP Relative to U.P. (Ratio)

(₹ crore)

Year	*U.P.*	*Gujrat*	*Haryana*	*Karnataka*	*Maharashtra*	*Punjab*	*Tamil Nadu*
1980–1981	2.182829921	1.025830362	0.472333737	0.874253605	2.354346888	0.693078099	1.124440934
1984–1985	2.769029192	1.513222842	0.610978041	1.257093433	2.938795368	0.94999556	1.548102776
1985–1986	3.047357635	1.48692869	0.714990717	1.275075013	3.269093699	1.031103579	1.690135278
1986–1987	3.226930062	1.644801926	0.719978485	1.403347894	3.366257806	1.086898572	1.813274759
1987–1988	3.495563601	1.56733269	0.773402478	1.553915121	3.81299807	1.240379775	2.083278382
1988–1989	3.771770756	2.013093512	0.930702103	1.652087581	4.162947512	1.304444507	2.132106456
1989–1990	4.034357311	2.057070676	0.978166128	1.788598851	4.776319388	1.481071211	2.354662202
1990–1991	4.540345829	2.183771755	1.14536562	1.965919074	5.355279696	1.566834692	2.625377683
1991–1992	5.196501669	2.435103778	1.344254147	2.473811941	5.898422019	1.836466785	3.020068197
1992–1993	5.368458869	2.824997371	1.43633241	2.551785777	6.613946234	1.971452105	3.086554975
1993–1994	5.869454592	3.521590011	1.607056419	3.060043275	8.420621491	2.239718008	4.273154909
1994–1995	0.471321955	4.127176094	1.611541792	0.739005467	9.423990785	2.381714822	5.081673006
1985–1996	6.723870752	4.472582827	1.597164717	3.62437433	10.19545454	2.478988583	5.65940821
1985–1997	7.514443121	4.970698322	2.100299784	3.891099339	10.63269646	2.620734572	5.301372415
1997–1998	7.699155769	4.952199539	2.173325061	4.150461853	11.05794252	2.762338518	5.940703842
1988–1999	7.991373147	5.395387397	2.304378909	4.73131199	11.19592447	2.980469431	6.351670401
1999–2000	8.139601851	5.21033892	2.423473853	4.782129012	12.2339074	3.063473763	6.355055124
2000–2001	8.180585741	7.75362905	2.628900038	5.07016499	12.26444494	3.194737096	6.839233758
2001–2002	8.033631298	5.176220648	2.727011519	4.928636438	12.04204732	3.227301665	6.497728259
2002–2003	8.42486206	5.782057792	2.872067293	5.192327298	13.12216838	3.225097874	6.756634961
2003–04	8.46169627	6.396754261	2.964246584	5.257396093	13.18093478	3.28077783	6.758491289
2004–05	6.959742483	5.171630968	2.497211851	4.482672446	11.13737157	2.679132437	5.668970994
2005–2006	7.49872418	5.582362224	3.009324633	5.060297972	11.64077248	3.015703732	6.202652219
2006–2007	7.684159688	5.887494288	3.364771231	4.941105546	12.35785365	3.095125797	6.500671851

So, an interesting question is, how does U.P. compare with the developed states of India? The figures in earlier table represent year on year changes, which may not capture the long term trends. They may be concealed or blurred in temporal fluctuations of the year on year growth rates. The growth of per capita SDP, rather than SDP, will show the true picture of development. Growth of per capita SDP is net of population growth.

We first consider the share of SDP of U.P. in the GNP, in comparison to the shares of SDP of six developed states of India during the same period. This will also reflect the status of the relative development U.P. A comparison of the share of U.P.s SDP in the GNP with the shares of the developed states' SDP in the Indian GNP, will highlight the relative position of the economic growth of U.P. in the comity of Indian states. The following table highlights the shares of the developed states' SDP in the Indian GNP relative to that of U.P.

Percentage shares of developed states' SDP in the GNP of India and developed states SDP relative to U.P.'s SDP share in NNP temporal changes in the SDP of U.P. are highly significant statistically.

A perusal of the this table reveals that (i) share of SDP of Gujarat relative to that of U.P. increased from 1.026 in 1981 to 5.89 in 2006–07. The share of SDP of Haryana, which was less than half that of U.P. in 1980–81, rose to 3.36 times of U.P. in 2006–07. Share of SDP of Karnataka, which was about 0.87 of U.P.'s share in 1980–81, which was 13 per cent less than that of U.P., has increased to 4.94 times that of U.P. in 2006–07. As against this, the share of SDP of Maharashtra was 2.35 in the base year, and has risen to 12.36 times that of U.P. the share of SDP of Punjab was hardly 0.69 relative to that of U.P. in 1980–81, thus it was 31 per cent lower than that of U.P.; but has increased to 3.1 times in 2006–07. Share of Tamil Nadu's SDP relative to U.P. was about 1.12 but has increased to 6.50 relative to that of U.P. in 2006–07. Gujarat, Maharashtra and Tamil Nadu are the fastest growing states of India and U.P. compares very poorly with the growth of these three states. Even moderately growing states like Punjab, Haryana and Karnataka, which compared poorly with U.P. in the base year, have left U.P. behind in the course of development. It is obvious that U.P. compares very poorly with all these states in the pace of growth. So it is not surprising that U.P. is called a sick state of India, which also pulls down the growth of the Indian economy.

The statistical significance of inter-temporal changes in the shares of SDP of states is evaluated by two factors ANOVA. The results are as in Table 4.

This table shows that the shares of SDP of developed states in the GNP relative to that of U.P. have varied significantly, both between the years, and among the states. So, these differentials are significant with respect to both time and space. These results confirm that U.P. lags significantly behind the developed states of India in economic growth. This thesis is further evaluated by more evidence.

Table 4: Two Factors ANOVA of Share of SDP of U.P. Relative to Shares of the Developed States ANOVA of States' Share of SDP in the NNP

Source of Variation	*SS*	*Df*	*MS*	*F*	*P-value*	*F crit*
Rows	565.6711	23	24.5944	19.08966	3.13E-32	1.607836
Columns	737.8162	6	122.9694	95.44626	1.25E-46	2.164893
Error	177.794	138	1.288362			
Total	1481.281	167				

Year on Year Growth Rates of SDP of States

A related question is as to when did the growth of SDP in U.P. begin lagging behind the growth of SDP in these states during all the years covered by the study? The periodic emergence of recession in the world and the Indian economy, also makes this question important. For answering this question, year on year growth rates of SDP are considered. Year on year growth rates of SDP also highlight the relative growth performance of U.P. during all these years separately. The following table depicts the year on year growth rates of SDP of selected states, and rates of growth of the Indian GNP.

Year on year growth rates, shown in the table, slow a great deal of variation both between the years and between the states. The following important features of year on year growth may be inferred from the table:

1. Annual growth rates of SDP of all states fluctuated between the years a great deal; these fluctuations almost verge on volatility;
2. On the whole, relative to the base year growth rate, the rates of growth of SDP of U.P. increased up to 1993–94, but thereafter, there is consistent decline, if the first and second parts of the time series are taken as a whole. Such fluctuating growth rates are not characteristic of a planned economy;
3. Gujarat recorded negative growth in two years, while U.P. and Karnataka recorded negative growth rate only in one year. No other state shows negative growth in any of the years covered by the study. So, U.P. has gone down compared to other states in this year;
4. An interesting point is that there is no state in this group whose year on year growth rate has been either greater or lower than the growth rate of SDP of U.P. consistently, in all the years;

Table 5: Year on Year/Short Run Growth Rates of SDP

S. No.	*Years*	*Gujarat*	*Haryana*	*Karnataka*	*Maharashtra*	*Punjab*	*Tamil Nadu*	*Uttar Pradesh*
1.	1985–1986	2.3816	21.9296	5.6824	15.9024	13.0877	13.7512	14.6649
2.	1986–1987	15.3360	4.9931	14.7549	7.3647	9.9078	11.8623	10.4098
3.	1987–1988	-1.5559	10.9758	14.3943	17.0204	17.8984	18.6932	11.9103
4.	1988–1989	41.0917	32.1916	16.7897	19.9314	15.5233	12.4243	18.5296
5.	1989–1990	8.4375	11.5311	14.8878	21.7549	20.4882	17.1963	13.5072
6.	1990–1991	11.5065	22.9910	15.4502	17.7689	11.1192	17.1130	18.2106
7.	1991–1992	13.0511	18.9877	27.5750	11.6653	18.8296	16.6245	16.0344
8.	1992–1993	22.3112	12.6521	8.7535	18.2198	13.1797	7.7514	8.9191
9.	1993–1994	32.0099	18.4846	26.9899	34.8247	20.3076	46.6089	15.7801
10.	1994–1995	24.7650	6.7552	-74.2902	19.1432	13.2075	26.6009	-91.4513
11.	1995–1996	16.2637	6.3278	426.1674	16.0674	11.6666	19.4821	30.5244
12.	1996–1997	20.1617	42.1800	16.0770	12.7571	14.3024	1.2801	20.8327
13.	1997–1998	4.1559	8.1799	11.5135	8.7262	10.1938	17.1529	7.1148
14.	1998–1999	16.2348	13.1204	21.6177	8.0183	15.1117	14.0675	10.7363
15.	1999–2000	2.7503	11.8984	7.5423	16.2639	9.3627	6.4562	8.3731
16.	2000–2001	54.7594	12.8116	10.2602	4.2559	8.4524	11.9196	4.5200
17.	2001–2002	-9.2328	9.9606	3.0454	4.0822	7.0850	0.7113	4.1002
18.	2002–2003	16.1640	9.5241	9.5563	13.3202	3.9215	8.1361	9.0568
19.	2003–2004	20.0486	11.9952	9.8723	8.9984	10.3859	8.5423	8.9869
20.	2004–2005	8.2157	12.7622	14.1271	13.0991	9.3050	12.2734	10.0926
21.	2005–2006	18.1981	31.9574	23.6116	14.4509	23.2578	19.8100	17.9816
22.	2006–2007	15.4989	22.4480	6.9334	16.2590	#REF!	14.7747	12.2210

5. The growth rates have not been uniform either in all the years, or in all states, in any year. So the growth rates seem to vary between the years and states in all the years;
6. Growth rates of SDP of U.P. also declined consistently from 1998–99 till 2003–04; Though the trend was reversed in 2004–05, yet the state did not record the rate of growth till the end, which could equal the base year rate;
7. Incidentally, growth rates of GNP also show fluctuations. But, fluctuations of growth rates of GNP of India have been smoother. The range of variations of growth of SDP of U.P. is from .486 to 41.7. Thus, the range of growth of SDP of U.P. is 41 per cent. As against this, the rates of growth of GNP of India varied from1.38 to 9.84, the variations being in the range of 7.47. The range is being defined as the magnitude of variation: Maximum-Minimum.

Volatility of Growth

Such fluctuation of growth rates in a narrow band, does not imply that the growth of GNP has been volatile. If we examine the desired range of variations and coefficient of stability, it may be inferred that the growth rate of GNP has been stable, since the variations lie in the range of 19.4575 to 4.74829. Thus the coefficient of stability is 14.709. It is obvious that the range of variations of India's growth rate satisfies the stability condition: But the actual range of variations of growth of SDP lie much beyond the stability, the range of U.P. is from 27.5119 to 6.27139 on the same criterion. Compared to U.P., the year on year growth rate of GNP of India has been stable. So far the rising trend has been maintained, by and large, throughout the period of study.

For an overall view and evaluation of statistical significance of the differences in the growth rates between the years and the states, two factors ANOVA without replication is used. Results are as follows:

Table 6: Two Factors ANOVA of Year on Year Growth Rates

ANOVA						
Source of Variation	*SS*	*Df*	*MS*	*F*	*P-value*	*F crit*
Rows	467377	20	23368.87	1.69201115	0.0436	1.6586801
Columns	63667.8	6	10611.3	0.76830542	0.5963	2.1750063
Error	1657356	120	13811.3			
Total	2188401	146				

These results show that the year on year annual rates of growth of SDP differ significantly between the years. The rates, however, do not differ significantly between the seven states.

These results do not furnish any evidence to show that the annual rates of growth of SDP of U.P. have been consistently lower and slower than the rates of growth of SDP of all developed states of India. However, the significant variations of annual rates of growth between the years implies that all these states, including U.P., are *not able to maintain consistency* in growth from one year to another year. Occurrences like inadequate rainfall or recession, or lower or higher investment in different years seem to account *for the significant variations* of annual growth rates between the years.

The slowing of growth of U.P. from 1998–99 onwards has increased the developmental differences between U.P. and India on the one hand, and differences of growth of U.P. and growth of most developed states of India on the other. This is an issue for planners and policy makers to address, otherwise regional development inequality will be further accentuated.

In 23 years covered by the data, on the whole, U.P has lagged behind Gujarat except in four years only (1985–86, 1990–91, 1995–96, 1999–2000). The minimum growth performance of U.P. relative to that of Gujarat has been 9 per cent, while the maximum has been seven times more in 1985–86 than that of Gujarat. Year on year fluctuations are affected partly by random factors and partly by international and other exogenous factors. *But long run growth is largely affected by systematic factors.*

After the adoption of NEP, the Indian economy has been among the big centers of attraction for foreign investors and MNCs. Compared to states such as Gujarat, Karnataka, Andra Pradesh, Maharashtra and Tamil Nadu, the U.P. government did not make much effort to attract foreign capital. Law and order conditions, poor infrastructure, lack of political will and corruption in U.P. drive away even domestic investors from U.P. to other states.

U.P. has lagged behind Haryana except in two years (1989–90, 2004–2005). The minimum growth performance of U.P. relative to that of Haryana is 27 per cent, while the maximum is 1.78 times than that of Haryana in 1986–87 only.

U.P. has also lagged behind Maharashtra except in seven years (1986–87, 1990–91, 1991–92, 1995–96, 1996–97,1998–99 2000–06) The minimum growth performance of U.P. relative to Maharashtra has been 26 per cent, while the maximum has been three times in 1995–96.

U.P. has lagged behind Punjab except in six years (1985–86, 1986–87, 1988–89, 1990–91, 2000–01, 2002–03). The minimum growth performance of U.P. relative to Punjab is 25 per cent and it was 1.36 times in 1990–91.

U.P. has lagged behind Tamil Nadu except in four years (1985–86, 1988–89, 1992–93, 1995–96). The minimum growth performance of U.P. relative to Tamil Nadu is 15 per cent, while its maximum is 2.15 times in 1995–96. It is obvious that U.P. performed far better on the growth front than other states from 1985 to 1986–87.

This empirical evidence reveals that the development performance of U.P. was relatively high when a stable and development oriented government ruled the state. *Good governance is a necessary condition for growth, but it is not a sufficient condition.* If we accept the assumption that growth is a function of good governance, both economic and political, then the growth trend and its revival may be attributed to the ruling party of the states during the period concerned. It shall be relevant for the country as a whole.

But year on year growth is often affected by transitory factors. Such factors lose importance in the long run. Therefore, the long run trend growth rates generally furnish more stable and reliable evidence for drawing firm inferences. This leads to the consideration of long run trend growth rates.

Long Run Growth of SDP of U.P. and Developed States

The earlier results reflect year on year changes in the relative share of SDP of U.P. which furnish only an idea about short term changes. Both cyclical and random factors affect such changes.

In view of the above, we first analyse the long run regression growth rates of seven states both in absolute and relative terms. The rates have been estimated by OLS from the following regression function:

$$\log Y_i = \beta_0 + \beta_1 X$$

Y depicts SDP, i = 1, 2,... 7, 8 shows state and X is time; β_1 measures the annual compound rate of growth. The OLS estimates of the growth rates derived from the above growth curve are reported as follows:

Table 7: Annual Compound Rates of Growth of SDP of States

State/UT	*Gujarat*	*Haryana*	*Karnataka*	*Maharashtra*	*Punjab*	*Tamil Nadu*	*Uttar Pradesh*
RATES	6.071	6.15	5.99	5.95	5.57	6.01	5.07
Relative	1.19810	1.21328	1.18137	1.17504	1.09982	1.18493	1

The table shows that the annual compound rate of growth of U.P. is the lowest among the seven states of India. U.P. has grown at an annual rate of 5.07 per cent whereas the annual rates of growth of all other states vary between 5.57 to 6.2 per cent. SDP of all other states has thus increased at rates ranging from 1.1 to 1.2 times the rate of growth of U.P. All six states other than U.P. listed earlier are considered as not only developed but also relatively more developed states, than most other states, including U.P. U.P. has been left trailing the growth of these states.

The question is whether these absolute and relative rates of growth vary significantly among the seven states. First, we examine the variations of absolute annual growth rates by one factor ANOVA the results of which are as in Table 8.

The calculated value of F is not only very high, but it is also statistically very significant. This indicates that the absolute growth rates have varied significantly among the seven states. The significant degree of divergence between the annual compound rates of growth of these states also suggests that U.P. must have slid down

Table 8: One Factor ANOVA of Absolute Rates of Growth of SDP of States

Source of Variation	*SS*	*Df*	*MS*	*F*	*P-value*	*F crit*
Between Groups	8.8E-05	6	1.4619E-05	65535	#NUM!	#NUM!
Within Groups	0	0	65535			
Total	8.8E-05	6				

substantially in per capita income below these states. This inference needs further evaluation. It is examined next. But these results do not highlight whether the relative rates also differ significantly. This is examined by two factors ANOVA the results of which are as follows. Two factors ANOVA without replication is used and the results are as follows:

Table 9: Two Factors ANOVA of Absolute and Relative Growth Rates of SDP

ANOVA						
Source of Variation	*SS*	*Df*	*MS*	*F*	*P-value*	*F crit*
Rows	4.174198	1	4.174198	1626.747	1.55E-08	5.987378
Columns	0.018858	6	0.003143	1.224885	0.405884	4.283866
Error	0.015396	6	0.002566			
Total	4.208452	13				

These results highlight the fact that (i) as expected, absolute rates of growth differ significantly from the relative rates of growth; and (ii) absolute rates of growth together with relative rates do not vary significantly between the states. This inference is, however, reversed, if we look at the results of one factor ANOVA which have already been discussed earlier.

Growth of Per Capita SDP

Data relating to per capita SDP of U.P. and other states are available only for a limited number of years. The following table shows the per capita SDP of U.P., and per capita SDP of developed states, and per capital GNP of India relative to the per capita SDP of U.P.

A perusal of this table reveals that, unlike the SDP, per capita SDP of all the states has increased consistently over the years during the entire period for which data are available. The following table of two factors ANOVA without replication shows the statistical significance of year on year growth rates of per capita SDP of states.

Table 10: Per Capita SDP of States

S. No.	*States*	*1980–81*	*1990–91*	*1993–94*	*1995–96*	*1996–97*	*1997–98*	*1998–99*	*1999–2000*	*2000–01*
1.	Gujarat	2089	6343	9796	13665	16153	16536	18815	18685	19228
	Gujarat/U.P.	1.49	4.52	6.99	9.75	11.52	11.79	13.42	13.33	13.71
2.	Haryana	2437	7721	11090	14244	16707	17749	19716	21551	23742
	Haryana/U.P.	1.74	5.51	7.91	10.16	11.92	12.66	14.06	15.37	16.93
3.	Karnataka	1644	4975	7838	10217	11670	12566	15420	16654	18041
	Karnataka/U.P.	1.17	3.55	5.59	7.29	8.32	8.96	11.00	11.88	12.87
4.	Maharashtra	2492	7612	12183	16152	17619	18954	20356	22604	23726
	Maharashtra/U.P.	1.78	5.43	8.69	11.52	12.57	13.52	14.52	16.12	16.92
5.	Punjab	2629	8177	12710	15471	17353	18762	21184	23254	25048
	Punjab/U.P.	1.88	5.83	9.07	11.03	12.38	13.38	15.11	16.59	17.87
6.	Tamil Nadu	1666	5541	8943	11866	13327	15404	17613	18623	19889
	Tamil Nadu/U.P.	1.19	3.95	6.38	8.46	9.51	10.99	12.56	13.28	14.19
7.	India (GNP)	132865	507487	780070	1069805	1247628	1388729	1601114	1771094	1902284
	India (GNP)/U.P.	94.77	361.97	556.40	763.06	889.89	990.53	1142.02	1263.26	1356.84
8.	Uttar Pradesh	1402	3937	5050	6299	7501	7779	8633	9323	9721

Table 11: Per Capita SDP of States

ANOVA						
Source of Variation	*SS*	*df*	*MS*	*F*	*P-value*	*F crit*
Rows	1.02844E+1	7	1.4692E+1	34.114059	5.55255E-18	2.178155558
Columns	4.02421E+1	8	503026448	1.1679975	0.334593739	2.108688484
Error	2.41178E+1	56	430674229			
Total	1.30986E+1	71				

The table reveals that (i) the rates of growth of per capita SDP of states differ significantly between the states; and (ii) the annual growth rates of per capita SDP, however, do not differ significantly between the years. This implies that the growth process has been stable with a rising trend.

The significance of the differentials of annual growth rate of per capita SDP among the states implies that the rates of growth of per capita SDP of developed states relative to the growth rates of per capita SDP of U.P. should also be significantly different. The following ANOVA table highlights the nature of these inter-state differentials of growth rates of per capita SDP of states relative to that of U.P.

These results confirm the earlier results for the absolute rates of growth of per capita SDP of states and that the relative rates of annual growth rates of SDP of states differ significantly among the states but the inter-temporal differences are not significant statistically. This also implies stability.

Table 12: Rates of growth of Per Capita SDP of States Relative to U.P.

ANOVA						
Source of Variation	*SS*	*df*	*MS*	*F*	*P-value*	*F crit*
Rows	5E+06	6	852635	34.1134	1.05951E-15	2.294601314
Columns	231973	8	28997	1.16014	0.342399002	2.138228827
Error	1E+06	48	24994			
Total	7E+06	62				

Long Run Annual Compound Rates of Growth of Per Capita SDP of States

As earlier, these long run annual compound rates of growth of per capita SDP have been derived from the growth curve. These annual compound rates of growth of per capita SDP and rates of growth of SDP of developed states relative to growth rate of SDP of U.P. are as follows:

Table 13: Annual Compound Rates of Growth of Per Capita SDP (Percentage)

State	*Gujarat*	*Haryana*	*Karnataka*	*Maharashtra*	*Punjab*	*Tamil Nadu*	*U.P.*	*India*
Growth Rate	5.13	5.02	5.34	5.07	4.98	5.59	4.31	5.93
Relative	1.19	1.16	1.24	1.18	1.15	1.30	1.0	1.38

The long run annual compound growth rate of per capita SDP of U.P. is the lowest among all the states and the per capita GNP of India. Per capita GNP of India has *grown at as fast a rate as 1.38 times the growth rate of per capita SDP of U.P.* This confirms that U.P. is left trailing much behind India in the development race. It is also confirmed that U.P. has lagged behind six developed states of India also in the long run growth of per capita SDP. This is evident from the perusal of the second row of the previous table that the annual compound rates of growth of per capita SDP of developed states have been 1.15 to 1.3 times the rate of growth of per capita SDP of U.P.

The results of two factors ANOVA, based on the previous table, are reported in Table 14.

The table shows that the absolute annual compound rates of growth of per capita SDP of states and per capita GNP of India differ significantly from the relative long run growth rates. But the annual compound rates of growth of per capita SDP of states and rates relative to U.P.'s growth rate, taken together, do not differ significantly among the states. However, the fact remains that the economy of U.P. has lagged behind the economy of India and economies of other developed states of the country.

Table 14: ANOVA

Source of Variation	*SS*	*df*	*MS*	*F*	*P-value*	*F crit*
Rows	63.083	1	63.083	949.348	9.79174E-09	5.591447848
Columns	1.2161	7	0.1737	2.61455	0.1140369	3.78704354
Error	0.4651	7	0.0664			
Total	64.765	15				

Conclusions

The main findings of the study are as follows:

1. SDP of all states, including SDP of U.P., has shown year on year variability both inter-temporally and between the states;
2. Year on year growth of SDP has varied significantly both inter-temporally and between the states;
3. During one phase/part of the period covered by the study, U.P. has shown a tendency of catching up, which was reversed in subsequent years;
4. On the whole, U.P. has lagged behind India and the six developed states in the growth of SDP;
5. U.P.'s share in GNP has also been declining;
6. Growth of SDP and per capita SDP of U.P. has been the lowest among the states included in the study;
7. Short run growth rates of SDP and per capita SDP have differed significantly among the states but the inter-temporal variations of growth rates is not significant which means that the states have recorded stable growth of SDP both in absolute and relative terms.

References

Myrdal, Gunnar (1956). *Economic Theory and Under-developed Regions*, Popular Prakashan, Mumbai

Prakash, Shri and Mohapatra, A.C. (1980). Economic Development in the State of Madhya Pradesh, India: A Study of Inter-Temporal and Intra-Regional Variations, *Third World Planning Review*, Vol. 2, No. 1, Liverpool University Press, U.K.

Prakash, Shri (1977). *Educational System—An Econometric Study*, Concept Publishing Co., New Delhi.

Prakash, Shri and Panigrahi, Ritisnigdha (2010). International Integration of Indian Stock Market and Impact of Slow Down on Indian Economy, *UPUEA Economic Journal*, Vol. 3, No. 4&5.

CHAPTER 6

Population, Work Force Profile and Economic Growth of U.P.

Shri Prakash and Gautam Negi

Introduction: Population

U.P. with an area of 0.24 million sq. kms and a population of 19.95 crores is the most populous state of the country. Although U.P. occupies only 7.3 per cent of the country's land area, it supports over 16 per cent of the country's population. Thus, the share of U.P. in the total population is slightly more than double its share in the land area. Naturally, the population density is more than twice the density of the population in India (828/382). The population density of India has increased three fold from 1951 to 2011, while for U.P. it has increased four-fold during the same period. The current high population of U.P. can partly be attributed to the high population growth rate of 25.85 per cent during the decade 1991–2001 and partly to the base effect. Population growth of U.P. is 4 per cent higher than the national average for the same period.

The growth rate of SDP relative to the growth of GNP of India also compares poorly. Developed states like Gujarat, Maharashtra, Tamil Nadu, Andhra Pradesh, Punjab and Haryana, taken together, account for slightly less than one third of the geographical area of India and support approx 32 per cent of the country's population. Thus, unlike U.P., these developed states support population in consonance with their share in the total land area of the country. The combined population of the SAARC countries, alongwith Thailand, Pakistan, Bangladesh, Myanmar, Nepal, Sri Lanka, Thailand and Maldives) is 52.33 crore. The population of U.P. is more than the most populous country of SAARC, that is, Pakistan (19 crores). Does this consonance or dissonance between the share in the land area, and proportion of population account for the relative underdevelopment of U.P. and the development of the other states of India?

Resource Base of Development

Resource availability is a necessary but not the sufficient condition for development. That is why books on the Indian economy in 1950s contained the sentence "India is a rich country inhabited by the poor". Israel offers an example of a resource scarce but economically developed country. However, the land endowment of U.P. relative to its population is scarce, though manpower endowment is abundant. Since human capital is considered to be a critical factor in development, U.P. should have been the most developed state, more so, as its land area is rich in agro climatic endowment. Scarcity of acreage is more than compensated by the location of the Ganges-Yamuna river belt in U.P. These are two biggest rivers in India and the quality of soil in U.P. is high in fertility. This is in addition to other rivers flowing through the state. This suggests that the problem of lower and slower growth of U.P. needs an explanation, in terms of factors, other than the natural resource base.

Economic development hinges upon efficient and intensive use of human resources, land and capital. Efficient and effective utilization of available resources is a necessary condition of growth. Efficiency is directly discernible from resource productivity. Productivity is a measure of efficiency with which resource inputs in production are converted into output of goods and services. Rising resource productivity is an outcome of the factor multiplication process of growth, which embodies an upward shift of the macro production function from the left to the right. The shift in the production function results from the use of better quality of factor inputs, improved organisation and better managerial techniques and superior technology (Prakash-Balakrishnan, 2008 and Amit Sharma, 2010). Such changes are generally centred on the improvement in human capital/resources and their productivity (Amit Sharma, 2011).

Basic Features of Human Resource Utilisation

In view of the abundance of human capital in U.P., a few important aspects to be considered are:

- What is the proportion of population in the labour force? This is shown by labour force participation rate
- What is the extent of employment? This is represented by workforce participation rate
- What is the household size and household income
- What is the SDP of U.P./per capita SDP
- What is the land productivity in U.P.
- What is the capital/labour productivity in U.P.
- What is the degree of industrialisation and urbanisation

Though U.P. accounts for 16 per cent of the Indian population, yet it accounts for only 13 per cent of the country's labour force. It implies that the dependency ratio in U.P. is more than that of India. Naturally, less number of people contribute to the SDP than the number of people who contribute to GNP. U.P. supports more people per rupee worth of SDP, than the people per rupee supported by GNP. So, U.P. is less developed than India, in terms of per capita income. Only if the total factor productivity of labour in U.P. was higher than that of India, U.P. would have been more developed than India. Since U.P. is less developed than India, the labour productivity in U.P. is likely to be lower than that of India. These inferences are supported by the following facts shown in Table 1.

Main and Marginal Workers in the Workforce

The following table highlights the main and marginal workers in U.P.'s work force and the work force of India and six developed states. A priori reasoning suggests that the *higher the proportion of the main relative to marginal workers, the greater is likelihood to be the stage of development of the state.* These data are reported in Table 1.

Table 1: Main/Marginal Workers as a Proportion of the Labour Force of U.P. and Developed States and India

States	*Total Population*	*% of Total Population*	*Labour Force*	*Labour Force as a % of Indian Labour Force*	*% Main Workers to Labour Force*	*% Marginal Workers to Labour Force*
India	1028610328	100%	402234724	100%	78%	22%
U.P.	166197921	16%	53983824	13%	73%	27%
Developed States Together	331668893	32%	142705953	35%	83%	17%
AP	76210007	7%	34893859	9%	83%	17%
Gujarat	50671017	5%	21255521	5%	80%	20%
Haryana	21144564	2%	8377466	2%	75%	25%
Maharashtra	96878627	9%	41173351	10%	84%	16%
Punjab	24358999	2%	9127474	2%	86%	14%
Tamil Nadu	62405679	6%	27878282	7%	85%	15%

The low literacy and work force participation rates with high birth rates are indicators of a lower stage of economic growth. These rates are directly related with low household incomes, poverty, illiteracy, low output, low SDP, higher crime rates and a high proportion of an unproductive population. A higher proportion of marginal workers in the labour force of U.P., relative to India, implies a higher incidence of unemployment or disguised unemployment, illiteracy and lower productivity in U.P. The inference is based on the fact that manual workers, employed mostly in the unorganised informal sector activities, are found mostly among marginal workers, and manual workers are largely illiterate or nominally educated. Their productivity and wages are also on the lower side, therefore it is no surprise that U.P. is among the less developed states of India.

Rural-Urban Divide of the Work Force

The rural-urban divide is also a factor of development or low development. The manufacturing and tertiary activities are mostly concentrated in urban regions. Besides, the rural areas also lag behind urban areas in social and economic infrastructure, especially, education, health, power, roads, banks, and a good communication network. This is unlike European countries, where social and economic infrastructure, do not differ significantly, either quantitatively or qualitatively, between the rural-urban regions. Southern states, Punjab and Haryana are also much ahead of U.P. in this respect. Hence, the rural urban divide is considered next. Table 2, shows a comparative picture of U.P. with India, with respect to the rural-urban divide.

Table 2: Rural and Urban Labour Force Participation Rates and Dependency Ratio for U.P. and India

	LFPR	*DR*	*LFPR*		*DR*	
			Rural	*Urban*	*Rural*	*Urban*
U.P.	32%	68%	34%	27%	66%	73%
India	39%	61%	42%	32%	58%	68%

Labour force participation rate (LFPR) is defined as the proportion of the population which is willing and available for employment and workforce participation rate refers to the proportion of persons who are employed. Dependency Rate (DR) is the proportion of the population, which is economically dependent due either to age, disability, being a housewife or unemployment or both. The labour force of the state is 13 per cent of the Indian rural labour force and 10 per cent of the Indian urban workforce. Thus, U.P. compares unfavourably with the proportion of the population of U.P. in the workforce, relative to the Indian population in the workforce.

The labour force participation rate is below the average of the country. It is 32 per cent compared to the national average of 39 per cent. The gap is higher for rural participation (U.P. 34 per cent and India 42 per cent) than for the urban labour force participation rate (27 per cent and 32 per cent). Low value of LFPR for U.P. implies a higher dependency ratio, relative to the national average. The dependency ratio is 68 per cent for U.P. as compared to 61 per cent for India. The relatively high dependency ratio and low labour force participation ratio may be among the major factors for U.P.'s relatively low development.

Male-Female Dichotomy in the Work Force

The differentials between male-female participation rates in the labour force highlights the degree of female empowerment on the one hand, and gender ratio and age structure of males and females in the state, on the other. The social and economic status of women is an indicator of the economic, educational and social development of a state. The greater the proportion of educated women, the greater tends to be the degree of women's empowerment, and hence, employment (Panigrahi, Riti Snigdha, 2011). The greater the women's participation in the work force, greater is their contribution to economic growth, and hence, economic and social independence.

Table 3: Male and Female Working Population in U.P., and Developed States and India

State	*Male Population*	*Male Working Population*	*%Male Working Population to Total Population*	*Female Population*	*Female Working Population*	*%Female Working Population to Total Population*
India	53,21,56,772	27,50,14,476	52%	49,64,53,556	7,28,57,170	15%
U.P.	8,75,65,369	4,09,81,558	47%	7,86,32,552	1,30,02,266	17%
Andhra Pradesh	3,85,27,413	2,16,62,192	56%	3,76,82,594	1,32,31,667	35%
Gujarat	2,63,85,577	1,44,77,286	55%	2,42,85,440	67,78,235	28%
Haryana	1,13,63,953	57,15,526	50%	97,80,611	26,61,940	27%
Maharashtra	5,04,00,596	2,68,52,095	53%	4,64,78,031	1,43,21,256	31%
Punjab	1,29,85,045	69,60,213	54%	1,13,73,954	21,67,261	19%
Tamil Nadu	3,14,00,909	1,81,00,397	58%	3,10,04,770	97,77,885	32%
Developed states	17,10,63,493	9,37,67,709	55%	16,06,05,400	4,89,38,244	30%

The male working population ratio for U.P. is 47 per cent, which is below the national average of 52 per cent. The female working population ratio for India is as low as 15 per cent. But, the female working population of U.P. is slightly higher than that of India at 17 per cent, though it is much lower than the ratio of developed states, taken together, as well as individually. This may partly reflect the traditional cultural trap of households in U.P. Less number of workers in gainful employment will decidedly contribute to slow economic growth.

The following table shows the gender wise workforce situation in U.P. and India. The table shows that U.P. is characterised by low work force participation for both genders as compared to India, which may also account for lower per capita income of U.P., relative to the national average.

Marginal and Main Workforce

The ratio of marginal workers to the total labour force for U.P. is low, as compared to India, for both the rural and urban workforce. Productivity of marginal workers is generally low, and they do not contribute to SDP as much as main workers due to productivity differentials, large or small numbers notwithstanding. A relatively large proportion of marginal workers in the work force may, therefore, be among the reasons for the relatively lower and slower growth of SDP of U.P., than the growth of GNP of India.

Table 4: Rural and Urban and Main/Marginal Workers in the Labour Force

States	*Rural/Urban*	*% of Total Population*	*Main Workers to Total Labour Force*	*Marginal Workers to Labour Force*
India	Rural	72%	74%	26%
	Urban	28%	91%	9%
U.P.	Rural	79%	70%	30%
	Urban	13%	87%	13%

U.P. is more rural centric than India. This is explained by two factors: (i) relatively more dependence on agriculture than manufacturing and tertiary production, and (ii) nearness to Delhi of western U.P. and to Kolkata of eastern U.P. This, among other factors, the geographical proximity of U.P. to Delhi and Kolkata has induced greater rural to urban migration from U.P. than other states. But, U.P. has more marginal than main workers, both in the rural and urban areas. As the contribution of marginal workers to SDP is less than that of main workers, this may also be considered to be a factor of the sluggish economic growth of U.P.

Investment in Industries

U.P. has less of overall investment of the country on the one hand, and even much less investment in the manufacturing and services on the other. As productivity of agriculture is lower than that of the tertiary and manufacturing sectors, it may be inferred that U.P. needs more investments in services and industries, than agriculture. A relatively lower proportion of manufacturing in SDP and industrial workers in the total work force may also partially, if not largely, account for the lower and slower growth of SDP of U.P., than the growth of SDP of other states of India.

U.P. has lagged behind considerably compared to the developed states of India, in attracting investments in the industrial sector. In the post liberalisation period from 1991 to Sept. 2011, the share of U.P. in total investments is only 2.77 per cent of total investments in the country. Low industrial development is accounted for by low overall investment. This accounts for the lower levels of development of U.P. than the development levels of India and other States. Table 5 highlights this aspect.

Table 5: Industrial Investment Proposals (Aug. 1991–Sept. 2011)

State	*Total Investment*	*% of Total Investment*	*Industrial Entrepreneurs Memorandum*			*LOI + DIL (Letters of intent + industrial licenses)*		
			No Filed	*Proposed Investment*	*Proposed Employment*	*No Granted*	*Proposed Investment*	*Proposed Employment*
India	8963742	100%	87326	8826641	20457187	4507	137101	966405
U.P.	248590	2.77%	6957	238634	1849558	377	9956	102492
AP	786710	8.78%	6706	770871	1297056	550	15839	100539
Gujarat	1025779	11.44%	10279	998245	1969928	471	27534	77760
Haryana	98974	1.10%	4228	94261	678858	252	4553	64539
Maharashtra	861331	9.61%	15959	842350	4094177	603	18981	140147
Punjab	119301	1.33%	3169	110948	735390	268	8353	86170
TN	381163	4.25%	7240	366835	2175458	874	14328	151559

The following inferences may be drawn from the table:

- The share of investment in U.P. is 2.77 per cent of the total investment in India, in the post liberalisation era. This is very low, considering the fact that U.P. accounts for 16 per cent of the population of India. This, in fact, apart from Haryana and Punjab, is the lowest proportion of total investments in any state of India. Gujarat and Maharastra, taken together, account for slightly more than one fifth of the total investment in India. Andhra Pradesh and Tamil Nadu account for another 10 per cent of the total investment in India during the same period.

- The amount of investment as per memoranda signed and filed in U.P. is also much smaller than that in Gujarat, Andhra Pradesh, Maharastra and Tamil Nadu. It is smaller than that of Punjab as well. Thus, the investment levels per production unit, highlights the fact that U.P. like Punjab and Haryana continues to host the SMEs.
- But both agriculture and small industries contribute much more to SDP in Punjab than U.P.
- Productivity and agricultural yield rates in U.P. continue to be lower than that of Punjab. One reason for the relatively lower levels of per hectare yield in U.P. seems to be the dominance of small farms, and even smaller farmers in U.P., than Punjab. This limits individual investment in yield raising inputs in agriculture. Public investment in agriculture in India has been extremely low during the globalisation era, and U.P. is no exception to this.
- U.P. compares favourably with the national average with regard to the number of Industrial Entrepreneurs Memorandum (IEM) filed, to the number of LOI/DIL issued. Both are close to 5 per cent of the total.
- Among the developed states, Punjab and Tamil Nadu have the best ratio for the number of proposals filed to sanctioned proposals.

Agriculture

The agriculture sector accounts for 20 per cent of the national GDP of India. In Punjab, Haryana and U.P. agriculture accounts for a much higher proportion of SDP. Thus, it is, but natural, that the per capita SDP of these states is linked to the agricultural productivity of the states. In view of this, the agriculture yield rate is shown in Table 6.

Table 6: Agricultural Productivity (yield per hectare) of U.P. and the Developed States Relative to that of Punjab

Rank	*State/Year*	*2000–01*	*2001–02*	*2002–03*	*2003–04*	*2004–05*	*2005–06*	*2006–07*	*2007–08*	*2008–09*	*2009–10*
	Punjab	1	1	1	1	1	1	1	1	1	1
3.5	Andhra Pradesh	0.52	0.52	0.44	0.51	0.53	0.59	1.64	0.61	0.65	0.59
5	Gujarat	0.21	0.35	0.29	0.41	0.35	0.39	1.05	0.43	0.38	0.38
1	Haryana	0.76	0.76	0.77	0.81	0.78	0.77	0.76	2.50	0.80	0.80
6	Maharashtra	0.19	0.19	0.22	0.22	0.22	0.21	0.24	0.69	0.27	0.24
2	Tamil Nadu	0.61	0.61	0.55	0.42	0.39	0.46	0.46	1.00	0.50	0.53
3.5	Uttar Pradesh	0.52	0.54	0.52	0.56	0.49	0.52	1.77	0.52	0.56	0.54
	All India	0.40	0.43	0.40	0.44	0.41	0.43	1.60	0.44	0.45	0.43

Growth of Agricultural Productivity

Analysis of crop productivity of agriculture is more complex than the analysis of productivity of manufacturing. The reason is that the (i) acreage allocation decisions of farmers are guided by net returns per acre than the yield rate in physical and monetary terms, (ii) relative monetary returns are based on (a) difference of yield rates physically of competing crops, and (b) per unit price differences of crops. Low physical yield, high value crops are allocated less physical yield and lower cost parts of holdings, which makes up the price differentials, while high yield low price, but more yield and high cost crops are allocated input intensive parts of holdings (Prakash, Buragohain and Sharma,... and Prakah, 2012). This is often overlooked by the analysis.

First, we examine the overall trend growth rates of agricultural productivity of the states, including U.P. This will reflect the overall picture of agricultural economies of the states over the years. The OLS estimates of exponential regression growth curves of agricultural productivity of the states are as follows:

Equation	R^2	Ranks according to growth rates	
$\log Y_1 = -0.329 + 0.0209\,X$, $t = (-3.1304)\ (1.2352)$	$R^2 = 0.1602$	Andhra Pradesh	= Rank 3
$\log Y_2 = -0.567 + 0.0285\,X$, $t = (-5.0796)(1.5807)$	$R^2 = 0.238$	Gujarat	= Rank 1
$\log Y_3 = -0.152 + 0.0171\,X$, $t = (-1.3822)\ (0.9651)$	$R^2 = 0.1043$	Haryana	= Rank 4
$\log Y_4 = -0.758 + 0.0276\,X$, $t = (-7.4727)(1.689)$	$R^2 = 0.2629$	Maharashtra	= Rank 2
$\log Y_5 = -0.284 + 0.002\,X$, $t = (-3.3989)\ (0.1506)$	$R^2 = 0.0028$	Tamil Nadu	= Rank 7
$\log Y_6 = -0.283 + 0.0108\,X$, $t = (-2.3915)\ (0.5665)$	$R^2 = 0.0386$	U.P.	= Rank 6
$\log Y_7 = -0.392 + 0.0141\,X$, $t = (-3.0397)\ (0.6804)$	$R^2 = 0.0547$	India	= Rank 5

Y_1 refers to Andhra Pradesh, Y_2 to Gujarat, Y_3 to Haryana, Y_4 to Maharashtra, Y_5 to Tamil Nadu, Y_6 to Uttar Pradesh, and Y_7 to India.

The growth curves reveal that the crop yields per hectare of these states relative to the yield rates of Punjab (i) have not grown significantly for any of the states and India. It means that the relative crop yield rates have been stagnating in all the states. Therefore, Punjab continues to remain the leading state, in so far as the crop yield rate is concerned, and growth of SDP, and per capita SDP of these states may largely be accounted for by non-agricultural sectors of the economy; (ii) annual compound rates of growth have, however, varied highly among the states; (iii) Gujarat tops in the growth of relative yields, and is followed by Maharashtra, Andhra Pradesh, Haryana, India, U.P. and Tamil Nadu in that order.

Non-significance of the growth of yield rates implies that the growth is not statistically different from zero. Therefore, it is not surprising that the state of U.P., whose economy continues to revolve around agriculture, but lags behind India, and developed states, in the development of manufacturing and tertiary production, continues to show slower and lower growth of SDP and per capita SDP.

Year on Year Changes in Crop Yields

These results relate to the long term trend growth; it does not highlight inter-temporal status of growth of crop yield rates. For this, year on year changes are examined.

The following inferences may be drawn from the previous table:

1. Gujarat and Maharashtra show the lowest yield rates in all the years except two, though the trend is positively rising over the years.
2. Yield rates of U.P. are higher than those of India. However, the yield rates in U.P., unlike that of Gujarat and Maharashtra, have remained almost stagnant over a period of one decade. This highlights the continued stagnation of agriculture which dominates the economic structure of U.P. notwithstanding the stagnancy of yield rates.
3. Tamil Nadu has registered a decline in the yield rates during the same period.
4. Andhra Pradesh and Haryana have registered some improvement in agricultural yield rates during this period.
5. Agricultural productivity of land in U.P. is only slightly more than half that of Punjab, though its rank is 3.5, and is tied with Andhra Pradesh. This runs against the favourable agro-climatic conditions and its location in the Ganges-Yamuna plains. The main reason seems to be the low size of holdings relative to that of Haryana and Punjab, and a large number of small and marginal farmers. Small and marginal farmers do not have resources to invest in yield raising inputs. Smaller holdings most of the times may also be further subdivided and fragmented from time to time. The state and central governments must come forward to promote investment in agriculture.

It is an empirical fact that private investment in health, education, irrigation and agriculture depends a great deal on public investment in these sectors. But, in the last decade of the twentieth century, public investment in agriculture, and irrigation in particular was negligible (Prakash, 1997; Prakash-Sharma, 2005; Amit Sharma, 2010; Hemlatha, 2009).

A graphical representation of agricultural productivity of U.P. and India relative to that of Punjab is shown by the Graph 1.

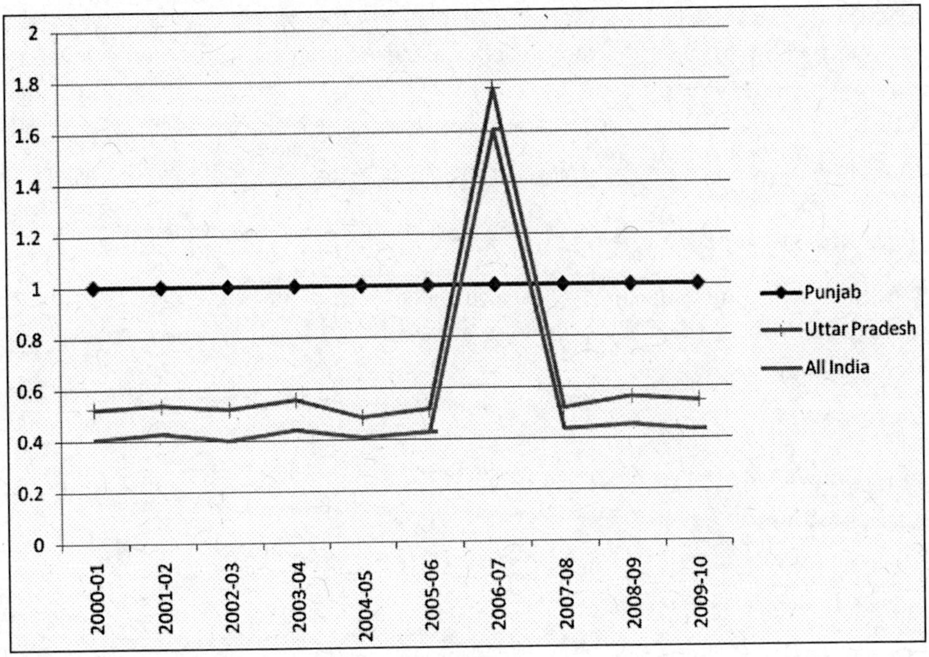

Graph 1

This diagram shows that agricultural productivity of U.P. rose above that of Punjab only in 2007, though it has been above the national average throughout.

The following deductions may also be drawn about agriculture productivity for the last decade of the twentieth century:

- Among the states and union territories, Punjab has the highest agricultural productivity;
- The agricultural productivity in U.P. has been half that of Punjab for the entire decade except for 2006–07;
- The agricultural productivity of U.P. has been slightly higher than that of India;

- 2006–2007 is the only exceptional year, when the agricultural productivity of Punjab was less compared to U.P. and India;
- Among the developed states, Haryana is the closest to Punjab in agricultural productivity, while Maharashtra is the most distant state from Punjab;
- During last three years, productivity has shown some rising trend in U.P.; and
- During the rest of the period, the agricultural yields of U.P. have stagnated, year-on-year fluctuations notwithstanding.

Thus, U.P. is characterized by high population relative to its share of the total area, low labour force participation rate, greater rural-urban divide, higher proportion of marginal workers, low capital investments and low agricultural productivity. In view of all these handicaps, it is natural that U.P. is a BIMARU state. The state of U.P. is characterised by all features of vicious circle of underdevelopment.

Growth of Per Capita SDP of U.P. and Per Capita GDP of India

The annual compound rate of growth of per capita SDP of U.P. and per capita GNP of India are estimated from the following growth curve:

$$\log Y_1 = \alpha_1 + \beta_1 X$$

$$\log Y_1 = \alpha_2 + \beta_2 X$$

where Y_i is per capita SDP/GNP, X is time measured in calendar years, and β shows unusual compounds growth rate.

$$\log Y_1 = 3.908 + 0.043\, X,\ R^2 = 0.9696,\ F = 255.497$$

$$t = (236.163)\ (15.984)$$

$$\log Y_2 = 4.136 + 0.0515\, X,\ R^2 = 0.9848,\ F = 519.872$$

$$t = (295.1364)\ (22.801)$$

The annual compound growth rates of per capita SDP of U.P and per capita GDP of India are 4.3 and 5.52 per cent respectively. Both these growth rates are statistically significant. But the growth rate of per capita SDP of U.P. is much lower than that of India. It means that U.P. has been left far behind the growth of per capita income of India, in spite of the significant rate of growth of its SDP.

These results and results reported in Table 7 suggest that the per capita SDP of U.P. must be less than the national average. U.P., in fact, has substantially lagged behind India in the per capita SDP and its growth. The high population of U.P. relative to other states, and the rapid population growth compared to India also account for the fact that the compound annual rate of growth of per capita SDP of U.P. is lower than the growth of per capita GNP of India, during the last decade. Per capita SDP of U.P. relative to GNP of India is shown in Table 7.

Table 7: Per Capita SDP of U.P. as Compared to India in the Last Decade

Year	*Per Capita U.P. (₹)*	*Per Capita India (₹)*	*U.P./India (%)*	*Gap*
2000–01	9828	16688	58.89	41.11
2001–02	9995	17782	56.21	43.79
2002–03	10648	18885	56.38	43.62
2003–04	11458	20871	54.89	45.11
2004–05	12196	23198	52.57	47.43
2005–06	14115	27123	52.02	47.98
2006–07	15865	31198	50.85	49.15
2007–08	17602	35820	49.14	50.86
2008–09	20004	40605	49.26	50.74
2009–10	23132	46492	49.75	50.25

This table reveals that:

1. Annual compound rate of growth of per capita SDP of U.P. during the decade has been only 4.2 per cent. Year on year growth rate shows that the per capita growth rate of U.P. has been higher than the national average in three out of 10 years in the last decade, though the overall average is much lower. 2001, 2002 and 2009–10 are the years of U.P.'s higher growth.
2. Per capita income of both U.P. and India has been rising year on year basis consistently.
3. Despite sustained growth over a period of one decade, per capita SDP of U.P. relative to GNP of India has declined continuously. In 2000–01, per capita SDP of U.P. was approximately 59 per cent of per capita GNP of India. However, it has declined to 49.75 per cent in 2009–10. This is a decline of almost 10 percentage points. In other words, U.P. has been sliding down below India by one percentage point annually. Obviously, U.P. has lagged behind India in the development race.
4. Correspondingly, the gap between per capita SDP of U.P. and per capita GNP of India has been rising on a year on year basis. It has increased from 41 in 2000–01 to 50 per cent in 2009–10; and

5. This decline may be accounted either by more rapid growth of GNP, rather than U.P.'s SDP, if growth of population of U.P. equals the national average. Alternatively, per capita SDP has declined relative to per capita GNP due to rapid growth of SDP and largely to more rapid growth of GNP or more rapid growth of population of U.P. than that of India. This is a more plausible reason. This is also supported the by the empirical evidence furnished by the rising share of U.P. of the Indian population. The government of U.P. has to address the problems of demography. A reduction in birth rates will also result in a reduction in the dependency ratio. Both these factors will contribute to accelerated growth of per capita SDP of U.P.

The year on year growth of per capita SDP and per capita GNP of India are shown in Graph 2:

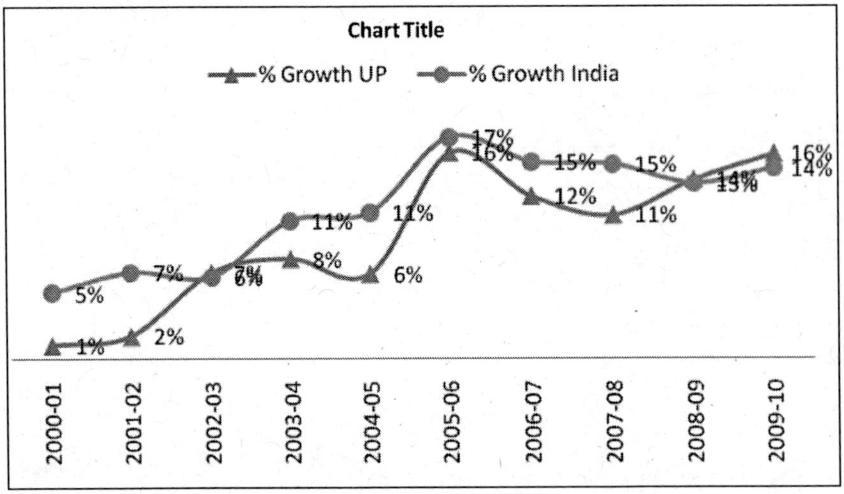

Graph 2: Growth of Per Capita SDP of U.P. and Per Capita GNP of India during the Last Decade

In terms of absolute value, the per capita income of India was 2.01 times more than the per capita income of U.P. in 2009–10. The status of U.P. relative to India compares poorly with 1999–2000 as the base, when per capita GNP of India was less than the per capita SDP of U.P.

A look at the graph shows that U.P. caught up with India in 2002–03. But, acceleration of growth of Indian GNP since 2003–04 pushed U.P.'s growth of per capita SDP below the national average. 2006 is another year when U.P. almost caught up with India. So, 2002–03 may be treated as an aberration, rather than a long from trend. This is supported by the fact that U.P. again caught up with India in the development race in 2008–09, but it again slid down. If we look at the overall context of growth, we find that U.P. tends to catch up with India whenever the Indian economy slides down below the long run growth trend, as in 1999–2000 and 2008–09, when the Indian economy was affected adversely by recession in the US in 1999–2000 and world-wide economic slowdown in 2008–09. A comforting thought is that U.P.'s economy is immune to international influences. This may partly be explained the by low share of U.P. in FDI/FI and exports from India. This needs policy interventions.

The utmost need of the hour is to transform the short term to the long term growth trend, if the state of U.P. is to maintain a relative growth position in the country. For this, a stable government with good governance, particularly a development oriented government, which does not allow law and order to become a deterrent for outside investors, assured power and water supply, good quality road network, high quality health and education services are made available. Appropriate and timely decisions and proper implementation of development strategies and policy are essential needs of growth. An important point is that states such as Andhra Pradesh, Gujarat, Haryana, Maharashtra, Punjab, Tamil Nadu have not only maintained their growth performance, but have also succeeded in accelerating the same. Induction of capital/investment has played the pivotal role in the relatively more developed states than U.P.

Conclusions

U.P.'s population size and its age and gender structure have been the constraints in rapid growth. Reduction of population size and dependency ratio, irrespective of gender and rural-urban divide, will impart momentum to growth by raising the labour participation rates. An important factor of slow and low growth of business and economy of U.P. is the unduly large proportion of marginal workers in the work force. Low literacy rates may also be accountable for this.

Stagnation of agricultural yield rates is another important factor for the low and slow growth of U.P. Yields per hectare have to be raised, say by 5 per cent per annum during next five years. This needs appropriate change in cultural practices, especially by small and marginal farmers, and heavy investments in yield raising inputs.

Greater emphasis has to be given to SMEs, which revolve around local human capital endowment. Investment, both Indian and foreign, has to be encouraged.

Power, water, quality of the road network, and improved law and order conditions and good governance are the needs of the hour.

Note

1. All data have been taken from the Internet.

References

Hemalatha, J. (2009). Private Cost of Secondary Education in India, Ph.D. Thesis, BIMTECH Center of Research Studies, Affiliated to B.R. Ambedkar University, Agra.

Panigrahi, Riti Snigdha (2011). Education and Women Empowerment in India, *Manpower Journal*, Jan.–Mar., IAMR, New Delhi.

Prakash, Shri (1977). *Educational System of India—An Econometric Study,* Concept Publishing Co., New Delhi.

Prakash, Shri and Balakrishnan, Brinda (2008). Input Output Modelling of Labour Productivity and its Human Capital and Technology Components in Indian Economy, *Bulletin of Political Economy,* Vol. 2, No. 2 (December 2008), pp. 137–164.

Prakash, Shri and Balakrsihnan, Brinda (2006). Managerial Approach to Conceptualization of Development and Growth—Convergence of Macro to Micro Theory, *Business Perspectives,* Vol. 8, No. 1.

Sharma, Amit (2007). Educational Development and Human Resource Qualifications in Indian Job Market, *Business Perspectives,* Vol. 9, No. 1, January–June.

Sharma, Amit (2011). Up-Gradation of Educational Qualifications in Selected Occupations: A Study of Higher Scientific and Technical Occupations since 1981 in the Indian Economy, Ph.D. Thesis, BIMTECH Center of Research Studies, Affiliated to University of Mysore, Mysore.

Sharma, Amit and Chaturvedi, H. (2007). Educational Development and Qualification Up-gradation in Indian Job Market—Analysis of Emerging Trend, *Manpower Journal,* Vol. XLII, No. 4, October–December, 2007.

Section–III

Educational Reforms and Higher Education in Uttar Pradesh

CHAPTER 7

Educational Reforms in Uttar Pradesh

Mohd Muzammil and Tabassum Khatoon

Economic reforms have set a new paradigm for educational development in India. The state's support for education is getting reduced and the role of the private sector is being strengthened. The plethora of private and public educational institutions have also posed grave challenges for the regulation and maintenance of the quality of education. The government, however, wants to continue having a role and the outcomes are mixed results across the states throughout India. In U.P., the challenge is even greater, because of its relative educational backwardness. Reforms in U.P. have squeezed the fiscal space and created more opportunities for the private providers and their participation even in the public domain of education in the state. State level reform-based success stories reveal that, in the case of Tamil Nadu, it is the political commitment (irrespective of the political party in power in the state), that has made the difference. In Kerala, the extraordinary performance of the education sector is credited to the efficient, honest and committed bureaucracy, Christian missionaries and the Sahitya Parishad. In Uttar Pradesh also, the better performance in literacy in the decade of the 1990s is largely because of the effective intervention in the education sector by the government.

Uttar Pradesh lags far behind in educational development, not for a single but several reasons.[1] These are related with poor performance of the state in almost all the social indicators of development. Educational backwardness has a long history, and progress over time has also been really slow.[2] Some improvement in educational development has been visible since the 1990s, which coincides with the economic reforms in India. This is despite the fact that, in the reforms period, the social sector allocations in general have been squeezed out.[3]

The capacity to spend on education of a state depends on the Gross State Domestic Product (GSDP), political will and commitment. The commitment to education is reflected in the ratio of the revenues of the budget allotted to education. The state government's expenditure on education (all levels) had gone up from 2.48 per cent of the State Domestic Product (SDP) in 1980–81 to 4.23 per cent in 1990–91. This ratio gradually came down to 2.75 per cent in 2003–04. But, it again recovered gradually to 3.34 per cent in 2006–07. It is far behind the normatively derived level of 6 per cent of the GSDP. The following table shows the year wise progression in the share of education in the GSDP. The period covered is from 1971 to 2006–07. However, there is one decade's gap in the data between 1971 and 1981, then the gap declines to five years from 1981 to 1996, then again there is an one year gap between 1995–96 and 1998–1999. Thereafter, the series is continuous up to 2006–07. These gaps are explained by the availability of the data with the authors.

Table 1: Share of Expenditure on Education in the State Domestic Product of U.P.

(Percentage)

Year	*Percent share in GSDP*
1970–71	1.76
1980–81	2.48
1985–86	3.13
1990–91	4.23
1995–96	3.28
1998–99	3.82
2000–01	3.78
2001–02	3.16
2002–03	3.12
2003–04	2.75
2004–05	2.94
2005–06	3.03
2006.07	3.34

Source: Calculated on the basis of the State budget data and state income data, published by the Department of Finance and Planning, U.P. Vide: GOUP: Uttar Pradesh ki Aya Vyaya ki Rooprekha (Outline of the Budget) 2008–09 and earlier issues.

The educational expenditure increased from 18 per cent of the budgetary expenditure in 1970–71 to 20 per cent in 1980–81. This compares very well with the lowest share for education, which was recorded in 1960–61, when the educational expenditure was only about 12 per cent of the total budgetary expenditure. By the close of the decade of 1980s, the share of educational expenditure rose to 24.2 per cent in 1989–90. Educational expenditure was ₹ 2,094 crores in 1990–91, which went up to ₹ 7,200 crore in 2004–05, showing an increase of more than three times. But, in relative terms, the share came down from approx 22 per cent to about 16 per cent during the same period.

Education in the Pre-Reform Period

It will be interesting to consider the progress of expenditure on education in the post reforms period, with expenditure in the post reforms period.

Table 2: Fiscal Allocation for Education and Total Budgetary Expenditure in U.P. (Pre-reform scenario)

(₹ crores)

Year	*Fiscal Allocation for Education*	*Total Budgetary Expenditure*	*(2) as % of (3)*
(1)	(2)	(3)	(4)
1950–51	7.10	51.84	13.70
1960–61	17.75	144.31	12.30
1970–71	74.84	413.86	18.13
1975–76	201.88	809.90	24.93
1980–81	345.87	1716.09	20.15
1989–90	1852.05	7654.05	24.20
1990–91	2093.81	9538.36	21.95

Source: Muzammil (2010e).

The post reforms phase in U.P. has witnessed a relatively declining share for education in general, and higher education in particular. The following table shows that the absolute amount on educational expenditure rose from ₹ 7,200 crore in 2004–05 to ₹ 12,300 crore in 2008–09 (BE); which was an increase of 1.7 times. But, the relative share remained virtually unchanged, at about 16 per cent.

Expenditure on Education during the Post Reforms Period

The progress of expenditure on education both in absolute and relative terms during the post reforms period may give an idea about the impact of reforms on education, so far as resource availability for education is concerned. It can also stand comparison with the pre-reforms period. Table 3 provides the data for this period.

The table shows that the educational expenditure during the reforms period has shown a relative decline both in terms of GSDP, and in terms of total budgetary expenditures.

This implies that the growth of expenditure on education has not kept pace with the growth of expenditure on other sectors of the economy, and segments of society.

Table 3: Fiscal Allocation for Education and Total Budgetary Expenditure in U.P. (Post Reforms Period)

(₹ crores)

Year	*Fiscal Allocation for Education*	*Total Budgetary Expenditure*	*(2) as % of (3)*
1	*2*	*3*	*4*
1990–91	2093.81	9538.36	21.95
1995–96	3360.92	17555.86	19.14
1997–98	4156.85	22195.03	18.73
1998–99	5840.15	27465.89	21.26
2000–01	6090.86	31032.61	19.63
2001–02	6018.15	31779.71	18.94
2003–04	6254.58	37943.72	16.48
2004–05	7200.10	44610.35	16.14
2005–06	8482.44	46617.14	18.19
2006–07	10471.54	55698.90	18.80
2007–08 RE	11599.85	67550.73	17.17
2008.09BE	12300.54	74828.67	16.44

Source: Muzammil (2010e).

Five year plans under the reform programmes witnessed increased allocation(s) for education in U.P. During the Eighth Five Year Plan, 8.5 per cent of budgetary expenditure was spent on education, and a similar ratio was also achieved in the Tenth Plan period. However, in the Ninth Five Year Plan, the allocation was reduced to about 5.4 per cent of the total. Non plan expenditure in this period went up greatly. The Eleventh Plan (2007–2012) allocation is very encouraging for educational development, as it accounts for over nine per cent of the total allocation of the Eleventh Five Year Plan.

Intra-Education Sector Allocation

The composition of the plan expenditure shows that the socially important segments like primary education get the largest share. Some 80 to 90 per cent of plan resources, and occasionally up to 95 per cent, is devoted for the expansion and improvement of the quality of primary education. Along with the efforts of the government, privatisation is also increasing at all levels of education in the state. Now, even the judiciary has cleared the decks for the greater involvement of the private sector in education. The new financing strategy also calls for innovative measures of funding education, and making the system of education better oriented for assuring employment with new opportunities in the liberal and open economy of the country (for more details see, Muzammil: 2010c).

Several measures of reforms in education have been undertaken in U.P. Due care has also been taken so that economic reforms also produce good results for the development of the social sector. Construction of school buildings in unserviced development blocks has been privatised, by making provision for non recurring grants to the private sector.

Decentralisation of educational administration has been done by giving more powers to village education committees, and by enlarging the area of their operations from appointing para-teachers to construction of school buildings. New schemes like Mid-day Meals (MDM) and Kasturba Gandhi Balika Vidyalaya (KGBV) were initiated for improving the nutritional health of children and retention in school, as well as for ensuring quality education. The FRBM Act under the reforms package at the state level puts a break on unproductive expenditure, thus saving resources for social sector development and reprioritisation of the expenditure for the primary levels of education and health service provisions.

Role of Governance and Political Commitment

State level success stories reveal that, in the case of Tamil Nadu, it is the political commitment irrespective of the political party in power at the level of the state government that accounts for educational development. In Kerala, the extraordinary performance is credited to the efficient, honest and committed bureaucracy. In Uttar Pradesh, the better performance in literacy in the decade of the 1990s, is because of effective government intervention in the educational sector.

The state of U.P., is moving in the direction of privatisation of education on a limited scale. The private sector is expected to participate in the construction of buildings, supplying educational inputs like computers and other materials like furniture and setting up of libraries. Experiments are also on for public private partnerships for supplying midday meals as well.[4]

The system of education is gradually moving from state control to a privately supported system. It has also been observed that with good governance and an efficient administration, even government intervention can produce better results in the changed circumstances.

Several steps have been undertaken to bring about reforms in the education sector in U.P. and also to ensure that measures of economic reforms produce favourable effects for the educational development of the state. The important reform measures are discussed as follows.

Privatisation of Construction of Buildings

Privatisation is the key word in the reforms package adopted in 1991. It has several connotations. The way in which it has come to play a role in the education sector in U.P. is the provision of non-recurring grants by the government to private management for opening of girls' high schools in unserviced blocks. This scheme was launched in 1994–95, when it became known that the government would be soliciting the private sector for providing educational infrastructure as well.

On the basis of a survey carried out for the purpose, the U.P. government identified 426 unserviced blocks. Therefore, a scheme named '*Non Recurring Grant to Private Management for Opening Girls High Schools in Un-serviced Blocks*' was started. Under this scheme, a non recurring grant of ₹ 10 lakhs (in two instalments of ₹ 5 lakhs each), now revised to ₹ 20 lakhs (Annual Plan 2006–07, p. 230) is given to private management under certain terms and conditions for the purpose as mentioned earlier. A total of 65 schools were opened by the U.P. Government through private management, and the remaining 361 schools were opened with financial assistance from the state government. Even in the disbursement of scholarships to SC/ST students in U.P., Basic Shiksha Adhikari (BSA's) office demands ₹ 50 and ₹ 75 per recipient for disbursement. Lots of data, relating to enrolments, are cooked up by principals in connivance of BSA's office at the school level to increase the number of SC/ST students to pay the payback to the BSA's office. The scheme will perform better if the scholarships are disbursed by cheque directly to the recipients.

Decentralisation and Strengthening Village Education Committees (VECs)

One of the most significant reforms in the decade of 1990s was the provision of more powers to the local bodies in rural and urban areas. The role of village panchayats was increased to ensure local participation and accountability. The 73rd and 74th Amendment of the Constitution of India enabled the local bodies a more prominent role in handling school education at the village level, and in urban areas.

The state government of U.P. constituted Village Education Committees (VECs) as statutory bodies under the U.P. Basic Education Act of 1972, which is popularly known as the Decentralisation Act. The government delegated the management of primary education to village panchayats. The VECs were further strengthened and more powers were delegated to them in 1999. This was a significant move to empower the local community to enable them to improve local school management and accountability.

Under the local body reforms in U.P., VECs are functioning as sub-committees of Gram Panchayats with a separate Shiksha Nidhi (Education Fund), which is empowered to address all local issues regarding elementary education. VECs have been made functional (GOUP: 2002, Vol. I, Part II, p. 255). VECs have the responsibilities of arranging the training of teachers of primary schools in the villages.

VECs have also been empowered for school construction work, school maintenance and development, engaging para teachers, that is, *Shiksha Mitra* and *Acharya Ji* for Education Guarantee Scheme (EGS) centres and payment of honorarium to them. Community based organisations like Mother Teacher Associations (MTAs) and Parent Teacher Associations (PTAs), Women Motivator Groups (WMGs) have also been constituted and sensitised in the project districts. Ward Committees (WCs) have also been constituted in urban areas.

Scheme for Nutrition and Retention

The decade of the 1990s has been significant from the viewpoint of new and innovative schemes to promote enrolments, and for increasing the retention of students in schools and thereby checking high dropout rates. One such scheme is the most celebrated Mid Day Meal (MDM) scheme, which was started in 1995 by the Government of India. Under this scheme, all students studying in to government and government aided primary schools, *Madarsas*, and EGS centres get free mid day meals which have 300 calories of energy. In the beginning, the students were supplied with 3 kilo of raw food grains per month for a period of 10 months in a year. The Supreme Court of India passed an order in November 2001 making it mandatory to supply cooked mid-day meals from September 2004, and gradually the whole state was brought under coverage. Misappropriation of grains meant for distribution among students led to this change in the scheme.

In order to implement this mandate, committees were set up from the state to the village level, for monitoring the progress of the scheme, and to provide necessary guidance. The responsibility of supplying mid day meals was given to Gram Pradhans in villages, and Ward Committees in city areas. In some cases, NGOs were entrusted with this task. The responsibility was given to Gramin Vikas Vibhag in villages, and to DUDA and SUDA in cities. Every school was allowed to buy utensils costing up to ₹ 2,000 from the school development fund. Cooks are appointed from among the

SC/ST and widows on a priority basis. The scheme is 100 per cent funded by the Government of India.

Special Quality Schemes

With a view to bringing about inclusive development of education, a new scheme, known as the Kasturba Gandhi Balika Vidyalaya Yojana, was launched by the Government of India in 25 educationally backward blocks. Under this scheme, residential schools have been established in these identified blocks to promote education of girls of the deprived sections. To begin with, the campuses of DIETs were used to run these schools. Seven Kasturba Gandhi Balika Vidyalaya (KGBV) schools are to be established by NGOs in U.P. (GOUP: 2005, p. 226). This step also indicates the influence of economic reforms in U.P., wherein the NGOs have been given an increased role for service delivery.

Fiscal Reforms in the State

The pace of fiscal adjustments and corrections at the state level gained further momentum during 2007–08. So far, 26 out of the 28 states have enacted FRBMAs. Sikkim and West Bengal are the two states yet to enact FRBMAs. This act has enabled the state government to check wasteful expenditure and allocate scarce resources on a priority basis to most important sectors that can provide greater pay offs and ensure greater welfare of the people, like expenditure on primary education and primary health care.

Debt Consolidation and Relief Facility (DCRF), formulated as per the recommendations of the Twelfth Finance Commission (TFC), has two components–consolidation of central loans (from the Ministry of Finance) and 24 out of the 28 states have been consolidated to the extent of ₹ 1,09,977 crores. Debt consolidation has provided interest relief to the states to the extent of ₹ 4,392 crores and ₹ 3,995 crores in 2005–06 and 2006–07 respectively. The fiscal gain to U.P. has helped consolidate its budgetary arrangements so that it is in a better position to fund the necessary expenditure on social services.

The second component of DCRF is debt waiver. For 2005–06, the consolidated debt of 14 states, amounting to ₹ 3,879 crore, was waived, off and for 2006–07, the debt of 19 states to the extent of ₹ 4,595 crore was waived. During 2007–08, 21 states are estimated to have got debt waivers of ₹ 4,812 crores. U.P. is among the main beneficiaries of this scheme. Debt consolidation and waivers have facilitated states in achieving targets of elimination of revenue deficits and containing fiscal deficits as a proportion of GSDP at three per cent well ahead of 2008–09. It also poses a challenge to states to sustain this momentum, and it provides an opportunity to leverage gains achieved to concentrate on social sectors, like education and health, to make the growth process more inclusive.

Reprioritisation of Educational Expenditure

As part of the expenditure reprioritisation strategy, public spending both in absolute and in relative terms on elementary education, primary and secondary health care and high priority areas of investment have been increased. The Government of U.P. has acknowledged that this will be possible only through substantial reduction in subsidies, and containing salary and pension expenditures and no budget support to loss making units of state enterprises. Recruitment of additional staff in the state is to be made very sparingly with the exception of *education,* police, and medical and health services (GOUP: 2004, p. 105, Emphasis added).

In pursuance of the provisions of Article 280 of the Constitution of India, the Thirteenth Finance Commission was constituted by the President of India under the Chairmanship of Dr. Vijay L. Kelkar vide a notification dated November 13, 2007. The Commission made recommendations covering a period of five years commencing on April 1, 2010. In making its recommendations, the Commission paid attention, among other considerations, to the impact of the proposed implementation of goods and services tax with effect from April 1, 2010, and the need to improve the quality of public expenditure to obtain better outcomes in the development of the social sectors.

Inter State Success Stories

The experience in the functioning of the social sectors and their performance has revealed that political support is an important prerequisite for effective programme delivery. When politicians care about a particular programme, they are more likely to insist on effective implementation by the civil servants. Civil servants, responsible for managing such programmes, are likely to be given more autonomy, as well as administrative and financial resources. Adequate provision of finance is a necessary condition for development, but it is not sufficient condition for success.

This is the reason that in certain schemes, even if there is less money allocated, commitment to produce better results, makes the difference. Programmes that enjoy political support are better positioned to ward off 'rent-seeking behaviour' by influential groups. Therefore, building political support is an important instrument for ensuring the success of an educational programme.

The Case of Tamil Nadu

The state of Tamil Nadu has performed better than Karnataka in human development since 1981; it, in fact, has overtaken the state of Karnataka. It would be useful to look into the underlying reasons of this extraordinary performance of Tamil Nadu.

At the outset, it appears that political support was a key factor in explaining Tamil Nadu's superior performance. In Tamil Nadu, political support took the form of a consensus between the state's two major Dravidian political parties, to promote policies and programmes designed to improve human development. For about three decades, both parties engaged in an active game of oneupmanship to extend the reach of these programmes for common ideological and electoral reasons.

The Nutritious Mid-Day Meal (NMM) programme was introduced in Tamil Nadu in 1982, covering pre-school and primary school children alike. This was soon expanded to include upper-primary and secondary students, as well as old-age pensioners (Seeta Prabhu, 2005). The programme employed about 200,000 people, mostly women, as organisers and cooks. At first, the government was mocked for the huge cost of the programme (estimated at ₹ 6.59 billion in 2002–03), but it clearly helped boost school enrolments, reduce dropout rates and improve nutrition. Teachers and parents were appreciative of the scheme, and its salutary effects, and on educational improvement. Its importance on the political agenda kept it relatively insulated from becoming another vehicle for patronage and rent-seeking. The NMM programme was so successful in Tamil Nadu, that the Supreme Court in 2001 ordered that all states adopt it. Consequently, cooked mid day meals came to be provided in primary schools in all states since that judgement of the apex court.

However, an aberration may be pointed out. In a senior secondary girls schools in Chennai, visited by an NIEPA team with an international delegation and with prior permission of the education secretary of Tamil Nadu and with advance information to the school principal, delegates were shown one half plate full of meal just outside a very small kitchen. Interaction with a large segment of students by the members of the delegation revealed that most of the girls brought meals from home. One is, therefore, not very sure whether the ultimate outcome is attributable to the midday meal scheme.

The Case of Kerala

The prime factor behind Kerala having attained the top position in human development, the top rank in literacy and top rank in the country's Education Development Index (EDI) with monotonous regularity, is the state government bureaucracy's receptivity and adaptability for innovative ideas in policy making, and in honest implementation of the same. (Prabhu, 2001) Other states have not been able to show this level of bureaucratic commitment and honesty. For instance, although Kerala's alternating state governments led by the Communist parties and the Congress parties tend to claim credit for the state's high literacy, the major providers of quality primary and secondary education in Kerala, are schools, run by the Syrian Christian and Roman Catholic churches. Yet, instead of discouraging private initiatives in school education, successive state administrations have co-opted them into the system, transforming most of them into 'aided' schools, eligible for enabling government grants.

A similar spirit of willingness to engineer public-private partnerships is evident behind the Kozhikode (Calicut) district administration's launching of a free online tutoring service for government school students, in collaboration with Learning Scholars-a subsidiary of a private limited company, which is a Kochi-based online tutoring firm.

The service is launched well before the state board's class X and XII Secondary School Leaving Certificate examinations, and designed to provide supplementary education to government school students at these examinations. Model question papers are answered online by the teachers of Learning Scholars, which provides e-tutoring services to students of classes IX and X. This is for the first time in India, that an online tutoring system has been introduced for school students, as a public-private partnership venture. It has started with three schools on an experimental basis, but gradually, all the 69 government schools in the district will be covered.

Concluding Remarks

The economic reforms at the state level have been slow. The results have been mixed, as the policies have differed from state to state. The invitation to the private sector to provide education stands out in many ways. However, the success of educational development in the decade of the 1990s was mainly the result of several government interventions, many of which had started in the late 1980s. For example, schemes like Operation Black-Board (OB), Sarva Shiksha Abhiyan (SSA), District Primary Education Project (DPEP), sponsored by the World Bank, Mahila Samakhya (MS), Education Guarantee Scheme (EGS), and the Mid Day Meal (MDM) programme, were started during this period. The effective implementation of these programmes have given very encouraging outcomes so far, as for as improvement in literacy is concerned.

Indeed, the improvement in literacy in the decade of the 1990s in U.P. was better than in many states and also compared to the national average. This once again proved that, if implemented sincerely and with less leakages, government intervention can produce better results even in states, where the political and administrative set up has not been so strong, over the last few decades.

Notes

1. For full details of argument, See for instance, the chapter: Vicious Cycle in Uttar Pradesh by Ajit Kumar Singh, Mohd. Muzammil and S. Nayak in Shovan Ray (Editor, 2010) *Backwaters of Development: Six Deprived States of India*, Oxford University Press.
2. For a brief historical review of pre and post independence India, the progress of education in U.P. along with the financial constraints and the political economy factors responsible for the same, see, Kingdon and Muzammil (2003), and Muzammil (2010).
3. See the article by Muzammil (2010). Shrinking Fiscal Space for Higher Education in Uttar Pradesh.
4. Editorial Observation: It is interesting to note that the success of the mid-day meal scheme in Gujarat. Administrations have found from experience that serving cooked food in schools involved disproportionately high school time and efforts of both teachers and students. This diluted both the amount and quality of learning-teaching, without having significant impact on attendance. This system was replaced by issuing of 10 kg grain (wheat/rice) per child enrolled. This led to larger enrolments and increased time for teaching-learning. Source-Information was given by the district education officer, Gandhinagar during the visit of the Editor Shri Prakash as Director of Survey of Schools in connection with the UNESCO's Project on Use of Sample Survey Techniques for Educational Statistics, NIEPA/NUEPA, New Delhi and UNESIO Paris.
5. Editorial Observation—In meetings of the Monitoring and Evaluation Committee of the Punjab State Planning Board, it was found that computers, and other scientific kits and reading material remained in the house of the Sarpanch. Principal/Head Masters and teachers were reluctant to use these due the fear of damage and ignorance. See Minutes of Evaluation and Monitoring Committee Meetings attended by Shri Prakash.
6. But there is more than what meets the eye in the attainment of hundred per cent literacy in Kerala. The District Collector of the district that piloted the success of the experiment in the nineties shared the mechanisms used for making the programme succeed in villages with the NIEPA team, comprising of Dr. Shri Prakash, Prof. K.G. Virmani and Dr. Sheel Chand Nuna. It was ordered that no money order shall be delivered to any person who does not know to sign. Nothing was to be supplied from fair price shops, if the person did not know how to sign. Those, who attended literacy classes regularly, were given free bus passes to travel within the district. On complaints lodged by women, the local wine shops/bars were eliminated from the villages in order to ensure that the regular drunkards and patrons of such shops/bars attended literacy classes and gave up drinking. All the women folk of the villages supported this initiative of the collector, and responded positively to the 100 per cent literacy campaign. Mr Rajendran, the District Collector and architect of the success of the programme, became an icon.

In repeated visits of Dr Shri Prakash and his NIEPa team to rural areas of the Ghaziabad district like Duhai, hardly 10–12 students used to be present in classes, though the enrolment register showed 70–75 enrollees. This escalated number was to ensure posting of more teachers. Besides, regular students of public and private schools were found attending classes of the non-formal system of education (NFSE) meant for school drop-outs. These classes ensured employment for one youth of the village, and provided additional coaching to those who were already enrolled in schools. Such distortions abound in the implementation of reforms.

References

Government of India (GOI) 2008, *Eleventh Five Year Plan* 2007–2012, Planning Commission, New Delhi, Volumes I, II and III.

Government of U.P. (GOUP) 1991, *Eighth Five Year Plan 1992–97 and Annual Plan 1992–93,* State Planning Commission, December.

Government of U.P. (GOUP) 1997, *Draft Ninth Five Year Plan 1997–2002 and Annual Plan 1997–98,* State Planning Commission, October.

Government of U.P. (GOUP) 2002, *Tenth Five Year Plan 2002–2007 and Annual Plan 2002–03,* State Planning Commission, April.

Government of U.P. (GOUP) 2004, *Annual Plan 2004–2005* Volume I (Part I) State Planning Commission, September.

Government of U.P. (GOUP) 2005, *Annual Plan 2006–2007* Volume I, State Planning Commission, November.

Government of U.P. (GOUP) 2007, *Eleventh Five Year Plan 2007–2012 and Annual Plan 2007–2008,* State Planning Commission.

Lecture, VHD College, Lucknow University, Lucknow, 5th January (mimeo).

Muzammil, M. (2010a). Challenges of Higher Education in India, *V.N. Vidyant Memorial.*

Muzammil, M. (2010b). Quantity, Quality and Equality—The Triangle in Indian Higher Education, Paper presented in the *International Seminar and Academic Administrators Workshop on "Envisioning Quality: Academic Professionalisation in Higher Education Based on Indo British Experiences",* organized by the Academic Staff College, AMU, Aligarh, 6–7 February 2010, sponsored by NUEPA and UGC, New Delhi.

Muzammil, M. (2010d). Higher Education in India: Challenges and Opportunities, *Keynote Address* at the TILT Biennial Conference organised by the Centre for the Advancement of Learning and Teaching (CALT) University College London (UCL) 5–9 July in the United Kingdom.

Muzammil, M. (2010e). Shrinking Fiscal Space for Higher Education in Uttar Pradesh, *University News,* Vol. 48, No. 28, July 12–18.

Muzammil, M. and Tabassum Khatoon (2005). Resource Constraints to Higher Education: Evidences from Uttar Pradesh, *University News (A weekly Journal of Higher Education),* Vol. 42, No. 52, December 27, 2004 – January 02, 2005.

Muzammil, M. (2001). Public Support for Education—Market based Approach, *Perspective in Education,* Vol. 17, No. 2, April.

Muzammil, M. (2010c). Higher Education and Development in the Era of, Globalisation, *Keynote Address* delivered at The National Seminar on Education and Economic Development in the Backdrop of Globalisation, Juhari Devi Girls PG College, Kanpur, 15th February.

Panchmukhi, P.R. (2000). 'Social Impact of Economic reforms in India: A Critical Appraisal' *Economic and Political Weekly*, Vol. XXXV, No. 10.

Panchmukhi, V.R. (1992). 'New Economic Policy and Social Sector' in *Indian Economy in Transition*, New Delhi, Deep and Deep Publications.

Prabhu, K. Seeta (1994). "The Budget and Structural Adjustment with a Human face' *Economic and Political Weekly*, Vol. XXIX, Nos. 16 and 17, April.

Prabhu, K. Seeta (1995). Structural Adjustment and Financing Elementary Education: The Indian Experience, *Journal of Educational Planning and Administration*, IX (1), pp. 27–43.

CHAPTER 8

Interstate Differentials of Development of General Higher Education with Special Reference to Uttar Pradesh

Shalini Sharma and Gunjan Bhatnagar

Introduction

Education is the cause, as well as the consequence of social and economic development. Modern economic growth revolves around the growth of productivity. But productivity depends on (i) Technology of production, and (ii) human capital. Development and successful exploitation of technology depends on the ingenuity and creativity of man. Education in general, and research in particular, is the base of development and commercial exploration of technology. (For an empirical analysis of the relationship between productivity, growth and education, see Sharma, Amit, 2011). Education is also the agent of social change, and change in the psychological mould of the people. Thus, human capital plays a catalytic role in development.

People are the greatest resources and agents of development. Human resources as pivots of development were recognised in the West, much later than in India. Since times immemorial, even illiterate and uneducated parents considered their children to be the most precious wealth, and the means of future security. The role of human resources in the modern knowledge economy has acquired even greater importance than before. Human, or intellectual capital, was recognised as the basic factor of production and growth formally by Vakil-Brahmanand (1956) and Schultz (1966).

Human resource development takes place basically at the household level initially (Rashmi Arora, 2010). Right from the day of conception, to the bearing and rearing of children, lot of investment is made in the children's uplift, and their growth as human resources by the family. Alfred Marshall (1892) estimated that £86 millions were spent by Britons in 1888 for child bearing and rearing. This includes both public and private investment. The £86 million of 1888 will amount to billions of pounds today. This would give an idea about the foundations on which human resources are developed, and accumulated over time. Of course, the quantum of investment will vary among households, and between the years. Investment and human resources grow, with the growth of income, both at the micro and macro levels. That is why Gary Becker postulated that marriage is a contract between the spouses to bear and rear children to accumulate human resources. This has been part and parcel of the Indian heritage for long; that is why new couples are expected to pay their debts towards their parents by bearing and rearing their own children. Elders bless the young by '*saying dudho nahao and puto fallow,* (May God bless you and bathe you in milk (symbol of wealth) and shower with sons'. This is what also accounts for the inter-generational transference of illiteracy and education (Prakaash, Shri, 1996; Arora, Rashmi Maini, 2010).

Human capital, in turn, depends on education, training and health. Therefore, it may be inferred that the more literate and educationally developed states are likely to be more economically and socially developed also. This thesis is supported by the fact that the rank correlation coefficient between the number of universities, and the growth rate of State's Domestic Product (SDP) of Indian states is 0.355, which is moderate in magnitude, but statistically significant; the corresponding value of 't' is 2.01. It is in view of this close relationship of education and economy, that we have selected higher education in Uttar Pradesh for a detailed study.

Background of the Study

University and collegiate education is at the top of the education hierarchy. However, growth of higher education can be sustained only if feeder level education, especially senior secondary education, grows at a commensurate rate. In turn, growth of senior secondary education depends on the growth of the secondary and below secondary school education. Basic education in India was, however, by and large, universalised in 2011. In the coming years, more children will be joining secondary and senior secondary education. This, in turn, will lead to increasing demand for seats in institutions of higher learning. Probably, this has prompted the Government of India to set the goal for universal senior secondary education by 2017. This policy goal might also be the result of the desire to compete in future with the developed countries, on an equal footing. Realisation of this goal will truly convert class education into mass education in India.

Once senior secondary education is universalised, the collegiate and university education will come under tremendous pressure. If plans for the expansion and diversification of higher education are not implemented properly, it will lead to serious problems in the job market as well. If senior secondary graduates neither get admission in colleges or universities, nor get jobs, then social tensions will rise. It may lead to serious social and political consequences. It has been observed that part of the trouble in the North East, Punjab and Kashmir is due to the unemployment among the educated.

Current Status

For analytical purposes, knowledge of the current status and past achievement may be useful. This aspect is taken up first for analysis.

Higher education is on the concurrent list, therefore both the central and state governments are responsible for its expansion and regulation. In 2009, India had 428 universities, of which 25 were central universities, and 403 universities were in the state sector. The universities are also classified into the following categories:

State Universities

1. Public universities in the state sector;
2. Deemed universities which are directly in the domain of the University Grants Commission (UGC); and
3. Private universities established by resolution in the state legislatures.

Pattern of Spatial Distribution

The patterns of spatial distribution of universities is highly skewed, and marked by high degrees of concentration. It is important to note that the existence of institutions of any level of education, including universities and colleges, at places of residence facilitates access to a majority of the people on the area. Non-existence of educational facilities in the neighbourhood, raises costs and inaccessibility. This applies to both state and central universities. The proposition of unequal distribution of universities and colleges is evaluated statistically.

Distribution of Central Universities in the States and Union Territories (2009)

Table 1 shows the state wise distribution of central universities. It highlights the high degree of concentration of central universities in India. This is being remedied now, with recent efforts of the central government to either establish a new university in the central domain, or take over some existing university in a state, with the objective that each state should have at least one central university. As many as eleven states do not have any central university as yet. U.P. in this case tops the list of states which have more than one central university.

Table 1: State Wise Distribution of Central Universities

One	*Two*	*Three*	*Four*
Mizoram	Assam	Andhra Pradesh	Uttar Pradesh
Nagaland	J&K		
Orissa	Madhya Pradesh		
Punjab	Manipur		
Rajasthan			
Sikkim			
Tamil Nadu			
Tripura			
Uttarakhand			
West Bengal			
Puducherry			

State Universities in India

The distribution of all 428 universities is also acutely skewed. Table 2 shows the state wise distribution of state universities in India. A perusal of the table reveals that five states, namely Tamil Nadu, Maharashtra, Uttar Pradesh, Andhra Pradesh and Karnataka, in that order, accounting for 40 per cent of the total universities in India. Five other states are in the second group accounting for 30 per cent of total universities in India. Thus, 70 per cent of the total universities are concentrated in 10 or slightly less than one third of the total states. This is the top group. As against this, 18 states account for slightly less than 20 per cent of total universities, and 21 states, taken together, account for less than 30 per cent of universities.

The following *Lorenz curve* highlights the degree of inequality in distribution (Figure 1).

Table 2: State Universities Data

Sl. No.	*States*	*No. of Universities*	*Sl. No.*	*States*	*No. of Universities*
1.	Tamil Nadu	50	17	Chhattisgarh	9
2.	Maharashtra	41	18	J&K	8
3.	Uttar Pradesh	38	19	Jharkhand	7
4.	Andhra Pradesh	33	20	Assam	6
5.	Karnataka	32	21	Himachal Pradesh	5
6.	Rajasthan	28	22	Sikkim	3
7.	Gujarat	24	23	Arunachal Pradesh	2
8.	West Bengal	20	24	Manipur	2
9.	Bihar	17	25	Tripura	2
10.	Madhya Pradesh	17	26	Chandigarh	2
11.	NCT of Delhi	16	27	Puducherry	2
12.	Uttarakhand	14	28	Goa	1
13.	Orissa	13	29	Meghalaya	1
14.	Haryana	12	30	Mizoram	1
15.	Punjab	11	31	Nagaland	1
16.	Kerala	10			

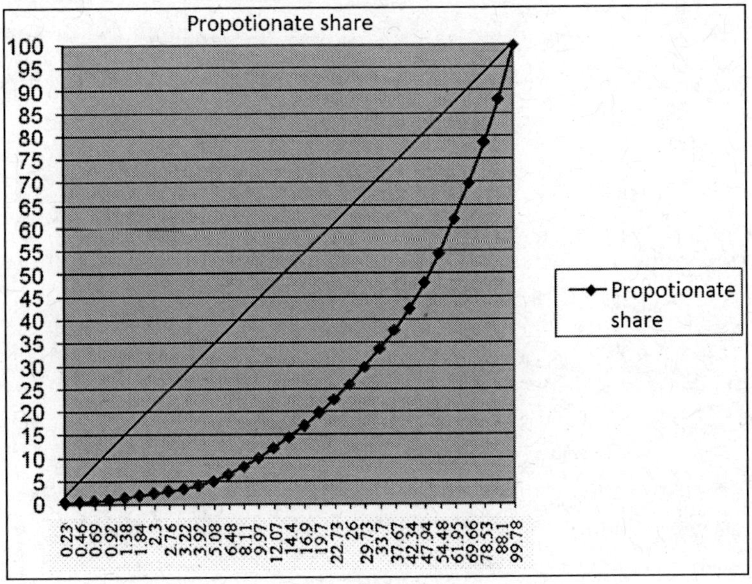

Fig. 1

That there is extremely high degree of concentration of universities among few states is clearly highlighted by the gap between the diagonal of the square and the Lorenz curve. The diagonal is the line of equal distribution.

Incidentally, Uttar Pradesh ranks third in India in the number of universities. It has as many as 38 universities, as against Tamil Nadu and Maharashtra, which boast of 50 and 41 universities respectively. U.P. thus accounts for roughly nine per cent of total universities in India. Out of 38 universities in Uttar Pradesh, 19 are public universities, and the other 19 are private universities. Thus, private enterprise in higher education accounts for 50 per cent of universities in Uttar Pradesh. Maharashtra also falls in the same category, where private enterprise and individual capital has played a pivotal role in the expansion of universities.

The median number of universities in India is 10. However, the actual number of universities equals the median number only in Kerala, while 15 states have more than the median number of universities; the number of universities in these states varies from 11 to 50. As against this, 15 states have less than the median number of universities.

Within both these groups, the number of universities varies greatly, and the range of variations differs sharply. In the first group, the range of variation is from 11 to 50, while in the second group, the range of variation is from 1 to 9. Interestingly, educationally less developed states, as indicated by the number of universities, also show a lower degree of intra-group inequality. The number of universities, however, is not normalised either by population, or the area to be served by the universities.

The degree of variation in the number of universities may also be gauged from the value of the coefficient of variation, which is as high as 102.5 per cent. The *Kurtosis* has a value of 0.56, which also indicates a high degree of concentration. The coefficient of skewness is 1.16, which is in consonance with the value of the coefficient of variation. These results highlight that (i) universities are not normally distributed; (ii) distribution of universities is positively skewed; and (iii) disproportionately high number of universities is concentrated in three states.

Most of the private institutions of higher education owe their existence either to politicians, or to successful businessman. Some businessman invest their money in order to discharge corporate social responsibility, whereas others enter the education field with their enterprise and capital, for having additional sources of income. The differentials of economic growth and diverse role of private enterprise in different states may partly account for differentials in the number of private universities in different states.

Distribution of Colleges in India

Colleges carry the main responsibility of imparting higher education. Table 3 shows the state wise distribution of colleges in India. The table reveals that:

1. Three states U.P., Maharashtra, and Karnataka account for more than 30 per cent of the total colleges in India;
2. If we add two more states to these three, and consider all five states, including Andhra Pradesh and Madhya Pradesh, having the maximum number of colleges then these five states account for approximately 50 per cent of the total colleges in 30 states and union territories taken together;

Table 3: State Wise Distributions of Colleges in India

Sl. No.	*States*	*No. of Colleges*	*Sl. No.*	*States*	*No. of Colleges*
1.	Uttar Pradesh	1055	19	Delhi	81
2.	Maharashtra	946	20	Manipur	54
3.	Karnataka	596	21	Himachal Pradesh	49
4.	Andhra Pradesh	457	22	Uttarakhand	46
5.	Madhya Pradesh	450	23	Meghalaya	34
6.	West Bengal	394	24	Goa	26
7.	Gujarat	386	25	Mizoram	21
8.	Orissa	379	26	Chandigarh	18
9.	Tamil Nadu	355	27	Tripura	16
10.	Bihar	338	28	Nagaland	14
11.	Rajasthan	252	29	Puducherry	12
12.	Assam	228	30	Arunachal Pradesh	8
13.	Kerala	228	31	Sikkim	5
14.	Punjab	218	32	A&N Islands	2
15.	Haryana	150	33	Daman Diu	1
16.	Chhattisgarh	145	34	D&N Haveli	0
17.	J&K	108	35	Lakshadweep	0
18.	Jharkhand	101			

3. The analysis also reveals that 20 out of the remaining states, taken together, account for 10 per cent of the total colleges only; and
4. Colleges are much more unevenly distributed than the universities. The Lorenz curve clearly highlights the high degree of spatial concentration of colleges among the states.

A perusal of the Lorenz curve and its comparison with the spatial distribution of universities will clearly establish this aspect (Figure 2).

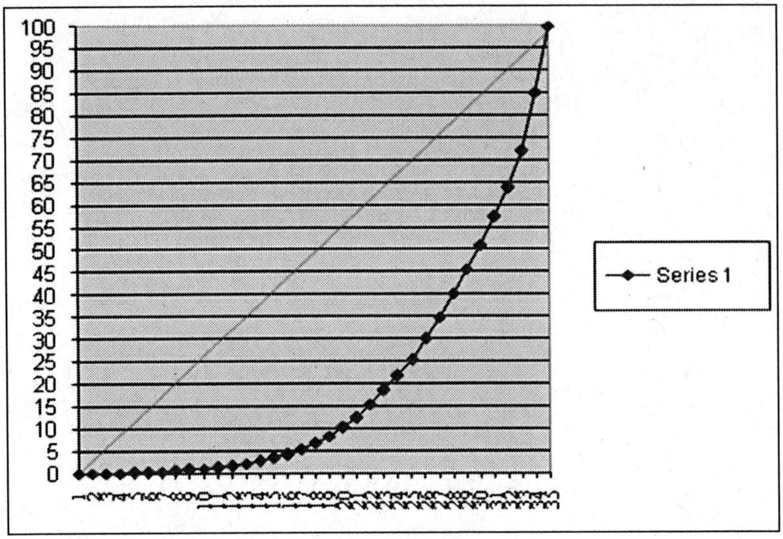

Fig. 2

Uttar Pradesh is among the leading states as for as the number of colleges is concerned; it has 1055 colleges. U.P. is followed by Maharashtra with 946 and Karnataka with 596 colleges. In Uttar Pradesh, 512 out of 1055 colleges are under *Section 2(f) and 12(B) and 543 colleges are not included under Section 12(B) of UGC* in operation now.

Thus, the state wise distribution of colleges also shows a highly uneven pattern of distribution. The mean number of colleges is 210.97, whereas the median is 104.5. This highlights the uneven distribution. The value of median is much lower than the mean, median and mode are equal in a normal distribution. Difference between the values of mean and median highlight the degree of departure from symmetry in distribution. The distribution is positively skewed and has a concentration of right side tail. This is obvious from coefficients of skewness and *Kurtosis*. The coefficient of variation of colleges is 80.85 per cent, which is again lower than the coefficient of variation of distribution of universities, but it is slightly higher than the coefficient of variation of enrolments in various universities. The pattern of distribution of colleges, like the spatial distribution of universities, also shows unevenness. The *Kurtosis* is as high as 3.39, while skewness is 1.80. These values highlight a very high degree of spatial concentration, and unequal distribution of colleges. The limited number of universities can obviously be distributed unequally. But, the establishment and running costs of colleges is generally lower than that of universities. Therefore, there may be less economic bottlenecks and population size in the command areas of colleges which may constitute lower leads of difficult barriers to cross compared to universities.

Enrolments and Faculty Size

Enrolments and faculty size are also relatively lower for colleges than for universities. Dispersal of colleges over wider areas, facilitates a much more even distribution of locations, and easier access to students/people. There has hardly been any definite policy of location of educational institutions in India even during the era of planned development. *Location decisions* have been guided by the push and pull factors (Prakash, Shri, 1977; Prakash and Shrivastava, D.K., 1992). For example, there was popular demand for the establishment of the Punjabi Suba. But, the decision was to establish the Panjabi University, Patiala. Such examples can be multiplied.

However, a deliberate attempt has been made to disperse facilities of higher collegiate education over a wider area, partly through government policies and partly by private initiatives. Consequently, in several towns/villages and small cities, the enrolment size of colleges is relatively small. This has compromised efficiency, in terms of unit cost and, in some cases, even the quality of education (Prakash, S., 1996).

It is interesting to note that Tamil Nadu, which tops in the number of universities, ranks ninth in the number of colleges. Uttar Pradesh, which ranks third in the number of universities, ranks first in the number of colleges. This suggests that overall development of higher education cannot be judged only on the basis of the number of universities. One has to consider universities and colleges together. It may be noted that the size of universities is much larger than colleges, in terms of expenditure, infrastructure, enrolments and faculty. Tamil Nadu seems to have concentrated more on the development of universities than colleges, whereas Uttar Pradesh has concentrated more on colleges than universities. A part of this can be explained by historical factors. During the British regime, Western education struck deep roots, and became an instrument of social and economic development, both at the household and community levels. Competition emerged in North India among the caste and religious leaders. Uttar Pradesh was no exception. The result was that numerous colleges with a caste nomenclature came into existence. Rajput, Jain, Vaishya, Khalsa, Jat colleges are the examples of this. The second nomenclature was based on religion. Aligarh Muslim University, Banaras Hindu University, Hindu College, Muslim College, Khalsa College are examples of such institutions, which came into existence due to caste and religion based competition. Christians were not far ahead in the race but their institutions were named mainly after saints like St. Joseph College, St. John's College, St. Stephens College are examples. Some colleges also carried the name Christian College and Presidency College.

However, after independence, competition shifted from religion and caste based leaders to political leaders. Since the 1980s, the competition is among business leaders and business houses. The Arya Samaj movement of social reforms in Hindu society focused on educational development also (Prakash, S., 1996). Consequently, Punjab, Haryana, Uttar Pradesh are dotted by many DAV schools and DAV colleges and colleges of similar denominations.

Enrolments

Existence of educational institutions represents the supply side of the equation. The degree of utilisation of the facilities depends on the demand for places in educational institutions. Enrolments reflect effective demand. Hence, enrolments in higher education are an appropriate indicator of educational development.

Table 4 shows enrolments in higher education in India. The pattern of distribution of enrolments also shows a high degree of spatial inequalities. Mean value of enrolments is as high as 40,12,296, while median enrolments are much lower than mean enrolments where the median has a value of 22,43,56.4. The coefficient of variation of enrolments is 76.62 per cent, which is much lower than the coefficient of variation of universities. It implies that the enrolment size of universities is much less uneven, than that of enrolments. *Kurtosis* is as high as 3.804, while the coefficient of skewedness is 1.91. These values highlight both the high degree of concentration and unequal distribution of enrolments among the states. It may be noted that the size of differentials by enrolments may be directly related to (i) size of the population in age group eligible for college, and university education; and (ii) demand for higher education. Demand for higher education depends on (i) affordability, and (ii) possession of conditions of the eligibility for admission. Incidentally, the opportunity cost constitutes a very high proportion of both public and private unit costs of education.

Table 4: State Wise Enrolment in 2009 in Higher Education

Sl. No.	*State*	*Number*
1.	Uttar Pradesh	21,70,516
2.	Maharashtra	18,13,942
3.	Andhra Pradesh	11,50,759
4.	Tamil Nadu	10,33,755
5.	West Bengal	9,03,103
6.	Karnataka	8,37,668
7.	Madhya Pradesh	7,50,745
8.	Gujarat	7,01,577
9.	Bihar	6,24,010
10.	Rajasthan	5,72,651
11.	Orissa	4,19,939
12.	Kerala	3,73,092
13.	Haryana	3,52,887
14.	Punjab	3,35,407
15.	NCT of Delhi	2,50,400
16.	Assam	2,34,124
17.	Chhattisgarh	2,26,105
18.	Jharkhand	2,22,608
19.	Uttarakhand	1,77,411
20.	Himachal Pradesh	1,18,194
21.	J&K	1,11,550
22.	Chandigarh	50,032
23.	Meghalaya	37,107
24.	Manipur	36,118
25.	Puducherry	31,595
26.	Tripura	25,884
27.	Goa	24,282
28.	Nagaland	22,057
29.	Arunachal Pradesh	12,670
30.	Mizoram	12,129
31.	Sikkim	5,841
32.	A&N Islands	2,600
33.	Daman&Diu	750
34.	Lakshadweep	300
35.	D&N Haveli	0
		1,36,41,808

Table 5: State-Wise Number of Colleges during the Year 2008–2009 and Increase in Number of Colleges from 2004–2005 to 2008–2009

State	*2004– 05*	*2005–06*	*2006–07*	*2007–08*	*2008–09*	*Growth Rate*
Uttar Pradesh	2037	2037	2047	2137	2181	1.61
Maharashtra	2598	2826	3052	3363	3849	4.17
Karnataka	1865	2096	2224	2436	2765	4.07
Andhra Pradesh	2296	2434	3026	3264	3648	5.31
Madhya Pradesh	1116	1116	1322	1524	1871	5.85
Tamil Nadu	1242	1242	1254	1297	1337	0.82

As expected the number of colleges and enrolments in states are almost perfectly related to each other. Rank correlation is statistically significant and its value is as high as 0.9718, and the t-value is 23.65. Thus the results are in consonance with each other.

The following Lorenz curve depicts the uneven distribution of enrolments among states (Figure 3).

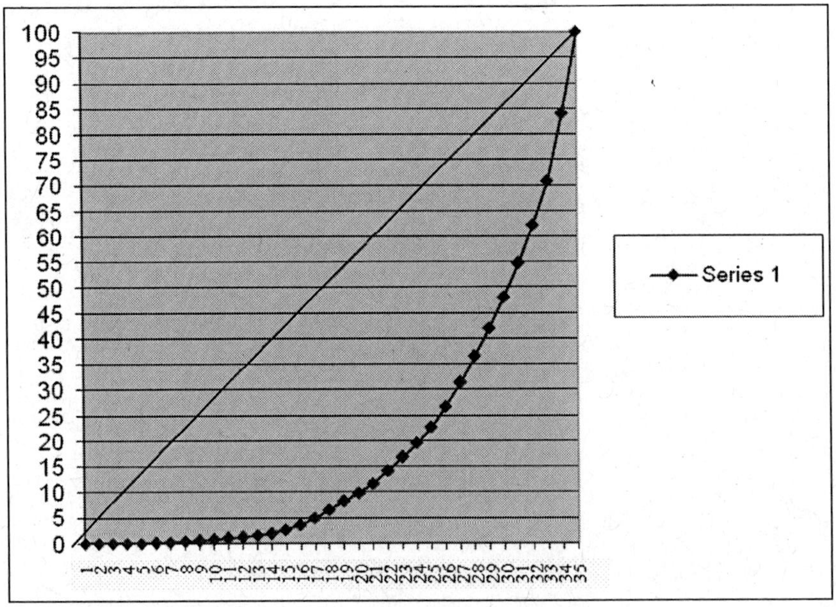

Fig. 3

Enrolments represent effective demand. If demand for places equals supply in an institution, the demand is defined as an effective demand. Therefore, high aggregate enrolments in Uttar Pradesh represent high effective demand for higher education.

However, institutional size is subject to intake restrictions, especially in institutions of professional education. Generally, big size of an institution denotes higher standing and prestige of a college among the institutions as well as the professions. It also shows a great deal of popularity among the students and parents. More prestigious an institution, the greater is the difficulty in getting into it. From this perspective, the number of colleges and universities in states represents only one side of the equation. Enrolments may generally be taken to represent the demand side (Shri Prakash, 1977).

One can expect the number of institutions to represent government funding and private enterprise in the field of higher education. Considering the number of institutions and the corresponding population size, then Uttar Pradesh can be expected to have a large average size of colleges. This is represented by enrolments per college. However, it may be due to expectations and wide spread/dispersal over space.

The first five states according to college size by enrolments are Uttarakhand, Delhi, Tamil Nadu, Chandigarh and Puducherry.

These results highlight an interesting feature. The smaller the area of the region, the larger is the enrolment size. The demand for places, and effective demand also depends on the patterns of locations. If colleges are established in small cities, semi urban and rural areas, the average size will be smaller. This is what accounts for the 12th rank of Uttar Pradesh in enrolments per college. But the earlier results contradict this.

Growth Profile of States

The following table furnishes a broad idea about the pace of growth of higher college education in India (Table 6).

The growth rates, shown in the table, have been derived from the exponential growth curve:

$$\log Y_i = a + bX$$

where Y_i, $i = 1, 2, 3, 4, 5$ represents the states in the table, X shows the time measured in calendar years and b shows the annual compound rate of growth. The equation is estimated by OLS.

Table 6

States	*Growth Rate*	*Growth Rate Relative to U.P.*
Uttar Pradesh	1.61	1
Maharashtra	4.17	2.59
Karnataka	4.07	2.52
Andhra Pradesh	5.31	3.29
Madhya Pradesh	5.85	3.63
Tamil Nadu	0.82	0.5

Growth of Colleges

This section focuses on the growth profile of collegiate education. The number of colleges and enrolments are used as important indices of growth. The number of colleges in India grew at an annual compound rate of 3.93 per cent, which is 2.44 per cent times more than the rate of growth of colleges in Uttar Pradesh. The rate of growth of colleges in Karnataka, Maharashtra, Andhra Pradesh and Madhya Pradesh exceeds the rate of growth in Uttar Pradesh by 2.59 to 3.63 times. Tamil Nadu is the only state among the top six states, having the maximum number of colleges, where colleges have grown at a sluggish rate compared to Uttar Pradesh. Thus, the growth of colleges in Uttar Pradesh has lagged behind not only the growth of colleges in India, but the state has lagged behind the other four developed states also. The growth rates appear to be affected partly by the base effect. Generally, higher the base, the lower the growth rate tends to be. Therefore, it may not be proper to infer on the basis of these rates, that the growth performance of Uttar Pradesh is not satisfactory. However, appropriate inference about the growth performance can be drawn from a comparison of the increase in the number of college education age group children and their actual enrolments. Availability of children eligible for admission is necessary, but not a sufficient condition for growth. The sufficient condition is economic affordability of cost, and eligibility for admission. Eligibility condition for admission in colleges requires successful completion of education up to class 12. But, the paucity of data at this time prevents us from examining this facet of growth of collegiate education.

Conclusions

The main findings of the analysis are that Uttar Pradesh ranks third, and first, in terms of state universities and number of colleges in India. It ranks first in enrolments in India. Uttar Pradesh accounts for 11.68 per cent of universities, 14.7 per cent of colleges and 15.91 per cent of enrolments in India. Thus, the share of U.P. in total enrolments in India almost matches its share of the Indian population. This is, however, only a crude measure. The growth of the number of universities in Uttar Pradesh has exceeded the rate of growth of colleges and universities only in Tamil Nadu, among the top six states, in terms of colleges in India.

The location of universities is highly uneven. Spatial distribution of colleges relative to universities is more even. In view of the huge population size, an extremely high number of illiterates and coverage by educational services in U.P., the state needs more accelerated development of education, especially higher education, if it has to catch up with the more developed states of India leave apart other countries. This needs enlisting the support of private enterprise on an increasing scale. If educational development is not taken care of, Uttar Pradesh will continue to grow sluggishly and lag behind other states in economic growth.

In view of the fact that human capital, especially higher educated human capital, holds the key to modern growth, it is no riddle that U.P. continues to lag behind other states in the development race. Under utilisation of human resources may partly account for this. Incidentally, a large number of highly educated persons migrated from U.P. to states such as MP, Haryana, Punjab, Rajasthan and North East in search of jobs in the sixties and seventies. The trend still continues, though at a slower rate.

References

Arora, Rashmi, Maini (2010). Inter-Generational Transference of Education: A Study of Capital Region of Delhi, Synopsis of Ph.D. Thesis, BIMTECH, Greater Noida.

Marshall, Alfred (1892). *Principles of Economics,* Macmillan, London.

Prakash, Shri (1977). *Educational System—An Econometric Study,* Concept Publishing Co., New Delhi.

Prakash, Shri (1996). *Cost of Education*, Anamika, New Delhi.

Prakash, Shri and Srivastava, D.K. (1992). Model of Location of Educational Institutions. In Nuna, Sheel Chandra and Raza, Munis (Editors) *Regional Development of Education in India*, NUEPA/NIEPA. New Delhi.

Schultz, T.W. (1966). *Economic Value of Education*, Columbia University Press.

Sharma, Amit (2011). Up-Gradation of Educational Qualifications in Selected Occupations: A Study of Higher Scientific and Technical Occupations since 1981 in the Indian Economy, Ph.D. Thesis, BIMTECH Center of Research Studies, Affiliated to University of Mysore, Mysore.

Vakil, C.N. and Brahamananda, P.R (1956). *Planning for an Expanding Econom: Accumulation, Employment and Technical Progress in Underdeveloped Countries,* Vora & Company, Bombay.

CHAPTER 9

Intra-Regional and Interdistrict Variations in the Facilities for Technical and Higher Education within Uttar Pradesh

Shalini Sharma and Gunjan Bhatnagar

Men have been learning from nature, experience and observation since the beginning of civilisation. The accumulated learning has been put to productive uses from time to time. At one time, stones were used to enhance human skills and effectiveness in hunting, stones were replaced first by arrows and then by guns. During all these changes, men remained at the centre stage of human life and society. With the evolution of civilisation, accumulation of layers upon layers of knowledge and its use for making men more efficient and productive, economic growth and social development has been taking place. All this while men have incessantly been exploring ways and means of storing labour and time in the form of capital to overcome the perishable nature of labour (Adam Smith, 1774). Machines and equipment, created through investments of financial capital, have been the carriers of not only labour and time invested in work relating to creation and production of machinery and equipment, but also to the store house of ingenuity, knowledge and skills of men that lie at the base of conceptualisation and implementation of scientific research into inventions and innovations (Sharma, Amit, 2012).

Financial capital is generally invested in machinery and equipment, which are the carriers of technology, and labour and time invested in the development of the same. Technology, however, owes its creation to scientific research and technological development. Innovations and inventions are, however, the main function of higher scientific, technical and professional education. This chapter focuses on:

1. The current status of higher scientific and technical education in Uttar Pradesh; and
2. Intrastate differentials within the state of Uttar Pradesh.

The globalised and liberalised Indian economy cannot maintain its current status and hope to be counted among the developed countries of the world in the future, unless it forges ahead in innovation and technological development; both these hold the key to the future. Incidentally, the first industrial revolution replaced the manual by mechanical processes of production, while the second industrial revolution replaced the mechanical by automatic processes of production. Processing of materials was involved in both these cases. The third industrial revolution revolves around the processing of information and knowledge rather than materials (Prakash, Shri, 1994). The super specialised skills, required for processing information and knowledge, need super specialised knowledge for creating the next generation technology. Scientific, technological and professional education is the hub of this new revolution. An important aspect of economic growth and social development, is that hardcore engineering and technological transformation cannot succeed without social engineering and institutional transformation. Education in general, and higher professional and technical education in particular, is the base for both economic growth and social transformation (Prakash, S., 1977). In view of this, the development of higher scientific and technical education is the most important aspect of development. But, paucity of resources and a proper academic environment for development of higher education, especially the feeder senior secondary institutions in the command area may restrict the diffusion of the regional development of education. This chapter examines the intra-regional differences of development of technical and professional higher education in Uttar Pradesh.

Sources of Data and Analytical Method

This chapter has been written on the basis of analysis of secondary data. The secondary data used in the chapter have been taken from the following sources:

1. Annual Progress Report of Uttar Pradesh Technical University; and
2. Reports of Higher Education in India.

Analysis of Data

The first section of the chapter has been organised in the following sections/parts:

The first part examines the total number of universities according to:

1. Intra-regional distribution between East and West Uttar Pradesh; and
2. Private and public ownership of institutions.

The second section of the chapter examines the number of institutes, other than universities, of higher technical and professional education in Uttar Pradesh, and their distribution between the Eastern and Western parts of the state.

The third section of the chapter deals with an analysis of the total enrolments in the state and their regional distribution.

The fourth section concentrates on the growth profile of institutes and enrolments therein.

SECTION I

Visweswarya (1931) highlighted that there is a positive relationship between education and economic development. But, the government plays a very important role in educational development. Education became an important subject for planned development after independence; it was included in the five year plans, and public investments in education were accorded high priority in all plans of development. Several universities were established in various parts of the country, although the British government of colonial India initiated the development of modern education during colonial rule over India.

Uttar Pradesh also moved in the direction of establishing universities. Both public as well as private universities were established. Banaras Hindu University (B.H.U.) and Aligarh Muslim University (AMU) came into existence due to the private initiatives of public leaders of British India. M.S. University, Baroda in Gujarat and Saugor University, Sagar in Madhya Pradesh were also the outcomes of private initiatives in British India in the field of university education. Numerous private colleges of higher education were established across the country due to private initiatives in the colonial period. But, the increasing role of the government in the field of education in independent India stultified private initiatives in education for quite some time. Private initiatives have now been revived after the adoption of the New Economic Policy in 1990–91, under which private investments in all fields of human activities, including education, has been encouraged to a great extent.

As the distribution of educational entrepreneurs is not evenly distributed, it is not surprising to find that the distribution of public and private universities is highly uneven in Uttar Pradesh. According to published data of 2008, 19 public universities were operating in Uttar Pradesh and 14 of these 19 public universities are located in Eastern U.P. Thus, Eastern U.P. accounts for approximately 73.68 per cent of the total public universities in U.P. This represents an extremely high degree of concentration, both from the viewpoint of Eastern U.P.'s share in total population and total area of the state. Only five public universities are located in Western U.P., which accounts for only 26.31 per cent of total universities. This is only a little more than one-fourth of the total public universities in U.P. in 2008. Region wise distribution of the universities is not available with the authors after 2008, though data relating to other facets are available up to 2011–12.

Another interesting facet of the growth of university education in U.P. is that many more private universities have been established in Western than Eastern U.P. Out of the nine private universities, seven universities are located in Western U.P. Thus, Western U.P. accounts for 77.77 per cent of all private universities in U.P. On the whole, Western U.P. accounts for 12 of the 28 universities in U.P., while Eastern U.P. has 16 of the 28 universities. Thus, Eastern U.P. has 25 per cent more universities than Western U.P.

The disproportionately high share of Western Uttar Pradesh in private universities and the measly share in public universities highlights two interrelated features of development of university education in Uttar Pradesh: (i) the Western region has more affluent and enterprising people, who are investing their money in university education; and (ii) neglect of the West and pampering of East U.P. by political establishment in university education. Bulging and ever rising demand for professional and technical education has induced and inspired many entrepreneurs to invest money in professional and technical education in Western U.P. They have well estimated returns on their investment in technical and professional education in this region of the state.

SECTION II

Schumpeter (1919) pointed out that a combination of qualitative improvement in labour and superior technology contributes to greater productivity. Technology and skills of men are needed for transformation of a poor and underdeveloped economy into the developed one. Similarly, Mr Masani, Vice Chancellor of Bombay University, in his convocation address in 1920, highlighted the urgent need for vocational and technical education to overcome the problem of unemployment among the graduates, and for the promotion of economic progress of the country (referred from Prakash, 1977). Thus, the need for development of technical education was recognised both at the international and national levels long back. Though technical and professional higher education progressed in colonial India, yet the progress was extremely limited. Even during the early years of expansion of education at all levels, and types in independent India, development of higher technical and professional education lagged far behind the progress of general higher education. But this scenario started changing in the mid-eighties. But growth of technical and professional higher education gathered great momentum after 1990–91 due largely to the freedom of entry provided to private entrepreneurs. Consequently, numerous institutions of higher professional and technical education have sprouted in different parts of the country. However, Maharashtra, Tamil Nadu, Karnataka, Andhra Pradesh and Uttar Pradesh have stolen a march over the rest of the states of India in the field of development of higher technical and professional education. Tremendous growth of higher professional and technical education in recent years in India is accounted mostly by private investments and educational entrepreneurs. Education seems to have emerged as a commercially viable and economically profitable industry in India in the new millennium.

So far as U.P. is concerned, 57.95 per cent of institutes of higher professional and technical education are in the Western region. This is an indicator that western U.P. has grown more rapidly than eastern U.P. in higher professional and technical education.

If we examine the background of this growth of technical education in western U.P., some important reasons for this growth can be pinpointed. Green revolution was triggered in western U.P. Aligarh was among the 14 districts of India selected for initiation of green revolution technology in the early sixties. Aligarh, Khurja, Bulandshahr, Hapur, Meerut, Muzzafarnagar and Saharanpur were considered to be the hub of agricultural development.

The pivotal role in the propagation, adoption and diffusion of the green revolution was played by the army connection of the people of western U.P., who went out to take up jobs in the army as a legacy; money flowed into the villages, which was invested in agriculture. This led to agricultural development of this region. If the population of a region depends largely on agriculture and becomes agriculturally developed, the region will attain economic development. The prosperity brought by agriculture influenced the development of education also. Although eastern U.P. is the abode of prestigious universities like B.H.U., Lucknow University and Allahabad University, yet the region lags behind western U.P. in human resource development.

Education in general and higher technical and professional education in particular improves productivity (Amit Sharma, 2012). For economic growth and social development on par with other states and regions within a state, higher technical and professional education is required for developing skills and competence.

Entrepreneurs of western U.P. after exploring commercial and industrial ventures turned their attention to investing in education, especially higher professional and technical education; now education has itself emerged as an industry for investment and returns on investment. Educational entrepreneurs are not only earning profits, but are also contributing to social as well as economic development.

SECTION III

This section examines the discipline wise growth of institutions of higher technical and professional education in three disciplines and enrolments in the state of U.P. from 2004 to 2011. We have been able to access data of only seven years from 2004–2005 to 2010–2011. These data are used to estimate the regression growth rates from the following growth curve:

$$\log Y_i = \beta_0 + \beta_1 X$$

where Y is the variable growth which is to be estimated and X is the time, measured in calendar years, i = 1, 2, 3 which stands for engineering, management and computer applications. β_0 and β_1 are parameters to be estimated by Ordinary Least Squares (OLS) technique of estimation.

The following table reports the estimated growth rates and their corresponding t values which are used for testing the significance of β_s, to determine whether the estimated values differ significantly from zero statistically. β_1 measures the annual compound rate of growth.

Table 1: Estimates of Growth Rates

Variables	*B.Tech*	*MBA*	*MCA*
Growth rate of institutes	11.33	12.29	3.35
t-values of institutes	9.65	8.72	4.24
Growth rate of enrolments	12.38	12.81	4.11
t-values of enrolments	9.98	9.10	4.99

Source: Authors' calculations based on data from reports of UPTU.

The growth rates pertain only to the first decade of the 21st century. The annual compound rate of growth of institutions of all three streams of technical and professional education, namely B.Tech, M.B.A., and M.C.A. taken together, is approximately 10.04 per cent which is highly significant statistically, since the calculated value of 't' is as high as 8.33, which is much greater than the critical value of 2 at 5 per cent level of probability. This growth rate shows that higher technical and professional education in Uttar Pradesh has grown more rapidly than the population and SDP and per capita SDP of the state.

However, growth of technical and professional education has varied both between the years and streams, but the overall trend is positive and highly significant. Maximum growth rate of institutions was observed in 2008–2009.

During the same period, enrolments in all three streams, taken together, have grown at an annual compound rate of 4.78 per cent which is highly significant statistically as the calculated value of t is 3.7 which exceeds the critical value of 2. But enrolments have grown at a rate which is much lower and slower than the growth of the number of institutions. Does it mean a decline in average enrolment size of institutions?

Like the number of institutions, growth of enrolments has also varied between the years and streams. But the highest growth in enrolments was experienced in 2007–08, which is a year before the highest rate of growth of institutions. It implies that the increase in the number of institutions in 2008–09 and 2009–10 was in response to the high growth of enrolments in 2007–08. This represents the catching up with the lag of growth of institutions behind enrolments in previous years.

The inferences relating to the variation of growth of number of institutions and enrolments between streams and years requires more empirical evidence. The following graph portrays the year on year growth of institutions and enrolments during the seven years for which data were available to us. All three streams of technical education are considered together in the following graph which will highlight variation of growth between the years alone.

Growth of Institutions and Enrolments in Technical Institutions

A perusal of the year on year growth of institutions reveals that (i) the number of institutes has been rising continuously; (ii) growth rate was accelerated from the third to the fourth and from the fourth to fifth year; (iii) but there has been a sharp decline from 2010 onwards, which is explained by the slowing down of growth of enrolments due largely to the difficulty in placements in the wake of world-wide economic slow-down and now the European debt crisis which has adversely affected the growth of the Indian economy. This is very well highlighted by the curve in the graph 1.

A perusal of the curve representing enrolments shows that (i) enrolments declined sharply from the first to second year; (ii) enrolments rose sharply from the second to third year; (iii) fourth year witnessed a little bit of slow-down in the growth of enrolments which coincided with the global economic slow-down; (iv) observations of the last two years have witnessed an extremely sharp decline in enrolments in technical and professional education.

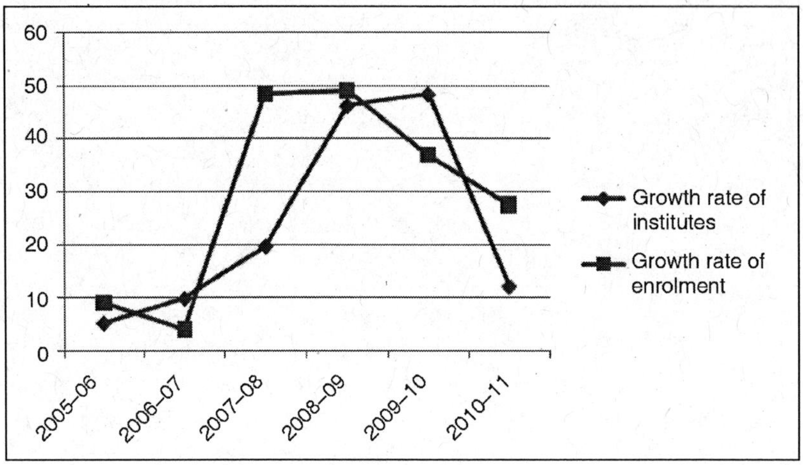

Graph 1

The deceleration in the growth of institutions and enrolments in technical and professional education seem to be accounted for by the sharp decline in the growth of GNP and consequently difficulties in placements of professionally and technically qualified personnel. Another factor to account for the decline in enrolments may probably be the prolific growth of institutions which was not warranted by the growth of enrolments at the senior secondary and graduate level on the one hand, and expansion of opportunities of employment. It has been observed that individuals, seeking higher education, tend to over-estimate their chances in the employment market even if unemployment prevails. This tendency is further accentuated in the face of scarcity of well qualified manpower in the market. This is a cobweb like swings in job markets across the globe (Prakash, 1977). Now the intensity of competition for attracting enrollees on the one hand, and exploration of opportunities of placements among the institutions has increased phenomenally on the other. One consequence of the growth of institutions ahead of growth of enrolments seems to be the decline in the enrolment size of institutions.

Inter-stream Growth of Institutions and Enrolments

Year on year growth of institutions, imparting education at the B. Tech., M.B.A. and M.C.A. levels, is considered and growth rates are reported in the table and are shown in the graph 2 below.

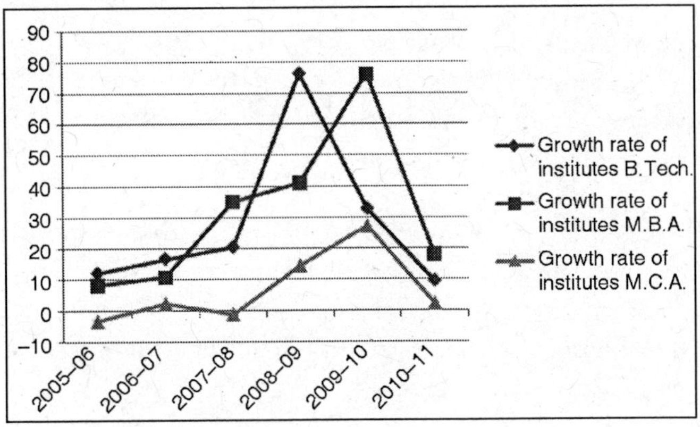

Source: Authors' calculations from reported data.

Graph 2

Growth of M.C.A. Institutions

A careful look at the graph shows that (i) the curve of growth rates of institutions of M.C.A. remained all along below the other two curves. The reason is that demand for computer education took off in the early eighties, when computer education was made a part of school education. Around the mid eighties more than 300 computer specialists, both hardware and software, were migrating to Middle-East daily from India. But the demand for such personnel dipped down sharply in the early nineties after the initial burst. However demand for this stream of education again received a push after liberalisation and globalisation in general and entry of private players in health, insurance and banking sectors in general and other financial services in particular. Emergence of business outsourcing and demand for medical transcription services boosted the demand for computer education including M.C.A.; (ii) 2007–08 saw a decline in growth of demand for places in the M.C.A. programme due largely to the global economic slow-down; (iii) years 2009 and 2010 experienced resurgence in the growth of demand for places in M.C.A. programme; and (iv) last year observations witnessed a reversal of trend in a big way when the growth rate touched minimum levels during the period of observation. This is accounted by the substantial fall in growth of the Indian economy under the impact of the European debt crisis.

Growth of Enrolments in Management and Engineering Institutions

The growth of enrolments in institutions of engineering, management and computer applications shows a trend almost similar to that of growth of institutes of engineering, management and computer applications. The following are specific features of year on year growth of institutes of management: (i) in the initial two years, management institutions grew more rapidly than those of computer applications, but at rates lower than those registered by engineering institutions; (ii) management institutions grew more rapidly than engineering institutions in 2007–08, but their growth rate went down below that of engineering institutions in 2008–09; (iii) in 2009–10 growth of institutions of management accelerated a great deal, with the result that the growth of engineering institutions was pushed below their own growth; (iv) during 2010–11, the rate of growth of institutions of both management and engineering nose-dived a great deal, though the rate of growth of management institutions remained a bit above that of engineering institutions.

The highest growth performance of engineering institutions among the three disciplines may be accounted for by the fact that the roots of engineering education are deeper than that of management education in India. Besides, the growth of manufacturing industries imparts an impetus to the growth of demand for engineers in the job market which, in turn, imparts momentum to the demand for places in engineering education. As against this, management post-graduates seek and find white jobs, especially in tertiary activities.

The need for management education was first realised with a sense of emergency only after the abolition of the Managing Agency System in 1969, though IIM Calcutta was established in 1961. Next to follow was IIM Ahmedabad in the 1970's. IIM Ahmedabad came into existence to obviate the need for going abroad for management education. However, real momentum was generated by the demand for management education in the 1980s with the emergence of private enterprise in higher technical and professional education and the partial opening up of the Indian economy. Expansion of professional and technical education, including management education, got an impetus. Maharashtra, Karnataka, Tamil Nadu and Andhra Pradesh have been in the forefront of the movement. Uttar Pradesh followed them much later. Naturally, these states got the advantage of early historical start over Uttar Pradesh.

Growth of Stream-wise Enrolments

Growth of stream-wise enrolments is shown in the following graph 3:

A careful examination of the graph highlights that (i) year on year growth of stream-wise enrolments seems to have mapped on to the growth of institutions of different streams that was discussed; (ii) all three streams of education registered acceleration and deceleration of growth from one to another year, in so far as acceleration is followed immediately by deceleration in the next year. There seems to be an autonomous self correction of excess demand for places; (iii) magnitudes of rise and fall in growth rates are almost equally high, which probably follows the cobweb like fluctuations in the job market, which is reflected in year on year changes in campus placements; (iv) magnitudes of rise and fall generally tend to decline from one to another year, that is, the troughs and peaks trace a rising curve. The reason for demand for B.Tech. education running ahead of demand for other two streams may partly be accounted for by the fact that good business schools on the one hand and employers on other give preferences to dual degree holders and work experience both in admissions and employment.

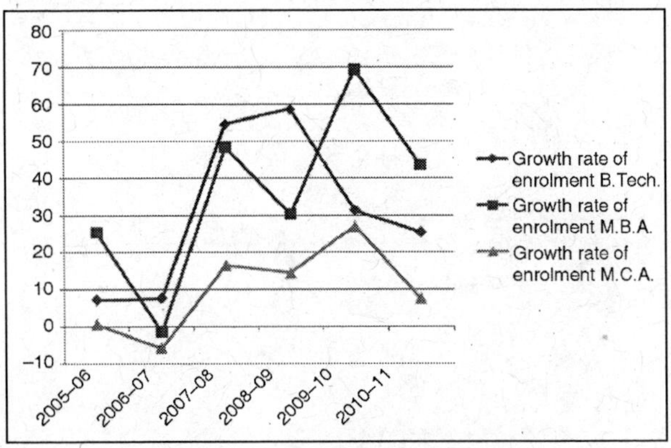

Source: Authors calculations on the basis of secondary data.

Graph 3

The accelerated growth of institutions has resulted in fierce competition for clientele both in education and job markets. The worldwide economy slowdown made placements extremely difficult during 2007–08, which resulted in a slackening of demand for places in educational institutions. This has further been complicated by the current debt crisis of several European countries. In 2010–11, for example, the total number of applicants in the Uttar Pradesh Technical University for management was nearly 20 per cent less than the available seats. Consequently, a large number of seats remained vacant in several colleges. The quality of enrollees has also gone down in this process, which will also affect the quality of placements. Great uncertainty about jobs after completion of post graduate education weakens the motivation to work hard. Private investors in education cannot afford to leave seats vacant, nor can they accept failure to place students after completion of education.

Spatial Distribution of Technical and Professional Colleges in Uttar Pradesh

As per the report of the Uttar Pradesh Technical University, it has 635 technical and professional colleges. 368 of these 635 colleges are located in western Uttar Pradesh.

Thus, west U.P. accounts for nearly 57.95 per cent of the total higher technical and professional educational institutions. Most of these colleges are owned and operated by private managements. Eastern Uttar Pradesh depended more on government funding of institutions, whereas private investors took the initiative in investing financial resources for professional and technical education. Interestingly, even in western Uttar Pradesh, technical institutions are concentrated in a few districts around Delhi. The following pie diagram, highlights spatial concentration in the distribution of institutions of technical education in western U.P.

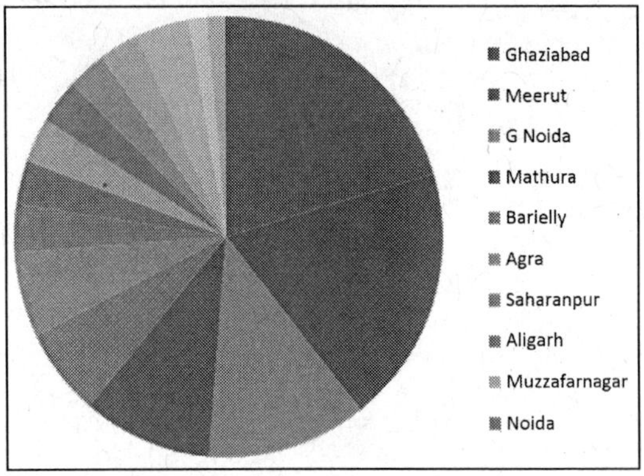

Diagram 1

The diagram 1 highlights spatial inequalities and a high degree of concentration in the distribution of technical and higher professional institutes which show great variations among the districts.

In western Uttar Pradesh, 61.14 per cent of the total institutes are located in four districts, namely Ghaziabad, Meerut, Greater Noida and Mathura. The remaining 38.85 per cent of the total institutes of professional and technical education are located in 13 districts of western Uttar Pradesh, which also includes Agra and Bareilly districts.

Private investors put more emphasis on buildings and infrastructure, which helps them in building brand image and brand positioning. Delhi, being the capital of India, has very high prices of real estate including land. This has induced several erstwhile Delhi based institutes to move into Ghaziabad, Noida, Greater Noida and Mathura, all of which are situated at the periphery of Delhi. Availability of land at affordable prices and easy reach from Delhi persuaded private investors to invest more money in institutions of technical and professional education in the National Capital region of Delhi. Thus, Ghaziabad, Noida, Meerut, Greater Noida and Mathura have become the hubs of technical and higher professional institutions. Thus, the advantageous location compared to other districts and administrative divisions have made these districts forge ahead of the rest of the state.

Once the message of concentration of institutes was floated, flocking takes place and more and more institutes are attracted in an already crowded vicinity. Due to concentration of institutions in one area, all institutes get the advantage of easy accessibility to visiting faculty. Thus, these locations help in coping with shortages of faculty in general, and visiting faculty in particular.

Location of institutes also depends on the location of industrial hubs and corporate houses. Presence of industries helps institutes to call people for institute–industry interface, summer projects and final placements. It also helps in getting trainees for MDPs and FDPs. All these benefits attracted private investors to come forward and invest money in technical institutions located in areas nearby Delhi.

Conclusions

The above analysis shows that (i) U.P. is adequately developed in the field of higher technical and professional education; (ii) the state is characterised by intra-regional inequalities of development of technical and professional education, irrespective of public or private ownership of institutions; (iii) Eastern U.P. accounts for a disproportionately high proportion of public universities, while western U.P. is the center of concentration of private universities and colleges of higher technical and professional education; (iv) even western U.P. a few districts in the NCR Delhi account for a major share of the total institutions not in only in the region but the state as a whole.

Policy Implications

There is an urgent need for policy interventions to remove inter and intra-regional inequalities of development of technical and professional education in U.P. The government may offer incentives to private investors to locate their institutions in the eastern parts of the state.

References

Prakash, Shri (1977). *Educational System—An Econometric Study*, Concept Book Publishing Company, New Delhi.

Prakash, Shri (1994).

Sharma, Amit (2012). *Upgradation of Educational Qualifications in Selected Technical and Professional Occupations in India*, Ph.D. Thesis, Department of Management, Mysore University, Mysore.

Smith, Adam (1774). *Nature and Causes of Wealth of Nations*, London.

Tables Appendices

Appendix Table 1: Private Universities

Amity University Uttar Pradesh	Gautam Budh Nagar	West
Jagadguru Rambhadracharya Handicapped University	Chitrakoot	East
Integral University	Lucknow	East
Sharda University	Gautam Budh Nagar gn	Wesr
G.L.A. University	Mathura	West
Mangalayatan University	Aligarh	West
Mohammad Ali Jauhar University	Rampur	West
Teerthanker Mahaveer University	Moradabad	West
Swami Vivekanand Subharti University	Meerut	West

Appendix Table 2: Public Universities

Allahabad University	Allahabad	East
Babasaheb Bhimrao Ambedkar University	Lucknow	East
Banaras Hindu University	Varanasi	East
Chhatrapati Shahu Ji Maharaj University	Kanpur	East
Chandra Shekhar Azad University of Agriculture & Technology	Kanpur	East
Deen Dayal Upadhaya Gorakhpur University	Gorakhpur	East
Dr. Ram Manohar Lohia Avadh University	Faizabad	East
Indian Institute of Technology Kanpur, Kanpur-208016, Uttar Pradesh	Kanpur	East
University of Lucknow	Lucknow	East
Mahatma Gandhi Kashi Vidyapith	Varanasi	East
Narendra Deva University of Agriculture & Technology	Faizabad	East
V.B.S. Purvanchal University, Jaunpur, Uttar Pradesh-222002	Jaunpur	East
Sampurnanand Sanskrit Vishwavidyalaya	Varanasi	East
Sanjay Gandhi Postgraduate Institute of Medical Sciences	Lucknow	East
Bundelkhand University	Jhansi	West
Aligarh Muslim University	Aligarh	West
Ch. Charan Sing University	Meerut	West
Dr. Bhim Rao Ambedkar University	Agra	West
M.J.P. Rohilkhand University	Barerily	West

Appendix Table 3: Distribution of Technical and Professional Colleges in West U.P.

Ghaziabad	75
Meerut	70
G. Noida	44
Mathura	36
Barielly	24
Agra	23
Saharanpur	13
Aligarh	12
Muzzafarnagar	12
Noida	12
Baghpat	11
Moradabad	11
Bijnor	9
Bulandshar	6
Etawah	5
Modinagar	5
Distribution of colleges in U.P. west	368

	Growth of Colleges			
	B.Tech	*MBA*	*MCA*	*Total*
2004–2005	75	86	90	251
2005–2006	84	93	87	264
2006–2007	98	103	89	290
2007–2008	118	139	90	347
2008–2009	208	196	103	507
2009–2010	276	345	131	752
2010–2011	302	407	134	843

	Growth in Enrolments			
2004–2005	24434	5803	5626	35863
2005–2006	26168	7270	5654	39092
2006–2007	28140	7161	5319	40620
2007–2008	43474	10620	6193	60287
2008–2009	68923	13830	7083	89836
2009–2010	90498	23400	8991	122889
2010–2011	113448	33570	9665	156683

	Growth Rates of Institutes		
	B.Tech	*MBA*	*MCA*
2005–2006	12	8.139	–3.33
2006–2007	16.66	10.75	2.29
2007–2008	20.4	34.95	–1.12
2008–2009	76.27	41	14.44
2009–2010	32.69	76.02	27.18
2010–2011	9.42	17.97	2.29

	Growth Rates of Enrolment		
	B.Tech	*MBA*	*MCA*
2005–2006	7.09	25.28	0.497
2006–2007	7.535	–1.499	–5.92
2007–2008	54.49	48.3	16.43
2008–2009	58.53	30.22	14.37
2009–2010	31.3	69.197	26.93
2010–2011	25.35	43.46	7.49

	Growth Rate of Institutes	*Growth Rate of Enrolment*
2005–2006	5.179	9.003
2006–2007	9.848	3.908
2007–2008	19.655	48.417
2008–2009	46.109	49.013
2009–2010	48.323	36.792
2010–2011	12.101	27.499

Section–IV

Employment, Sectoral Growth and Entrepreneurship in Uttar Pradesh

CHAPTER 10

Economic Transformation of Uttar Pradesh: The Role of Grassroots Level Entrepreneurship

M.L. Pandit

Introduction

This chapter highlights the role of entrepreneurs, and their innovations, in ending the stagnation in the economic history of mankind. Innovations are the key to any meaningful and sustained economic transformation; entrepreneurs lead this change. The study argues that the promotion of grassroots entrepreneurship is the key to rapid economic transformation of Uttar Pradesh. A plan for promoting grassroots entrepreneurship and innovations is also outlined.

Backdrop of Modern Economic Growth

The history of mankind, especially of major civilisations, is proof enough of varied human potentialities and accomplishments. However, until the Eighteenth Century these potentialities and accomplishments blossomed and flourished primarily in the non-economic spheres like art and architecture, languages and literature, philosophy, war and warfare, and so on. The economic history, by and large, continued to remain one of sustenance and stagnation, until the eighteenth century industrial revolution. In fact, real per capita GDP (in 1990 US dollars) of the world economy recorded a marginal decline from US$ 444 to US$ 435 from the beginning, to the end of the first millennium. Per capita GDP even during the next eight hundred and twenty years, increased marginally from US$ 435 to US$ 667, or by a mere fifty per cent. Incidentally, the decline in the per capita GDP during the first millennium was higher for the present day developed world, in contrast to the rest of the world. For example, the per capita GDP of Western Europe during the millennium declined from US$ 450 to US$ 400. For Asia (excluding Japan), per capita GDP at the beginning and end of the millennium remained unchanged at US$ 450. Although economic stagnation continued its impact the global economy, the Western world began to reap economic dividends from the middle of the second millennium, on account of two significant developments. First and the foremost development, was the discovery of some major sea routes across the globe, and the consequent opening up of international trade. The second development, again led by the Western Europe, especially England, was in scientific knowledge and experiments. These developments, especially on account of the virtual monopoly of the growing international trade, enabled some European countries to colonise and exploit economically, most of the rest of the world. No wonder, therefore, that Western Europe recorded a three-fold increase in their real per capita GDP from the beginning of the second millennium till 1820. However, a three-fold increase in per capita GDP over such a long period of time, does not represent any major economic transformation. The figures referred to here are in 1990 MS dollars, and have been compiled painstakingly by Maddison (2007). Keynes (1931), after an overview of the long economic history of the present day developed world, sums this up as follows:

> *"From the earliest times of which we have record-back, say, to two thousand years before Christ-down to the beginning of the eighteenth century, there was no very great change in the standards of living of the average man living in the civilised centers of the earth."*

Entrepreneurship and Innovation as Breakers of Economic Stagnation

Between 1820 and 1998, the world population increased 5.6 times and the world's real per capita GDP 8.5 times. If we consider the already developed world separately, the increase in the latter indicator is many times more. Life expectancy, an indicator of the quality of life, also recorded impressive gains; it rose from 26 to 66 years during the period referred to earlier. Besides, these indicators have further gained impressive magnitude since 1998.

The question is why could not the long global economic stagnation be overcome anywhere, until the second half of the eighteenth century? How could some countries accomplish major strides in economic transformation, rather economic miracles thereafter? Keynes, again, provides some insights in this regard, by identifying the two most important causes of the long-term economic stagnation: "*This slow rate of progress, or lack of progress, was due to two reasons—to the remarkable absence of important technical improvements and to the failure of capital to accumulate.*"

Since the techniques and systems of production and distribution repeated themselves year after year, rather millennium after millennium, there was no end to economic stagnation. A breakthrough was possible only after the foundation of scientific thought, knowledge and experiments came to be laid during the sixteenth and seventeenth centuries in Western Europe, especially England. This is how the foundation for a series of unprecedented technical inventions and innovations to transform agriculture, manufacturing, energy, trade, transport, and many other segments of the economy, was laid in the second half of the eighteenth century. While technical inventions resulted from scientific knowledge and experiments, mostly in laboratories, identification of commercially viable inventions and innovations among all such advances, and their exploitation for business and profits are undertaken generally by entrepreneurs. Entrepreneurs may or may, not have a scientific background, but they have the ability, or knack to identify and exploit commercially viable opportunities thrown open by technical inventions, or even otherwise. This, no doubt, exposes them to considerable risks and uncertainties, associated with exploring new techniques and products. While the risks are formidable, the rewards are likewise high, if their endeavours turn out to be successful. But, entrepreneurs are the people with a very high appetite for risk taking, associated with exploring new business opportunities.

The industrial revolution, pioneered in England, and made possible by an unprecedented series of major technical inventions in the second half of the eighteenth century, was essentially an outcome of the efforts of a large class of petty craftsmen, who assumed the role of entrepreneurs to seize the emerging new business opportunities. The revolution laid the foundations for ending the long economic stagnation that mankind had not been able to overcome till then. The period of the revolution also coincided with the mitigation of the scarcity of the capital. The supply of capital was facilitated and supported by declining interest rates in England, around the time of the industrial revolution. This lends support to the view that the period was 'propitious for invention and expansion' (Ashton, 1972). As already stated, growing international trade and colonisation of some parts of the globe by countries where the revolution came to be pioneered and extended initially, had played a supportive role in the success of the revolution. Major technical improvements made possible by the revolution, coupled with the increasing supply of capital and the growth of international trade, enabled mankind to accomplish rapid and sustained economic growth, thereby denting the long global economic stagnation, though not everywhere. It is a different matter why this revolution and the consequent economic transformation remained to be extended and completed for most of the third world even two centuries after the breakthrough. The explanation for this failure lies primarily in the inability of this world to swell the ranks of entrepreneurs to the required levels. In fact, economic transformation of the developed world also did not happen simultaneously. The transformation has been like a movement, extending as and when its pre-conditions were met. This feature of the revolution and modern economic growth has been aptly captured by Ashton (1972) as follows:

> *"The industrial revolution is to be thought of as a movement, not as a period of time. Whether it presents itself in England after 1760, in the United States and Germany after 1870, or in Canada, Japan, and Russia in our own day, its character and effects are fundamentally the same."*

This aspect of the revolution continues to be reinforced till this day as rapid and sustained modern economic growth continues to encompass regions and countries where its pre-conditions are satisfied. For instance, some East-Asian countries shaped an economic miracle in about a quarter-century after the 1960s by creating favourable conditions for it to happen. China, perhaps inspired inspired by this miracle, also followed suit by introducing economic reforms favourable for rapid, and sustained economic growth. India also introduced some major economic reforms a decade later, to accelerate her economic growth. Similar instances are available from Africa as well as South-America.

Economic transformation of the third world is no longer dependent on shaping new technical inventions and innovations. This complex task has already been performed. Most of the new technologies are generally readily available for exploitation to the developing world. Similar is the case with business knowledge and management practices. Easy availability of technology and business knowledge, coupled with the ease with which capital can be mobilised within, and outside a country presently, have greatly facilitated the task of poverty eradication and economic transformation. Dwindling investment opportunities in the Western world are also translating into Third World opportunities, as more and more capital from the first world is being invested in the developing world. This investment is also accompanied by technology transfers on favouable terms. Moreover, the developed world offers a vast market for Third World exports, although the latter world, by itself, has tremendous potential to absorb its growing output of goods and services, provided faster growth also translates into rising incomes for its vast population. Growing prospects of imitating modern Western technology and easy access to capital and markets have reduced significantly the time span over which an economy can transform itself. Such possibilities have come to be referred to as 'Economic catch-up is accelerating.' The essence of this catch-up can be had from the following quote (A Game of Catch-up, 2011):

> *"Britain's economy doubled in size in the 32 years from 1830 to 1862 as increased productivity spread from cotton to other industries. America's GDP doubled in only*

17 years as it overtook Britain in the 1870s. The economies of China and India have doubled within a decade."

Entrepreneurs as Agents of Transformation of the Economy of Uttar Pradesh

Since the Third World has opportunity of imitating and adapting the already developed Western technologies to their factor endowment and socio-economic realities, what kind of pre-conditions do the Third World countries have to create for rapid economic transformation and poverty eradication? The answer lies primarily in the ability of each country to create a favourable business environment, so that entrepreneurs and their operatives can function efficiently. Since the availability of capital and marketability of products are no longer formidable challenges, swelling the ranks of the entrepreneurs emerges as the main pre-condition for speedy economic transformation. Entrepreneurs, as a class, prosper when economic reforms create a level playing field for them to rise to the occasion, operate, compete and prosper. Economic reforms world-wide, including in China and India, have essentially been in the direction of ending excessive state regulations and controls of economic activities, which had resulted in slow and lopsided economic growth. The outcome of such reforms, rather market liberalisation, has not only been encouraging, but path breaking in accomplishing economic miracles. Since entrepreneurs hold the key in any rapid and sustainable economic transformation, any country seeking such transformation has naturally to facilitate their emergence and success.

What applies to countries holds good for a state as well. The economic transformation of Uttar Pradesh likewise can also be accomplished by widening and deepening the prospects of entrepreneurship among its vast and varied human resources. The main thrust of this study is on exploring the possibilities of accomplishing this task. Given the vastness of the state and its varied resource base, the study focuses on the promotion of entrepreneurship at the grassroots level so as to impact the entire state. If entrepreneurs succeed in enhancing the efficiency of all the resources at the level of every village and block, there is no reason why the economy of the state cannot witness unprecedented economic growth, and complete economic transformation over a quarter century. An attempt to explore as to how the state can exploit its hidden entrepreneurial potential is the subject matter of the following discussion.

Entrepreneurs currently hold the key in generating rapid and sustained economic growth, until an economy reaches the middle income plateau. Reaching this level is possible simply by imitating important technical improvements as well as business practices from the developed world, provided access to capital and markets does not pose formidable challenges. Given the relative ease with which capital can be mobilised and output marketed presently, economic growth of a region to a considerable extent is determined by its ability and success in swelling the ranks of entrepreneurs at all levels, to exploit its economic potentialities innovatively.

How can entrepreneurs make this possible? The answer lies in the very role entrepreneurs are best known for. Since literature on the meaning, scope and traits of entrepreneurship is vast and varied, we highlight the following pioneering definition of J.B. Say for our purposes here. He, incidentally, had coined this term around 1800 (Drucker, 1993, p. 21):

> *"The entrepreneur shifts economic resources out of an area of lower and into an area of higher productivity and greater yield." It is this shift, which enables any lagging economy to surge ahead economically. It is important to stress, that this shift must begin at the grassroots levels and encompass the entire resource base of an economy. Consequently, the major focus has to be on entrepreneurs of modest means and missions. High priority has to be accorded to encouraging and grooming people to assume entrepreneurial roles in their already familiar areas of activity or engagement. The effort has to begin virtually at the household, village and block levels. The focus of such an effort is not on one or two activities, but as far as possible, the entire sphere of grassroots level economic activities spreading over all sectors, so that productivity and yields of the entire resource base is enhanced.*

The state can accomplish economic prosperity and high standards of living by shifting its vast population from low to high productivity activities. This shift does not necessarily imply changing the area of economic activity, but enhancing the productivity within each of the activities the prospective entrepreneurs are already engaged in and are familiar with. Grassroots level innovations to raise the productivity of resources can be easier to explore, when entrepreneurs are encouraged to concentrate their efforts within their existing range of economic activities. They have to be guided and encouraged to think of improving the quality of their products and services, or even of introducing a new product within their familiar sphere of productive activity. Exploring the scope of new raw materials, better technical and business processes, or the extension of markets provide very fertile grounds for conceiving productivity enhancement packages at the grassroots levels. The task is made easier, when the area of activity remains the same as before. The entrepreneur with experience in an area is bound to have many ideas as how his area or product quality and range, can be improved. Motivation and encouragement to experiment with feasible ideas is most likely to yield handsome dividends in terms of innovations and productivity gains. The experiment, rather its tasking, is made easy as the required manpower and skills are already available locally. In fact, even the work force already engaged in a low productivity activity can offer useful suggestions to enhance their productivity, to enrich their work profile.

Swelling the Supply Pool of Entrepreneurs

Before attempting to answer this question, it is important to clarify as to what kinds of people can comfortably assume the roles of entrepreneurs. The following passage (Habakkuk, 1958) broadly sums up the commonly observed entrepreneurial traits:

> *"A flair for identifying and seizing opportunities for profit, an eye for the possibilities of new products, unexploited raw material supplies, untapped markets; willingness to take considerable risks; vision, drive and initiative; ability to devote their whole energies completely to attain their ends."*

These attributes enable entrepreneurs to conceive and shape innovations. We would, however, confine our attention here on how productivity of resources at the village or block levels of Uttar Pradesh can be increased. An overview of the traits listed earlier reveals that most of these may be present among a large section of the people, but these may not surface in most of them on their own. Moreover, history is witness that whenever and wherever opportunities and the environment for the emergence of entrepreneurs have become propitious, their supplies have mushroomed. For instance, when some important technical improvements took shape in England in the eighteenth century, petty craftsmen and owners of cottage industries assumed entrepreneurial roles on a large enough scale, to shape the path breaking industrial revolution. Likewise when some East Asian countries opened up their economies after independence, entrepreneurs of the region accomplished an 'economic miracle' in a quarter century. After China created space and opportunities for its entrepreneurs to transform her virtually stagnant economy in 1978, the outcomes have been unprecedented. India has also witnessed unprecedented economic growth after the 1990–91 economic reforms paved the way for greater degrees of freedom for entrepreneurs to invest and operate. Thus, entrepreneurs and their traits are by themselves nourished by emerging economic opportunities and favourable business environment. Fortunately, entrepreneurial traits are no longer regarded as in-born only. These traits can, and have been favourably impacted by training and exposure, and above all, opportunities. The task becomes far easier when entrepreneurs have to confine their roles to activities they are already dealing with, at the levels of small towns and villages. Moreover, the very success of the first generation of entrepreneurs generates waves of such people, by bringing to the surface their dormant traits referred to earlier. This feature has been evident in almost every successful economic transformation, the world over.

Uttar Pradesh is the most populated state of India. With 199 million people, it accounts for 16.49 per cent of the Indian population. But, her share in the national GDP in 2010 at 8.34 per cent was half the share of her population. In other words, the state is half way economically, even by national standards. The state ranks 18th in the HDI index among Indian states. Although, the state already has 2.3 million small scale industrial units, yet this number, at 12 per cent of the all India figure is far below the share of the population. The scope for revitalising such units through some grassroots minimal innovations remains very high. The primary sector, expectedly, continues to account for over one-third (36.25 per cent in 2004–05) of the net state domestic product. The scope for innovations and consequent productivity gains in this sector are virtually unlimited.

Way to Begin

Since the state of U.P. has a huge population, the pool from which entrepreneurs can be identified, groomed, guided and launched is naturally vast and diverse. Why are people, especially the educated unemployed, reluctant to assume entrepreneurial roles here? The answer lies essentially the because of the lack of awareness about the scope and prospects of productivity enhancement in routinely ongoing economic activities. Risks and uncertainties associated with such roles, though not formidable, may also bother some of the prospective entrepreneurs. We do not stress capital needs as a prime cause, as the scope of mobilising tiny sums of capital for grassroots level innovations from the financial institutions and government sponsored development agencies remains wide open. As already stated, prospective entrepreneurs have to be motivated to venture into familiar activities to minimise the element of risk and uncertainty, associated with their intended innovations. How can this be done?

The task has to begin at the village and block levels. A group of experts has to be constituted for each block of the state. This group has to be charged with the responsibility of identifying the occupational and productivity profile of the people. This exercise should enable the group to identify the block level resource endowment, including skill and specialisation sets. The experts then have to identify skills and occupations where productivity levels are far below the state and national averages, but where the scope for improvement with minimum efforts and capital is enormous. This identification would take care of the risk and uncertainty apprehensions among the prospective entrepreneurs.

Once the exercise of mapping the resource endowment and their productivity levels at the village and block levels is completed, the next step has to be singled out for those activities, where the locality can claim some advantage, in terms of a specific resource or skill. Such activities should constitute the base for the grassroots level innovations to raise productivity levels A pilot project to launch some of the motivated youngsters into entrepreneurial roles must begin in some identified low productivity activities with considerable potential for innovation. This project must receive guidance and assistance of an expert group, as well as state sponsored developmental agencies. The pilot project must begin in all the major sectors of the village, and the block. Once some members of the first batch of entrepreneurs are able to accomplish some productivity gains in their respective activities in a village, or a block, the task of swelling the ranks of entrepreneurs would be greatly eased and facilitated. It is important to stress that each block must begin with activities where it enjoys some advantage in terms of some resources, especially skills. Unless the workforce is able to excel in its tasks, entrepreneurial success cannot be guaranteed. Since the exercise involves imitating the techniques and systems in operation in localities, where higher productivity levels have already been accomplished within, or outside the state, the prospects of success are fairly bright. It is again important to stress, that a level playing field for the prospective innovators is critical for the success of the pilot project. Policy makers and administrators have to accord high priority to this area of activity. The process of registering tiny enterprises has not only to be made cheap and convenient enough but transparent as well. Moreover, in case an entrepreneur does not feel comfortable in running his enterprise, the process of de-registration and closure must be equally easy and owner friendly. Unless the word red tape is made to disappear from the vocabularies of the grassroots level entrepreneurs, the suggested pilot project for innovation and productivity enhancement, cannot be made to succeed and take roots.

An illustration would be imperative here. The state's share of national GDP is half its share of the population. This implies that if the state can raise its productivity levels to even current national standards, the GDP of UP can easily be doubled. As national standards of productivity can be achieved by imitating the techniques and methods readily available within the country, risks and uncertainties associated with entrepreneurship get nearly eliminated. Even the providers of capital can feel secure when making advances to enterprises, which are going to imitate already successful experiments.

The exercise of identifying the most potential grassroot economic activities for productivity enhancement, has to extend to all sectors of economic activity like agriculture, horticulture, manufacturing, trade, transport, education and so on. Once the state is able to raise standards of productivity in all the sectors initially to national averages, the ranks of entrepreneurs are bound to swell to take these levels to still higher levels. Some areas and sectors of the state have already attained even higher than the national levels of productivity and the lagging regions, or sectors, have to copy the same for their risk free transformation.

The suggested framework for transforming the economy of Uttar Pradesh through grassroots level innovations is not new, or unique. Similar experiments elsewhere have already yielded dividends in terms of economic prosperity. Historically, first generation entrepreneurs have made the easey and availability of local skills as their guiding principle of product selection, rather than regional specialisation. While the evidence to this effect is vast and varied, it may suffice to refer briefly to just one, or two instances. Punjab, for example, has two major specialisations, namely, commercial agriculture and engineering industries. While commercial agriculture is the outcome of its vast fertile and irrigated land, the foundation of the engineering industries was laid after independence, on the basis of the abundance of blacksmithy types of skills among large sections of the work force (Pandit, 1978, 1985). No wonder, the state and its entrepreneurs made full use of these skills, to lay the foundation of many engineering and related industries. A chain of industrial training schools were established to help the work force to perfect and diversify their skill sets. The handicraft and handloom sector in Jammu and Kashmir also began to grow and diversify fast after the state government launched massive training programmes in handicraft skills. Utter Pradesh must also adopt this very principle in the suggested grassroot level innovative endeavours. Venturing into unknown economic activities at the start of economic transformation exposes the entrepreneurs to considerable risks and uncertainties. Once a region's entrepreneurs have gained considerable experience and confidence in productivity enhancement in conventional sectors, venturing into new and unknown areas becomes less risky.

There is no better guarantee to secure the new generation of grassroot level small scale entrepreneurs and their workers. For instance, the people of Kashmir are at ease with handicraft and tourism related activities. It is, therefore, imperative for development and employment promotion agencies in Uttar Pradesh, to identify the product, or service specialisations of each region, and then focus on their productivity upgradation. In fact, it would be worthwhile if non-governmental organisations, engaged in promoting the rural economy of the state, offer their assistance in identification of activities where the scope of productivity enhancement is high, and untapped.

References

Ashton, T.S. (1972). "The Industrial Revolution 1760–1830", Great Britain, Oxford University Press, pp. 48, 114.

Drucker, Peter F. (1993). *Innovation and Entrepreneurship*, New York, First Harper Business Edition, p. 21.

Habakkuk, J. (1958). "The Entrepreneur and Economic Development", in I. Livingstone (Editor, 1971), *Economic Policy for Development*, Penguin Books, Great Britain, p. 39.

Keynes, J.M. (1931). "The Economic Possibility of our Grandchildren" in Essays in Persuasion, London, Macmillan, p. 360.

Maddison, Angus (2007). *The World Economy*, New Delhi, OECD and Academic Foundation, Indian Edition, chapter 1.

Pandit, M.L. (1978). "Less known factors behind industrial change in Punjab and Haryana", *Economic and Political Weekly*, Vol. XIII, 1978.

______ (1985). *Industrial Development of the Punjab and Haryana*, New Delhi, BR Publishing Corporation.

The Economist, Special Report, The World Economy, September 24th, 2011, p. 5.

CHAPTER 11

Economic Growth and Promotion of Social Welfare: Evaluation of Selected Employment Generation Schemes in U.P.

Nimisha Singh and Ajeet Singh Rauthan

Introduction

Per capita income is an index of the level of development of an economy, and any rise in the per capita income over time, relates to the process of growth. Social welfare, that is, welfare of the people, depends largely on the development stage of the economy and patterns of income distribution on the one hand, and policies of the government on the other. But, market oriented economies are generally characterised by inequalities in the personal distribution of income. Besides, regional inequalities reflect the unequal distribution of the gains of development among regions. The poverty of the people is a reflection of unequal distribution of income at a given point in time among the people, and among the regions, and its perpetuation reflects the continuation of the process of unequal income distribution, and uneven growth of the regions. Growth and development of market economies generally involves mortally differential development benefits for different segments of society. It further accentuates the degree of income inequalities through time. Poverty alleviation, therefore, cannot be left to market forces. Public policy interventions are is needed for the prevention of further deterioration of the condition of the poor on the one hand, and reducing poverty on the other.

Background

The Government of India, recognising the role of infrastructure in poverty eradication, has taken up a massive programme for the construction of rural infrastructure under different programmes and projects in the past. Creation of infrastructure, both physical and social, provides opportunities for improved living conditions as well as a means of livelihood for people through employment generation.

The Departments of Rural Development of the state governments have implemented a number of a programmes in the rural areas for poverty eradication, employment generation, development of rural infrastructure, and provision of minimum basic services, etc. The basic thrust of such programmes is the generation of employment in the infrastructure sectors to take care of the earlier goals.

These schemes cover all aspects of employment, including organisation of the rural poor into self help groups, and their capacity building through training, and the planning and execution of economic activities. The centre and states have together allocated funds for infrastructure development, and financial assistance to the poor through bank credit, and subsidy for productive activities. Creation of infrastructure, both physical and social, has been given greater thrust than over before, in the Tenth Five Year Plan. The thrust in the Eleventh Five Year Plan is social inclusion, in combination with the provision of improved livelihood opportunities. This approach puts emphasis on education, health and other basic facilities. Human resource development is also an important aspect of these schemes, which plays a pivotal role in the growth process. The following are some of the important schemes for the promotion of welfare and growth in all the states, including U.P.

Swarnjayanti Gram Swarozgar Yojana (SGSY)

The Swarnjayanti Gram Swarozgar Yojana (SGSY) is an important self-employment programme for the rural poor. It is designed to stimulate self-employment activities. The *Yojana*, which came in to effect in 1999, aims to achieve this objective by encourageing families to engage in income-generating activities; government provides assistance through a combination of wages, technical capacity building, and a package of financial assistance. Financial assistance includes both institutional credit and subsidy. The centre and state together provide loans and subsidy for *swarojgaris* in the ratio of 75:25.

The scheme falls under the purview of the Ministry of Rural Development and is implemented by the District Rural Development Agencies (DRDA), with the active involvement of *panchayats*, banks and non-governmental organisations. The progress of the scheme is now discussed to delineate its current status. The progress is classified broadly into financial and physical terms.

Mahatma Gandhi National Rural Employment Guarantee Act (MGNREGA)

The Mahatma Gandhi National Rural Employment Guarantee Act (MGNREGA) is a job providing scheme; legislation for the scheme was enacted in September, 2005. The objective of the Act is to enhance security livelihood of in rural areas, by providing at least 100 days of guaranteed wage employment in a financial year to every household, whose adult members volunteer to do unskilled manual work.

This Act was introduced with the aim of improving the purchasing power of the rural people, engaged primarily in semi or unskilled work in rural India. It does not matter *whether the persons are, or are not below the poverty line*. The Act was initially called the National Rural Employment Guarantee Act (NREGA), but it was renamed on 2 October 2009.

MGNREGA marks a paradigm shift from all precedent wage employment programmes. Unlike the earlier wage employment programmes, that were allocation based, MGNREGA is demand driven. It provides a rights-based framework for wage employment. Employment is dependent on the workers exercising the choice to apply for registration, obtain a job card, and seek employment for the time and duration that the worker wants. The Act is designed to offer an incentive structure to the states for providing employment as ninety per cent of the cost for employment provided is borne by the Centre.

The NREGA Act was notified in 200 districts in the first phase with effect from 2 February 2006, and was then extended to on additional 130 districts in the financial year 2007–2008; 113 districts were notified with effect from 1 April 2007. But in U.P. only 17 districts were notified with effect from 15 May 2007. Thus, U.P. accounts for even less than 8 per cent of the total districts, which are covered by the scheme in India. This is not in consonance with either the population size, or incidence of poverty in U.P., or the total number of districts that the state has got.

Performance of Employment Schemes

Progress of the schemes being studied are evaluated year wise both in financial and physical terms.

Financial Progress of SGSY in Current Prices

The analysis discusses both allocation and achievement in terms of expenditure incurred on the implementation of the scheme. First, we discuss allocation. Achievements under the scheme largely depend on allocation. Performance under this head reflects the allocation efficiency. As against this, actual achievement/realisation of the goal reflects utilisation efficiency. Under this scheme, funds provided by the Government of India to states go directly to the District Rural Development Agencies (DRDA) of the states.

There has been an increase in the funds available over the years to promote the scheme to provide livelihood. The total amount allocated for the implementation of the scheme increased by only 1.5 per cent from 2003 to 2004. But, there was a sharp increase of 21.87 per cent in allocation in 2005, though funds available in 2006 for the scheme came down by 4.29 per cent in comparison to 2005. Then, the allocation grew by 39 per cent in 2008 and the growth of allocation again declined by 8 per cent in 2010. *Thus, the financial allocation for the implementation of the scheme shows wild fluctuations over the years even during a limited period (medium run) of seven years.* This shows volatility and may adversely affect both the allocation and utilisation efficiency. May be allocation of funds depends upon demand for employment under the scheme.

Allocations in Real Terms (Constant Prices)

This period of seven years is split into two plan periods. So, part of the increase may be accounted for by the carryover funds from the preceding into subsequent plan period. The other point to note is that the financial allocations are in current prices. If we adjust these figures for inflation, the picture will be drastically different. Since the focus of the scheme is on the poor, who spend a major proportion of their income on food, the food inflation rate is the appropriate deflator. The allocation in real terms and corresponding growth rates are reported in Table 1.

Table 1: Swarnjayanti Gram Swarojgar Yojna Financial Progress in Current Prices[1]

Year	*Total Funds Available*	*Total Expenditure*	*Expenditure Against Available Funds (%)*	*Growth in Funds Available (%)*	*Growth in Expenditure (%)*
2003	18725.36	9206.13	49.16		
2004	19018.95	12286.39	64.60	1.57	33.46
2005	23178.12	21376.10	92.23	21.87	73.98
2006	24171.46	19495.88	80.66	4.29	–8.80
2007	26294.95	20137.97	76.58	8.79	3.29
2008	36698.71	25357.49	69.10	39.57	25.92
2009	45392.41	31833.61	70.13	23.69	25.54
2010	49313.18	35153.04	71.29	8.64	10.43
2011	60164.58	40742.43	67.72	22.01	15.90

Proportions and growth rates as per authors' calculations.

Source: Department of Rural Development, Government of U.P., RuralSoft (http://ruralsoft.up.nic.in)

SGSY Financial Progress in Constant 1993–94 Prices

The range of variations of allocation of funds in current prices is ₹ 60,164–18,725, whereas in constant prices, the range of variations is 291–174. This highlights the following important features of the allocation of funds:

1. The differences between current and constant price allocations indicates the magnitude of the inflationary pressure in the economy;
2. Allocation of funds for the scheme shows a rising trend. However, allocated funds current prices seem to have changed much more rapidly than the sums allocated constant prices. Thus, it embodies money illusion;
3. The role of a systematic policy is critically evident from the consistent but slower rate of growth of the series in constant rather than in current prices;
4. If we look at the year on year growth of the series in constant prices, it is evident that it follows the pattern of growth of the series in current prices.

Year on Year Fluctuations of the Allocated Funds

From a perusal of the growth of allocation in constant prices under the scheme, the following features are observable:

1. Year on year fluctuation shows that the allocation declined from 2003 to 2004 and from 2009 to 2010;
2. In the remaining years, the year on year growth is positive, for both nominal and real amounts of funds allocated, but it fluctuates;
3. The fluctuation in the growth rate of the allocated funds in constant prices ranges from 0.98 to 29.64 per cent. As against this, the growth of allocation of funds in current prices ranges from 1.57 to 39.57 per cent. *Two ranges of variations of allocated funds highlight the impact of inflation that creates money illusion;* and
4. The highest growth rate embodies the base effect.

Year on Year Fluctuations in Expenditure/Utilisation

1. Year on year growth in the actual expenditure in constant prices is negative in two consecutive years, that is, from 2006 to 2007 and from 2007 to 2008. This was despite an increase in expenditure in current prices. This may reflect the twin effects of the worldwide economic slowdown and inflation;
2. In the remaining years also, the year on year growth of expenditure in actual prices fluctuates a great deal, and the range of these changes is 1.4 to 67.5 per cent, which is extremely high; and

3. These growth rates highlight the haphazard nature of allocation, which directly affects expenditure.

The year on year growth rate may conceal rather than reveal long term trend, which is supported by the fact, that the allocation of funds in constant prices has increased at a statistically significant annual compound rate of 3.87 per cent, whereas the actual expenditure in constant prices has increased, at 4.6 per cent per annum. *Actual expenditure tends to grow more rapidly than allocated funds.* This shows mitigation of the bottleneck effect of low allocation, and greater efficiency in utilisation rather than the efficiency of allocation.

Thus, actual expenditure under the scheme shows a consistently higher rate of growth than the rate of growth of allocation of funds. This facet may imply that the growth of expenditure for employment is greatly constrained by the funds allocated for it. Delayed release of funds may often lead to accelerated growth of expenditure under the scheme.

The thesis is well supported by empirical evidence. Tables 1 and 2 show that:

1. Expenditure always lags behind allocations;
2. Proportions of the allocated funds in nominal and real terms, accounted for by the expenditure vary greatly between the years. This shows the volatility of efficiency of resource utilisation; and
3. Range of variation of expenditure is as high as 49 to 98 per cent.

Table 2: Swarnjayanti Gram Swarojgar Yojna Financial Progress in Constant 1993–94 Prices[1]

Index HSP	*Fund Allocation*	*Expenditure*	*Exp. Against Available Funds (%)*	*Growth in Fund Allocation (%)*	*Growth in Expenditure (%)*
174	107.62	52.91	49.16		
181	105.08	67.88	64.60	–2.36	28.30
188	123.29	113.70	92.23	17.33	67.50
194	124.60	100.49	80.66	1.06	–11.62
209	125.81	96.35	76.58	0.98	–4.12
225	163.11	112.70	69.10	29.64	16.96
247	183.77	128.88	70.13	12.67	14.36
269	183.32	130.68	71.29	–0.25	1.40
291	206.75	140.01	67.72	12.78	7.14

[1]Proportions and growth rates as per authors' calculations.

Long Term Trend Relation between Expenditure and Allocation

The degree and dimension of the hypothesised long term relationship between allocated funds and their utilisation is shown by the following regression relation the OLS estimate of which is reported:

Current Prices

$$Y_1 = 1232.9735 + 0.675\ X_1,\ R^2 = 0.9395,\ F = 108.79 > F^{*}1.62E{-}05$$
$$t = (0.52) \qquad \ldots (10.43)$$

Constant Prices

$$Y_2 = 4.6945 + 0.6811\ X_2,\ R^2 = 0.7752,\ F = 24.1342 > F^{*}0.001728$$
$$t = (0.224) \qquad \ldots (4.913)$$

where Y_1 and Y_2 are actual expenditure in current and constant prices, and X_1 and X_2 are total allocation under the series in current and constant prices respectively.

Both the functions fit the data well, and the explained proportion of variation ranges from 77.52 to 93.95 per cent of the total changes in expenditure in current and constant prices respectively. The regression coefficients in both equations are highly significant statistically. These relations lend credence to the thesis stated earlier. These functions highlight the fact that out of every increase of ₹ 100 in allocation, ₹ 68 are spent for the implementation of the scheme. It means that the utilisation of the allocated funds is only 68 per cent of the total. The message is that, those who administer the scheme should raise their efficiency of utilisation of allocated funds in order to press their claim for higher allocation in subsequent periods, since unspent funds are often carried forward to the next year, and non-utilisation of allocated funds may affect the allocation for the succeeding year. However, the imbalance between allocation and expenditure may also be explained by the administrative expenditure, and relatively low/high efficiency in execution, which is quite high.

These results also lend support to the thesis that allocated funds constrain expenditure under the scheme. If more jobs are to be generated for the poor, allocation need to be increased. But, this also requires an increase in the efficiency of the utilisation of the allocated funds.

Actual Expenditure under SGSY

If we go by past experience with regard to plan targets and actual achievement during the entire era of planned development, it should be noted that the actual achievements tend to fall short of plan targets in most of the cases. It is, therefore, not surprising that the actual expenditure also falls short of plan allocation in these cases. It is also not surprising that physical targets remain partially unfulfilled. In view of this, we have also analysed the actual expenditure, both in current and constant prices. If allocated funds are not exhausted by expenditure, then plan targets cannot be realised.

Growth Performance of the Scheme

If we consider the period as a whole, year on year fluctuations will be ironed out. The following growth curve shows that despite the year on year fluctuations of the growth of funds and expenditure, the allocated funds have increased at an annual compound rate of 6.72 per cent.

$$\log Y = 4.154 + 0.0672X, R^2 = 0.96, F = 175.53 > F^* = 3.26E\text{–}06$$
$$t = (145.47)\ (13.25)$$

where, Y = total funds available, X stands for time.

This highlights the overall long run rising trend of allocation of funds for the scheme, annual grow fluctuations of notwithstanding.

In 2003, the expenditure as a percentage of available funds was 49 per cent (Table 1). Actual expenditure under the scheme thus fell short by as much as 51 per cent. Naturally, financial constraints could not be blamed for this shortfall. Is it then explained by an inefficient administration of the scheme at the grassroots? Or, does it relate to the lackadaisical approach of the administration towards the poor of society? Or, does it relate to delayed release and receipt of funds in the districts? Answers to these questions require information, which we do not have. *This may need an independent investigation.*

Incidentally, poverty is caste based, but religion neutral. Does the shortfall in expenditures reflect bias against caste or the poor in the administrative set-up? Expenditure kept growing every year with 80 per cent funds utilisation under the scheme in 2006. In the following years, the expenditure against available funds started to decline, and came down to 70 per cent in 2009 and 71 per cent in 2010. This shows the shortfalls in the use of the allocated funds. Such shortfalls affect achieving physical targets.

Expenditure as a proportion of the allocated funds in 2004 rose by 15.44 and in 2005 by 25.8 percentage points, whereas the growth in available funds has only been 1.5 per cent. This suggests that the administration of the scheme at the grassroots alone may not account for the inefficient utilisation of the allocated funds. This has been the phenomenon, where growth in expenditure has been more than the growth in available funds except for the years 2006, 2007 and 2008, when growth of available funds was more than the growth in expenditure.

Financial Progress of MGNREGA

Funds for the MGNREGA scheme increased by 51.53 only from 2008–09 to 2009–10. In 2010–11, available funds grew by only 1.24 only. With the increase in available funds, expenditure also grew by 80.5 per cent in 2009–10 and by –4.55 per cent in 2010–11. Even though available funds grew in 2010–11, expenditure went down by 4.55 per cent. Of the total funds available, the major expenditure has been on wages, which were 65.18 per cent, 62.22 per cent and 65.11 per cent in 2008–09, 2009–10, 2010–11 respectively. The remaining expenditure is accounted by administrative and materials related expenditure. Thus, 25–38 per cent of the total expenditure is accounted for by the administrative costs which seem to be quite high.

Physical Achievement of the Schemes

SGSY Physical Achievement

The long run trend of actual expenditure under the scheme for the promotion of employment is much better than the allotted funds for the scheme. Long run annual compound growth rate of expenditure is as high as 7.36 per cent. Interestingly, the growth rate of the actual expenditure constant prices on promotion of employment under the scheme is 4.50 per cent. Growth in constant prices is invariably lower than the growth rate in current prices.

The liberal allocation of funds has mitigated the resources constraint, which in turn has facilitated the growth of actual expenditure. These results suggest that the actual utilisation of funds is directly related to funds made available for the scheme. But the timely release of funds also affects the efficiency of utilisation. The interrelation between the two variables is as follows:

$$\log Y = 3.9700 + 0.0736X,\ R^2 = 0.9172,\ F = 77.58 > F^* = 4.91E\text{–}05$$

$$t = (84.48)\ (8.81)$$

where Y is total expenditure and X is time.

SGSY Physical Progress

Since its inception in 1999, *Swarnjayanti Gram Swarozgar Yojana* (SGSY) has provided assistance to both SHG *swarojgaris* and individual *swarojgaris*.

In 2003, the total number of beneficiaries was 58,121, which increased to 94,784, i.e. by 63 per cent in 2004. The year 2005 saw growth of 105 per cent, which dipped to 0.18 per cent in 2006. In the following year, growth was 3 per cent, followed by 13 per cent the next year and going up to 21 per cent in 2009. The year 2010 had 2,73,213 beneficiaries, which showed a decline in comparison to 2009 by –1.6 per cent.

Group/Caste Composition of the Beneficiaries (SGSY)

Out of the total 58,121 *swarojgaris* in 2003, 49 per cent were SC/ST, 30 per cent women and 0.82 per cent disabled. Despite the scheme having separate components for the disabled poor, the number of disabled *swarojgaris* has been below 1 per cent till 2008 which rose to 1.23 per cent in 2009 and stayed at the same level in 2010. This may partly be accounted for by the total number of persons in this category. The number of SC/ST *swarojgaris* was at its highest in 2003, accounting for 49 per cent, which saw a decrease till 2005, accounting for 45 per cent of total *swarojgaris*. From 2006 to 2009, and the number of SC/ST *swarojgaris* remained stagnant, but registered an increase in 2010, accounting for 48 per cent of the total beneficiaries of the scheme.

There has been a gradual increase in the number of women *swarojgaris* from 30 per cent in 2003 to 38 per cent in 2010, except for the year 2005, when the number came down to 29.3 per cent.

The Physical Growth Performance of the SGSY Scheme

Despite the year on year fluctuations in benefits of the *swarojgaris*, the total achievement of the scheme has grown at an annual compound rate of 7.94 per cent. This highlights the long term trend in the impact of the scheme on the rural population.

The long term annual compound growth rate of achievement under the scheme for promotion of employment is significantly high at 7.94 per cent compared to the annual compound growth rate of 6.72 per cent of available funds. This suggests that over the years, awareness about the scheme has increased, which has stimulated self-employment activities among the beneficiaries. The following is the growth curve.

$$\log Y = 4.867 + 0.079X, \ R^2 = 0.805$$
$$t = (58.72)\ (5.389)$$

where Y is total achievement and X is time.

$$\log Y = 4.154 + 0.067236X, \ R^2 = 0.961$$
$$t = (145.47)\ (13.25)$$

where Y is available funds and X is time.

Beneficiaries According to Categories

$$\log Y_1 = 4.536 + 0.081X, \; R^2 = 0.834$$
$$(59.26) \quad (5.94)$$

$$\log Y_2 = 4.3107 + 0.096X, \; R^2 = 0.8839$$
$$(58.070) \quad (7.282)$$

$$\log Y_3 = 2.5696 + 0.1283X, \; R^2 = 0.8808$$
$$(25.599) \quad (7.1903)$$

Y_1= SC/ST, Y_2= Woman, Y_3= Disabled and X = time.

Despite year on year fluctuations in the allocation of funds, actual expenditure and achievement, the benefit to SC/ST grew at an annual compound rate of 8.10 per cent; the benefit to women grew at annual compound rate of 9.6 per cent, and benefit to the disabled grew at 12.8 per cent. The long term trend in benefits to the disabled is significant, *indicating inclusive growth with provision for self-employment* activities geared towards women, SC/ST and disabled.

Variations in the Total Employment and Employment of Different Categories

Results furnished by the year on year and differential trend growth rates highlight a very high degree of variations between the years as well as categories of the poor beneficiaries. In view of this, ANOVA has also been used.

ANOVA

Source of Variation	*SS*	*df*	*MS*	*F*	*P-value*	*F crit*
Rows	54823768900	8	6.85E+09	5.607936	0.000457831	2.355081
Columns	1.926E+11	3	6.42E+10	52.53617	1.07126E–10	3.008787
Error	29328313521	24	1.22E+09			
Total	2.76752E+11	35				

The results of ANOVA show that both between the rows and column the variations are statistically significant. It means that the total employment and employment of all three categories has differed significantly between the categories as well as between the years. This highlights the variability and differences of benefits between the years and categories.

We have examined the relationship between the financial expenditure and funds allocated for the scheme. But, the test of the pudding is in the eating. So, the degree of success of the scheme should be measured by outcomes of its implementation. Outcome is in terms of employment generated for the poor. The following regression relation shows the interdependence between the financial expenditure incurred under the scheme and the number of beneficiaries, who got the jobs.

$$Y = 13109.188 + 8.037X, \; R^2 = 0.9416, \; F = 113.02 > F^* = 1.42701E\text{-}05$$
$$t = (0.66) \qquad (10.63)$$

where Y is total achievement of employment and X depicts expenditure.

The regression function fits the data well. The estimated regression coefficients are statistically significant. The regression function shows that an increase of one unit in expenditure leads to the employment of eight more persons. This is an important result. It can be used to plan for the generation of jobs to eradicate unemployment among the eligible poor persons available for employment under the scheme.

Different Categories of Employment in SGSY

A perusal of the Table 3, showing shares of SC/ST, women and disabled, highlights that the SC/ST account for 45–49 per cent of total employment generated under the scheme, whereas, women account for 29–40 per cent of the total employment generated. As against this, the share of the disabled is hardly 0.1 per cent. Second, whereas, the share of the SC/ST shows a slightly declining trend, the other two categories indicate a rising trend. Shares of different categories in employment may be directly related to (i) proportion of eligible persons of a category seeking jobs, and (ii) persons who come forward to avail of the benefits under the scheme. It may be stated that, as per newspaper reports, several would be beneficiaries sell/hand over the job cards to the village headman who s/he sell them to other beneficiaries. Those, who do not avail of the job opportunities under the scheme, generally migrate to cities to benefit from the higher wages of employment in the cities. This highlights three related aspects: (i) the actual benefits may accrue to the unintended beneficiaries, (ii) delegation of power to panchayats has not eliminated corruption, and (iii) the benefits may be mis-delivered.

Incidentally, employment among SC/ST is not reported according to gender. We suspect that a part of employment of SC/ST may include women also. But, the low share of disabled seems to be accounted for mainly by the low share of disabled in the working age group population.

Table 3: Swarnjayanti Gram Swarojgar Yojna Physical Progress of Employment in Numbers (SC/ST, Women, Disabled)

Year	*Total*		*SC/ST*			*Women*			*Disabled*		
	Achieve-ment	*Growth %*	*Achieve-ment*	*%age*	*Growth %*	*Achieve-ment*	*%age*	*Growth %*	*Achieve-ment*	*%age*	*Growth %*
2003	58121		28536	49.1		17434	30		475	0.82	
2004	94784	63.08	43771	46.18	53.39	28970	30.56	66.17	375	0.4	–21.05
2005	194164	104.85	88113	45.38	101.30	56943	29.33	96.56	1476	0.76	293.60
2006	194526	0.19	92192	47.39	4.63	63174	32.48	10.94	1401	0.72	–5.08
2007	202100	3.89	95362	47.19	3.44	65983	32.65	4.45	1948	0.96	39.04
2008	228749	13.19	107770	47.11	13.01	81279	35.53	23.18	2107	0.92	8.16
2009	277811	21.45	132798	47.8	23.22	98658	35.51	21.38	3406	1.23	61.65
2010	273213	–1.66	131736	48.22	–0.80	104232	38.15	5.65	3359	1.23	–1.38
2011	327204	19.76	160046	48.91	21.49	131389	40.16	26.05	4577	1.4	36.26

Source: Department of Rural Development, Government of U.P., RuralSoft (http://ruralsoft.up.nic.in)

Table 4: MGNREGA

Employment provided to households	14.83265 Lakhs	
Persondays [in lakhs]	Total : 531.64	
SCs	290.77	[54.69%]
STs	16.64	[3.13%]
Women	105.29	[19.81%]
Others	224.23	[42.18%]
Total Funds	2374.36 Crore	
Expenditure	826.26 Crore	
Total Work Taken up	159501	
Work Completed	46543	
Work in progress	112958	

Source: http://www.mgnregaup.in/Home.aspx

However, the SC/ST seems to have gained more than their share in the total population. But, it is also a fact that SC/ST constitute the largest proportion among the poor of the country as well as in U.P. The growth of shares of different groups in total employment is determined as follows:

Growth of Shares of Different Categories in SGSY

The earlier thesis regarding the trend growth may be judged by the following regression functions:

$$Y_1 = 46.65 + 0.166\,T,\ R^2 = 0.141,\ F = 1.152 > F^* = 0.319$$
$$t = (53.73) \qquad (1.073)$$

$$Y_2 = 27.25 + 1.313\,T,\ R^2 = 0.914,\ F = 74.57 > F^*5.58E\text{-}05$$
$$t = (31.830) \qquad (8.635)$$

$$Y_3 = 0.440 + 0.099\,T,\ R^2 = 0.77,\ F = 23.43 > F^*0.001877$$
$$t = (3.812) \qquad (4.840)$$

where $Y_{1,}$ $Y_{2,}$ and Y_3 are employment categories of SC/ST, women and disabled respectively.

Though, the share of SC/ST shows a positive rising trend, but is not statistically significant. The change in SC/ST *in the total employment is statistically as good as zero.* Therefore, it may be inferred that the employment of the *SC/ST under the scheme has remained static* during a decade. This may be accounted for by the allocation constraint, or the number of persons seeking jobs under the scheme.

As against SC/ST, the share of women has increased positively and significantly. The share of women in total employment has increased by an annual compound nation about 1.31 per cent.

Like the share of women, employment of the disabled has also increased at a low but significant rate of 0.1 units per annum.

These inferences are also supported by the following results of the ANOVA table, based on shares of three different categories in employment.

Two Factors without Replication

ANOVA

Source of Variation	*SS*	*Df*	*MS*	*F*	*P-value*	*F crit*
Rows	61.84464251	8	7.730580314	1.937598	0.12382	2.5911
Columns	10300.66926	2	5150.334631	1290.884	2.1E-18	3.63372
Error	63.83639893	16	3.989774933			
Total	10426.3503	26				

The share of employment between categories has changed significantly, though within categories variation over the years is not significant. Non-significance of the growth of the share of SC/STs seems to account for the non-significance of variation between the years.

Physical Progress of the MGNREGA Scheme

Since its inception in 2007, NREGA has provided employment to 14.83265 lakh households. Out of the total beneficiaries, 54.69 per cent are SC, 3.13 per cent are ST, 19.81 per cent women and 42.18 per cent belong to other categories. Women and other beneficiaries seem to overlap. Out of the total funding of ₹ 2374.36 crore available for the NREGA project, only 826.26 crore has been spent on this scheme. Expenditure accounts for only 34.8 per cent of the total available funds. *This rate of utilisation of allocated funds is indicative of a high level of inefficiency. Administrative inefficiently needs attention.* This affects not only the mitigation of poverty, but also the growth of the economy of the state.

Over a period of time, the number of households, who demanded employment, has increased. 2009–10 saw growth of 30 per cent and 2010–11 saw growth of 16 per cent in the number of households demanding and getting employment under the scheme.

With the increase in the number of households getting employment, the percentage of SC availing this benefit rose to 56.41 per cent in 2009–10 from 53.56 per cent in 2008–09. However, 2010–11 saw a decline in the percentage of SC participation to 53.96 per cent.

18.11 per cent women participated in this employment programme in 2008–09, which rose to 21.67 per cent in 2009–10 and slightly slipped to 21.42 per cent in 2010–11.

The total number of households that availed of 100 days employment saw growth of 23 per cent in 2009–10 and registered a decline by 24.64 per cent born 2009–10 to 2010–11.

In 2008–09 and 2009–10 close to 14 per cent of the households availed 100 days of employment under the scheme. In 2010–11 only 9.3 per cent households availed of 100 days of employment. It may be noted that 100 days in a year is only partial employment during the agriculturally slack seasons. He does not guarantee continued employment thought the year who are unemployed even in peak season.

Growth Performance of MGNREGA Scheme

Ever since its inception in 2006 for the promotion of employment, the scheme has seen fluctuations in the year to year allocation of funds and expenditure. The annual compound rate of growth in allocated funds by 9.93 per cent highlights the long term trend, annual fluctuations notwithstanding. The long term trend growth of actual expenditure on providing employment under the scheme is almost the same as the growth of allotted funds for the scheme. This reflects effective utilisation of available funds. Long tem annual compound growth rate is 9.90 per cent.

Utilisation of Allocated Funds

The liberal allocation of funds and increased awareness about the scheme facilitated the growth of actual expenditure. These results suggest that the actual utilisation of funds is directly related to funds made available for the scheme. The interrelation between these two variables is as follows:

$$Y = 5.49 + 0.099\,X,\ R^2 = 0.7717$$

$$t = (51.35)\ (1.84)$$

where Y shows expenditure and X denotes allocated funds.

The results highlight that actual expenditure is not significantly related to the allocated funds for the scheme. Corresponding to a unit increase in allocation, expenditure rises only by 0.1, that is only one tenth of the increased allocation is actually used. This reflects very low utilisations efficiency. This result reinforces earlier finding.

This again highlights inefficiency in the utilisation of allocated funds. It may not be wrong to suggest that inter-scheme transfer of unutilised funds should be allocated to raise efficiency of utilisation of allocated funds.

The following questions need to be answered in connection with the scheme:

1. Why have only a portion of the rural poor applied for job cards?
2. Why do those, who got job cards, did not seek employment yet?
3. Why are all the households, who demanded employment, did not get jobs?

This is the list of questions which we are not in a position to answer on the basis of the data available to us. The administration may be in a position to provide answers to these questions. Researchers can attempt to answer such questions on the basis of field surveys.

Table 5: MGNREGA Outcomes (Financial)

Year	*Financial Outcomes (` in lakhs)*									
	Central Release	*Total Funds Available Including O.B*	*Total Exp.*	*% Age of Exp. Against Total Available Fund*	*Expenditure on Wages*	*% Age of Expenditure on Wages*	*Expenditure on Material*	*% Age of Expenditure on Material*	*Administrative Expenditure*	*% Age of Administrative Expenditure*
2008–09	393390.12	470692.85	356887.72	75.82	225446.52	65.18	120413.84	34.82	11027.36	3.09
2009–10	531887.16	713268.05	590003.88	82.72	354123.08	62.22	214995.2	37.78	20885.6	3.54
2010–11	526658.86	722148.1	563120.12	77.98	351965.3	65.11	188575.15	34.89	22579.67	4.01

Source: http://164.100.12.7/Netnrega/mpr_ht/nregampr_dmu.aspx?fin_year = 2010-2011&month = Latest&flag = 1&page1 = S

Table 6: Mahatma Gandhi NREGA Outcomes (Physical: Employment)

Year	*No. of Households who have Demanded Employment*	*No. of Households Provided Employment*	*Percentage in Lakhs*								*Average Person Days per Household*	*Number of Households Availed 100 days of Employment*
			Total	*SCs*	*% Age of SC Participation*	*STs*	*% Age of ST Participation*	*Women*	*% Age of Women participation*	*Others*		
2008–09	4338490	4336466	2272.21	1216.90	53.56	44.57	1.96	411.46	18.11	1010.74	52.40	647525
2009–10	5667644	5483434	3559.26	2007.86	56.41	52.74	1.48	771.36	21.67	1498.66	64.91	796929
2010–11	6581786	6431213	3348.97	1806.99	53.96	70.48	2.10	717.27	21.42	1471.50	52.07	600559

Source: http://164.100.12.7/Netnrega/mpr_ht/nregampr_dmu.aspx?fin_year = 2010–2011&month = Latest&flag = 1&page1 = S

Conclusion

The analysis of data highlights the following aspects of the implementation of the employment generation programme for promoting the welfare of the poor in Uttar Pradesh:

1. Allocation of funds in current prices for different schemes has been rising consistently;
2. Growth of allocation of funds in constant prices has grown at a much lower and slower rate than the growth in current prices. Inflation has neutralised the growth of funds to a large extent;
3. Actual expenditure, both in current and constant prices, has substantially lagged behind the allocated funds. Thus, for any given allocative efficiency, efficiency of utilisation needs improvement;
4. Physical achievement in terms of persons employed has shown considerable growth.
5. Share of SC/ST in total employment is the highest, but has not increased significantly over the years;
6. Share of women in employment has registered the maximum growth.
7. Disabled have lagged behind both these groups; and
8. Spending of allocated funds under—NREGA shows a very high degree of inefficiency.

Thus, some aspects of inclusiveness of growth have not gained momentum under these schemes.

References

Lubhaya, R. (2008). *Implementation of NREGA—The Rajasthan Experience,* Rural Development and Panchayati Raj Department, Government of Rajasthan (www.rdprd.gov.in).

Sharma, A. (2009). *Evaluating Performance of National Rural Employment Guarantee Act, NCAER-PIF Study*, Public Interest Foundation. http://www.ncaer.org/downloads/reports/NCAER-PIFstudyNREGA.pdf

Goparaju, Srikanth and Shome, Samik (2011). What Next for MGNREGA?, *IIM Journal of Management Science,* Vol. 2, No. 1, Jan–June.

CHAPTER 12

Cost Efficiencies of Principal Crops: A Comparative Study among Indian States

G.N. Patel and A. Bose

Agriculture is a source of livelihood for the majority of the population in India. Food grains are the single largest contributors to agriculture output. The agricultural sector contributes 18.5 per cent to the Gross Domestic Product (GDP), in spite of the rapid rise of the secondary and services sectors in the economy.

Uttar Pradesh has the largest population in the country, and it is also the biggest producer of food-grains. Western parts of Uttar Pradesh, comprising the fertile Indo-Ganges plains is considered to be a part of the green revolution belt. In addition to 4.10 crore tonnes of food-grains, U.P. produces 1.30 crore tonnes of sugarcane and 1.05 crore tonnes of potato, contributing almost 40 per cent to India's total produce of these.

Land Grab by Government and Industry: Alarming Portents

This state probably prompts the government to acquire land on an increasing scale. Devinder Sharma in an article titled "Who will feed Uttar Pradesh?" writes, 'Out of the total area of 1.98 crore hectares under food-grain crops in Uttar Pradesh, one-third or roughly 66 lakh hectares is planned to be shifted from agriculture to non-agriculture activity. Much of the fertile and productive lands of western Uttar Pradesh will therefore disappear, to be replaced by concrete jungles. In addition to wheat and rice, sugarcane and potato would be the other two major crops whose production will be negatively impacted'.

As per rough estimates, 66 lakh hectares that would be taken out of farming would mean production loss of 140 lakh tonnes of food-grains. In other words, Uttar Pradesh will be faced with a terrible food crisis in the years to come, the seeds for which are being sown now. Add to this the anticipated shortfalls in potato and sugarcane production, since the area under these two crops will also go down drastically, the road ahead for Uttar Pradesh is not only dark but laced with social unrest.

Already lagging behind most other states in socio-economic development, Uttar Pradesh will surely see a surge in hunger, malnutrition and under-nourishment. We can only imagine the socio-political fallout of the misadventure that the government is attempting, with such a massive takeover of fertile land.

Other analysts have also been drawing attention to the impact of urbanisation on transfers of land from agricultural to non-agricultural uses (e.g. Prakash, S., 2009, 2011).

Uttar Pradesh has a total area of 31.29 million hectares out of 231 million acres of cultivable land in India. Of this, almost 62.44 per cent, that is 19.54 million hectares is used for the cultivation of paddy, wheat and maize alone. Sugarcane is a major cash crop grown in U.P., and almost 50 per cent of the total area under cultivation of sugarcane in India is in U.P.

We examine the performance of Uttar Pradesh vis-à-vis other states in the production of these principal crops. In the absence of more recent data, we consider the data from the archives of the Directorate of Economics and Statistics, Ministry of Agriculture, for 2007–08. For each of the five major crops, we examine the relative efficiency of the top five Indian states. The data pertaining to the per hectare cost of cultivation, per quintal cost of production and yield in quintals per hectare for the five major states producing each of these crops. This analysis clearly shows that agricultural efficiency, as measured by factor costs, viz., production costs and cultivation costs per quintal of yield of the respective crops shows U.P. lagging behind the other major producers.

Paddy

Paddy is one of the most important foodcrops grown in India. Cultivation costs per hectare for paddy differs from state to state, as does the production costs per quintal of paddy. The following data show the cultivation and production costs and respective yields of paddy in 2008 for the top five states of India (Table 1).

It is interesting to note that while the cultivation cost is high in Punjab though lower than in Andhra Pradesh, the production cost per quintal is the lowest. Per hectare yield in Punjab is the highest among the top states.

Table 1: Factor Costs and Relative Efficiency for Paddy (2007–08)

State	*Cultivation Cost (per hectare)* ₹	*Production Cost (per quintal)* ₹	*Yield (quintal/hectare)*
Andhra Pradesh	37443.61	638.56	55.11
Orissa	21713.38	599.68	32.03
Punjab	34781.20	505.92	68.01
Uttar Pradesh	22301.17	600.73	35.00
West Bengal	28141.88	668.34	36.70

To compare the cropping efficiency with respect to cultivation and production, we convert both cultivation and production costs to the rupee costs per quintal crop yields. This results in the following data for paddy production (Table 2).

Table 2: Factor Costs and Relative Efficiency for Paddy (2007–08)

State	*Cultivation Cost/Quintal* (₹)	*Production Cost/Quintal* (₹)	*Efficiency*
Andhra Pradesh	679.43	11.59	0.75
Orissa	677.91	18.72	0.75
Punjab	511.41	7.44	1.00
Uttar Pradesh	637.18	17.16	0.80
West Bengal	766.81	18.21	0.67

It appears that Punjab is doing better than the other states in using less inputs to produce an unit output of paddy. By the same token, Uttar Pradesh is lagging behind Punjab, though it is ahead of Andhra Pradesh, West Bengal and Orissa.

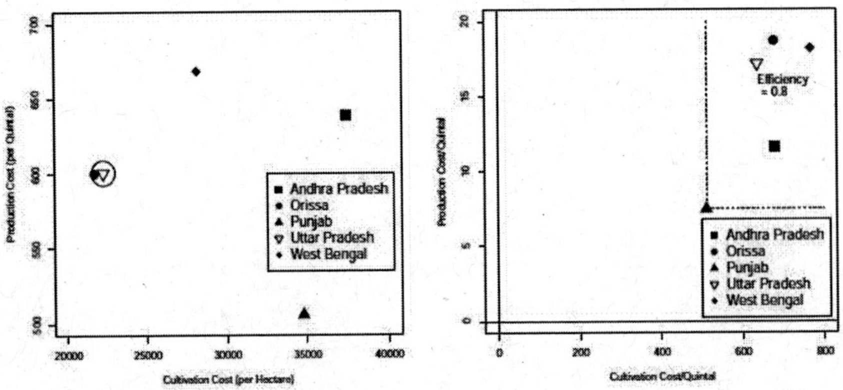

Fig. 1: Paddy: Uttar Pradesh vs. Other Major Paddy Cultivating States

The DEA efficiencies in the last column bear out these observations. The efficiency of 0.80 for Uttar Pradesh implies that it should be possible for Uttar Pradesh to either reduce its input costs by 80.26 per cent without reducing the yield of paddy, or, using the current level of inputs, to increase the yield to 1.25 times the current levels. Punjab, with the highest efficiency provides the benchmark.

We also observe that, with respect to the benchmark of Punjab, the cultivation of paddy in Uttar Pradesh is operating at an average efficiency of 511/637.18 = 80.26 per cent. The production of paddy in U.P. is operating at 7.44/17.16 = 43.34 per cent efficiency.

Thus, major gains in Paddy cropping by way of cost reductions or increase in output would be through improvement of production techniques.

Wheat

Cultivation costs per hectare and the production costs per quintal of wheat differ widely from state to state. The following data show the cultivation costs, production costs and respective yields of paddy in 2008 for the top five states of India. The production costs for wheat are low and more or less equal for Punjab, Rajasthan and U.P., but the cultivation cost is the lowest in Madhya Pradesh. However, the yield of wheat is very low in M.P., while Punjab has a significantly higher yield than the other states. Barring the very low yield in M.P., U.P.'s yield of wheat is the lowest among the major wheat producers (Table 3).

Table 3: Factor Costs and Relative Efficiency for Wheat (2007–08)

State	*Cultivation Cost (per hectare)* ₹	*Production Cost (per quintal)* ₹	*Yield (quintal/hectare)*
Haryana	32380.45	673.46	41.99
Madhya Pradesh	21450.07	779.37	23.86
Punjab	32826.96	647.95	46.47
Rajasthan	25729.27	649.77	33.39
Uttar Pradesh	25529.15	651.14	33.29

To compare the cropping efficiency with respect to cultivation and production, we convert both cultivation and production costs to the rupee costs per quintal crop yield. This results in the following data for wheat production (Table 4).

Table 4: Factor Costs and Relative Efficiency for Wheat (2007–08)

State	*Cultivation Cost/Quintal* (₹)	*Production Cost/Quintal* (₹)	*Efficiency*
Haryana	771.15	16.04	0.92
Madhya Pradesh	899.00	32.66	0.79
Punjab	706.41	13.94	1.00
Rajasthan	770.57	19.46	0.92
Uttar Pradesh	766.87	19.56	0.92

It is clear that Punjab is doing better than all other states in using less quantity of inputs to produce an unit output of wheat. Uttar Pradesh, which lags behind Punjab, is operating at the same level of efficiency as Haryana and Rajasthan, with all three states having an efficiency of 0.92. The DEA efficiencies in the last column bear out these observations. The efficiency of 0.92 for Uttar Pradesh implies that it should be possible for Uttar Pradesh to either reduce its input costs by 92.12 per cent without reducing the yield of wheat, or, using the current level of inputs, to increase the yield to 1.09 times the current levels. Punjab, with the highest efficiency provides the benchmark.

We also observe that, with respect to the benchmark of Punjab, the cultivation of wheat in Uttar Pradesh is operating at an average efficiency of 706.41/766.87 = 92.12 per cent. The production of wheat in U.P. is operating at 13.94/19.56 = 71.29 per cent efficiency.

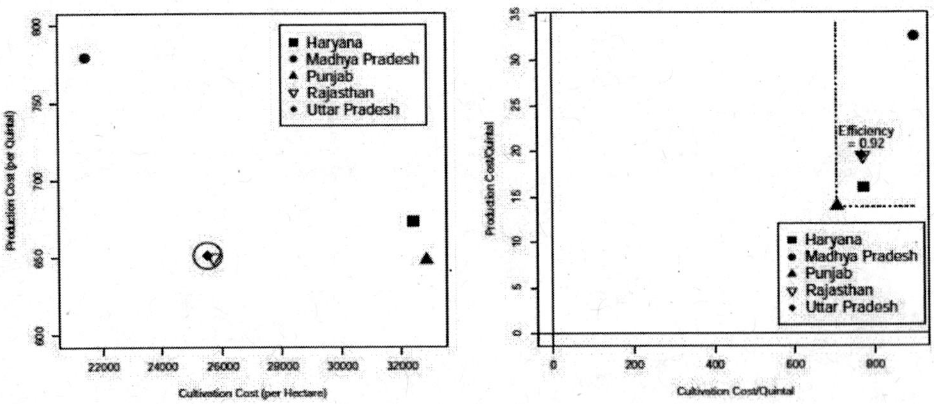

Fig. 2: Wheat: Uttar Pradesh vs. Other Major Wheat Cultivating States

Thus, marginally greater gains in Wheat cropping by way of cost reduction, or increase in output would be by the use of improve techniques of production to reduce production costs and attain higher efficiency in production.

Maize

Statistics for maize for the major states of India show a large range of variations of cultivation and production costs as well as yields. The following data show the cultivation and production costs and respective yields of maize in 2008 for the top five states of India. Cultivation cost is the lowest in Karnataka, with not too much difference among the other major states. Only Andhra Pradesh has very high maize cultivation costs. For production cost too the range is wide, with Bihar and Karnataka having the lowest costs, while Uttar Pradesh has the highest cost of production. Interestingly, the yield is by far the highest in AP, Bihar comes next. The yield of maize is the lowest in U.P. (Table 5).

Table 5: Factor Costs and Relative Efficiency for Maize (2007–08)

State	*Cultivation Cost (per hectare)* ₹	*Production Cost (per quintal)* ₹	*Yield (quintal/hectare)*
Andhra Pradesh	26728.22	611.10	41.50
Bihar	18586.90	429.07	37.92
Karnataka	15568.85	465.07	29.95
Rajasthan	17729.11	690.80	21.07
Uttar Pradesh	16709.03	842.75	17.01

For comparing efficiency of cultivation and production, we convert both cultivation and production costs to the rupee costs per quintal crop yields. This results in the following data for maize production. It is clear that Bihar is doing better than other states in using less quantity of inputs to produce one unit output of maize (Table 6).

Table 6: Factor Costs and Relative Efficiency for Maize (2007–08)

State	*Cultivation Cost/Quintal* (₹)	*Production Cost/Quintal* (₹)	*Efficiency*
Andhra Pradesh	644.05	14.73	0.77
Bihar	490.16	11.32	1.00
Karnataka	519.83	15.53	0.94
Rajasthan	841.44	32.79	0.58
Uttar Pradesh	982.31	49.54	0.50

Uttar Pradesh is lagging behind all major producers, with high production costs being the concern, ₹ 49.54 per quintal as against ₹ 11.32 per quintal in Bihar. The DEA efficiencies corroborate the above observations. The efficiency of 0.50 for Uttar Pradesh implies that it should be possible for U.P. to either reduce its input costs by

49.90 per cent without reducing the yield of maize, or, using the current level of inputs to increase the yield to 2 times its current levels. Bihar, with the highest efficiency provides the benchmark.

We also observe that, the cultivation of maize in Uttar Pradesh is operating at an average efficiency of 490.16/982.31 = 49.9 per cent with respect to the benchmark of Bihar. The production of maize in U.P. is operating at 11.32/49.54 = 22.84 per cent efficiency.

Thus, significantly greater gains by way of cost reductions or increase in output would be through improvement of maize production techniques.

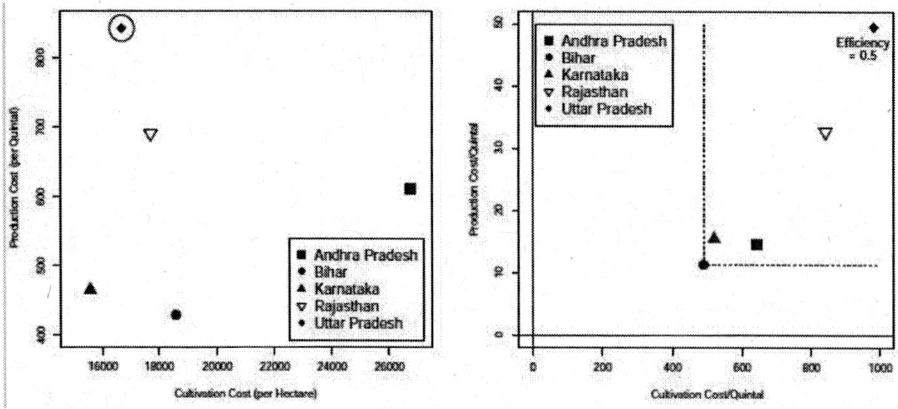

Fig. 3: Maize: Uttar Pradesh vs. Other Major Wheat Cultivating States

Sugarcane

The following data show the cultivation and production costs and respective yields of sugarcane in 2008 for the top five states of India. Uttar Pradesh has almost half of India's cultivated area for sugarcane (Table 7).

Table 7: Factor Costs and Relative Efficiency for Sugarcane (2007–08)

State	*Cultivation Cost (per hectare)* ₹	*Production Cost (per quintal)* ₹	*Yield (quintal/hectare)*
Andhra Pradesh	83204.91	106.06	782.50
Karnataka	43752.91	48.46	887.30
Maharashtra	73056.97	76.29	875.36
Tamil Nadu	83081.91	73.45	1109.07
Uttar Pradesh	40843.89	73.35	523.37

This is reflected in low cultivation costs, arising out of economies of scale. However, the production costs is high compared to the benchmark of Karnataka, and more significantly, the yield is abysmally low, less than half that of Tamil Nadu (Table 8).

Table 8: Factor Costs and Relative Efficiency for Sugarcane (2007–08)

State	*Cultivation Cost/Quintal (₹)*	*Production Cost/Quintal (₹)*	*Efficiency*
Andhra Pradesh	106.33	0.14	0.46
Karnataka	49.31	0.05	1.00
Maharashtra	83.46	0.09	0.63
Tamil Nadu	74.91	0.07	0.82
Uttar Pradesh	78.04	0.14	0.63

To compare the cropping efficiency with respect to cultivation and production, we convert both cultivation and production costs to the rupee costs per quintal crop yield. This results in the following data for sugarcane production. Karnataka seems to be doing better than other states in using less quantity of inputs to produce an one unit output of sugarcane. Uttar Pradesh ranks below Karnataka and Tamil Nadu, and efficiency-wise, it is at par with Maharashtra.

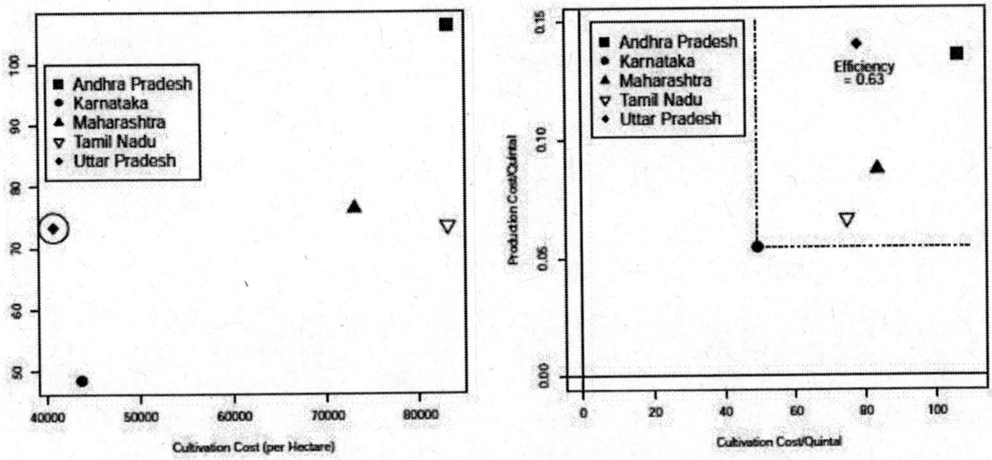

Fig. 4: Sugarcane: Uttar Pradesh vs. Other Major Sugarcane Cultivating States

The efficiency of 0.63 for Uttar Pradesh implies that it should be possible for Uttar Pradesh to either reduce its input costs by 63.19 per cent without reducing the yield of maize, or, using the current level of inputs, to increase the yield to 1.58 times its current level. Karnataka, with the highest efficiency, provides the benchmark.

We also observe that, cultivation of sugarcane in Uttar Pradesh is operating at an average efficiency of 49.31/78.04 = 63.19 per cent in relation to the benchmark of Karnataka. The production of sugarcane in U.P. is operating at 0.05/0.14 = 38.97 per cent efficiency. Thus, significantly greater gains in sugarcane cropping by way of cost reductions or increase in output could be through improvement of production techniques.

Conclusions

It is clear that the cropping efficiency is poor in Uttar Pradesh as compared to the other major crop growing states of India. With agriculture being the mainstay of a major section of the population, there is huge potential for improving the state of development of U.P. by addressing the shortcomings in cropping technology. It is also quite evident that the production costs are relatively high in Uttar Pradesh among the five major states.

The efficiencies compared to the respective benchmarks for the four crops studied are (Table 9):

Table 9

Crop	*Benchmark State*	*Efficiency of Uttar Pradesh Compared with Benchmark*	
		Cultivation (%)	*Production (%)*
Paddy	Punjab	80.26	43.34
Wheat	Punjab	92.12	71.29
Maize	Bihar	49.9	22.84
Sugarcane	Karnataka	63.19	38.97

Reasons for Poor Agricultural Efficiency—Indiscriminate Exploitation of Ground Water

The excessive pumping of ground water for irrigation purposes in intensively cultivated areas of western Uttar Pradesh has caused lowering of the ground water levels in certain pockets. This has raised production costs due to higher energy requirements for pumping water from greater depths. As against this, the vast potential of ground water in eastern Uttar Pradesh remains untapped.

Issues Related to Cropping Systems for U.P.

Rice-Wheat

Rice-Wheat system is the most widely adopted cropping system in the country and has become the mainstay of production in Uttar Pradesh. Despite the enormous growth of this cropping system, there is stagnations in the productivity of these crops, with possible declines in production in the future. Important issues that have emerged as a threat to the sustainability of rice-wheat system are:

1. over mining of nutrients from the soil;
2. disturbed soil aggregates due to puddling in rice;
3. decreasing response to nutrients;
4. declining ground water table;
5. build up of diseases/pests;
6. build up of Phalaris minor;
7. low input use efficiency in the north western plains;
8. low use of fertiliser in eastern and central parts; and
9. want of appropriate varietal combinations.

Maize-Wheat

Poor maize-wheat yield has been reported from eastern Uttar Pradesh. The most significant reasons for poor maize-wheat yield are:

1. sowing time;
2. poor plant population;
3. poor weed management;
4. poor use of organic and inorganic fertilisers; and
5. large area under rain-fed cultivation.

Most of the area in maize-wheat system is in rain-fed, conditions, when uncertainty of rainfall is a major limitation. This also acts as a deterrent for farmers to adopt intensive input use, leading to deterioration of soil health and depletion of major plant nutrients from the soil. Farmers in general tend to grow low yielding traditional varieties. Maize is very sensitive to water logging and drought. Any delay in weed control in maize can reduce the yield significantly. Declining yield trends in maize-wheat system can be attributed to deficiencies of multiple nutrients. Continuously over-mining of nutrients from the soil, and imbalance in use of fertilisers in maize-wheat system are some of the many reasons for such decline.

Sugarcane-Wheat

Some of the common problems in sugarcane-wheat mixed cropping system are:

1. late planting of sugarcane as well as wheat;
2. unbalanced and inadequate use of nutrients.

Since majority of farmers apply only N in sugarcane, the use of P and K is limited. The emerging deficiencies of P, K, S and micro-nutrients are limiting productivity directly, and through interactions with other nutrients:

1. poor nitrogen use efficiency in sugarcane;
2. build up of Trianthema partulacastrum and Cyprus rotundus in sugarcane; and
3. stubble of sugarcane poses tillage problems for succeeding crops and need to be managed properly.

Western Uttar Pradesh has been witnessing major problems in agriculture also due to the following reasons, which are generally attributable to population growth:

1. decreasing size of land holdings;
2. decreasing underground water; and
3. degradation of land fertility.

There is an urgent need to address the problems in their totality. Addressing the technical issues leading to low production efficiency (or high production costs) would need a sufficiently thorough scrutiny of the major shortcomings, which lead to low agricultural outputs and high costs. Issues of land grab by government and industry should be deliberated after thorough examination, and with appropriate alternatives offered to the affected farmers.

References

Charnes, A., Cooper, W. and Rhodes, E. (1978). Measuring the Efficiency of Decision Making Units, *European Journal of Operational Research*, 2: 429–444.

Charnes, A., Cooper, W. and Rhodes, E. (1981). Evaluating Program and Managerial Efficiency: An Application of Data Envelopment Analysis to Program Follow Through. *Management Science*, 27: 668–697.

Cooper, W., Seiford, L. and Tone, K. (2007). Data Envelopment Analysis, Springer, 2nd Edition.

Directorate of Economics and Statistics (2001). Agricultural Statistics at a Glance, Govt. of India.

Farrell, M.J. (1957). The Measurement of Productive Efficiency, *Journal of the Royal Statistical Society*, 253–281.

IASRI, N.D. (2002). Agricultural Research Data Book, N. Delhi.

Sharma, D. (2010). Who will Feed Uttar Pradesh? d-sector.org, Making Sense of Development.

Section–V

Foreign Direct Investment and Finances of Uttar Pradesh

CHAPTER 13

Foreign Direct Investment in Uttar Pradesh

Pooja Misra, Jaya Gupta and Tom George

Introduction

First the concept of foreign direct investment has been explained and clarified.

Concept

Foreign Direct Investment (FDI) is an instrument by which residents of one country (the source country) acquire ownership of assets for controlling production, distribution and other activities of a firm in another country (the host country). The International Monetary Fund defines FDI as 'investment that is made to acquire a lasting interest in an enterprise operating in an economy other than that of the investor. The investor's purpose is to have an effective voice in the management of the enterprise'. The United Nations 1999 World Investment Report (UNCTAD, 1999) defines FDI as 'investment involving a long term relationship which reflects a lasting interest and control of a resident entity in one country (foreign direct investor or parent enterprise) in an enterprise resident in an economy other than that of foreign direct investor (FDI enterprise, affiliate enterprise or foreign affiliate). The word 'long-term' distinguishes FDI from portfolio investment by institutional investors for short term gains. Portfolio investment is short term in nature, and involves a high turnover of securities.

The common feature of these definitions of FDI relates to 'control' and 'controlling interest'; it is the most important feature that distinguishes FDI from portfolio investment. A portfolio investor does not seek control or lasting interest. There is no agreement, however, on what constitutes a controlling interest. Generally, a minimum of 10 per cent of shareholding for influencing (potentially, or actually exercised) the key policies of the underlying project is considered necessary. Sometimes, another qualification is used to highlight FDI, which involves transferring capital from a source country to a host country.

For this purpose, investment activities abroad are considered to be FDI when:

1. There is control through substantial equity shareholding; and
2. There is a shift of part of the company's assets, production or sales to the host country.

However, this may not necessarily always be the case. A project may also be financed totally by borrowing in the host country. Thus, the distinguishing feature of FDI is the element of control over management and policy decisions. Many firms are unwilling to invest in other country unless they have 100 per cent equity ownership and control over the recipient unit. Others refuse to make such investments unless they have at least a majority control (that is a 51 per cent stake). In recent years, however, there has been a tendency for making FDI co-operative arrangements, where several firms participate, and no single party holds a majority control (for example joint ventures).

But, what exactly does 'control' mean in the definition of FDI? The term 'control' implies that some degree of discretionary decision making by the investor is present in the management policies and strategy. For example, this control may occur through the ability of the investor to elect, or select one, or more members on the board of directors, of the foreign company's subsidiary. The non-equity forms of FDI include subcontracting management contracts, franchising, licensing and product sharing. Lall and Streeten (1977) argue that majority shareholding is not a necessary condition for exercising control, as it may be achievable with a low equity share, and even without an explicit management contract.

So, it is possible (in theory at least) to define and characterise FDI. But measuring FDI in practice is a totally different 'game'. There are inherent problems in measuring FDI, particularly when the investment takes the form of machinery, or capitalised technological contributions. There are also gaps in the FDI statistics available from the source and the host countries. Most countries do not publish comprehensive information on the foreign operations of their companies for reasons of secrecy. Because of these problems, inconsistency between measures of FDI flows and stocks is the rule rather than the exception.

Interest in FDI, which has motivated attempts to come up with theories to explain causes and effects is attributed to the following reasons. The first reason is the rapid growth in FDI and the change in its pattern, particularly since the 1980s. In the 1990s, FDI accounted for about a quarter of international capital outflows, having grown more rapidly, relative to other forms of international investments since the 1970s. The rapid growth of FDI has resulted from global competition, as well as from the tendency to free financial, goods and factor markets. It has been observed that FDI flows continue to expand even when world trade slows down. For example, when the growth of trade is retarded by trade barriers, FDI may increase, as firms attempt to circumvent the barriers to exports. It has also been observed that even when portfolio investment dried up in Asian countries as a result of the crisis of the 1990s, FDI flows were not affected significantly. The latest available OECD figures show that FDI inflows to OECD countries increased from US $ 249 billion in 1996 to US $ 684 billion in 1999, whereas FDI outflows increased from US $ 341 billion to $ 768 in during the same period.

The second reason for interest in FDI is the concern it raises about the causes and consequences of foreign ownership in the host country. The views on this issue are so diverse, falling between the extremes of regarding FDI as symbolising new colonialism or imperialism, and at the other extreme of viewing it as something without which the host country cannot survive. Most countries show an ambivalent attitude towards FDI. Inward FDI is said to have negative employment effects, retards home-grown technological progress and worsens the trade balance. A substantial foreign ownership often gives rise to concerns about the loss of sovereignty and compromise over national security. Outward FDI is sometimes blamed for the export of employment, and for giving foreigners access to domestic technology. This brief discussion of the concept and role of FDI may facilitate the understanding of the role of FDI in U.P. But, first we consider the basic profile of the economy of Uttar Pradesh.

Profile of Uttar Pradesh

Uttar Pradesh is a key hub for IT and ITes industries, including software, captive business process outsourcing (BPO) and electronics. It is also a leading agricultural state of the country; it is amongst the top producers of major agricultural goods, such as wheat, rice and sugarcane. The state offers a wide range of subsidies, fiscal and other policy incentives and assistance for business under the Industrial and Service Sector Investment Policy, 2004. The state also has well drafted sector-specific policies for IT, biotech and tourism. Besides, the state has a large skilled labour force, making it an ideal destination for knowledge-based industries. The state also has a large pool of semi-skilled and unskilled work force.

Uttar Pradesh has witnessed high infrastructural growth in the past few years. There has been considerable increase in the number of industrial clusters and public-private partnerships in the infrastructural domain. It has good connectivity through four national highways, six airports and rail links to all major cities. With reference to the political environment, there is political stability with a single-party government. The state government is committed to creating a rich business climate through several policies and incentives.

The following Table 1 highlights the relative status of U.P. in India.

Table 1: Uttar Pradesh in Figures ... (1/2)

Parameter	Uttar Pradesh	All-states	Source
Economy			
GSDP as a percentage of all states' GSDP	8.7	100.0	CMIE, as of 2007-08, current prices
Average GSDP growth rate (%)*	9.6	11.8	CMIE, 2000-01 to 2007-08, current prices
Per capita GSDP (US$)	453.7	992.5	CMIE, as of 2007-08, current prices
Physical infrastructure			
Installed power capacity (MW)	9,983.7	159,398.5	Central Electricity Authority, as of March 2010
GSM cellular subscribers (No)	58,818,203#	456,586,162	Cellular Operators Association of India, as of June 2010
Broadband subscribers (No)	238,791	4,981,976	As of October 2008
National highway length (km)	6,774	70,548	Ministry of Road Transport & Highways, Annual Report 2008-09
Airports (No)	6	133	Airport Authority of India
Social indicators			
Literacy rate (%)	56.3	64.8	Census of India, 2001
Birth rate (per 1,000 population)	29.1	22.8	Ministry of Health and Family Welfare, RHS Bulletin, March 2008

*Calculated in Indian rupee terms

#Includes Uttarakhand

Source: www.ibef.org

The following Table 2 also shows the relative status of U.P.

Table 2: Uttar Pradesh in Figures ... (2/2)

Parameter	Uttar Pradesh	All-states	Source
Ease of doing business			
FDI inflows (US$ billion)	0.1*	120.2	Department of Industry Policy & Promotion, April 2000 to May 2010
Outstanding investments (US$ billion)	85.2	1,972.6	CMIE, as of March 2010
Industrial infrastructure			
PPP projects (No)	12	515	www.pppindiadatabase.com
SEZ (No)	17	363	Notified as of July 2010, www.sezindia.nic.in

PPP: Public private partnership. SEZ: special economic zone

#Includes Uttarakhand.

Uttar Pradesh has certain latent advantages due to its natural landscape, and availability of rich resources pool. The thrust of the state has been concentrated in certain specific industries, which suits its natural resources.

Key Industries in Uttar Pradesh

The following figure shows the industries under policy thrust:

Key industries with policy thrust and factor advantages

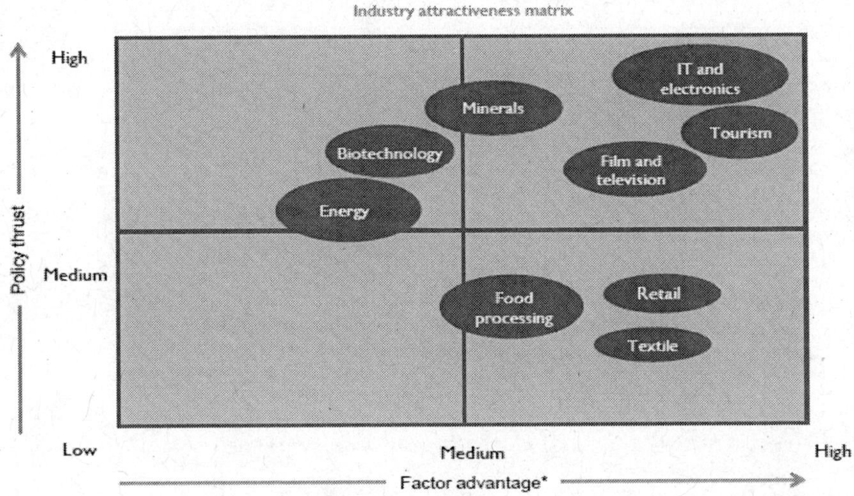

Resource advantages include the talent pool, natural resources and geographical location. The key industries of Uttar Pradesh, which give a comparative advantage to U.P. over other states, are IT, agriculture, agro-processing, textiles, leather goods, tourism and sports goods. The Uttar Pradesh State Industrial Development Corporation (UPSIDC) and the Department of Infrastructure and Industrial Development are jointly responsible for the development of the industrial infrastructure in the state. The state government has set up an "Udyog Bandhu" to facilitate investments in the industrial and service sectors. The organisation has a three-tier structure, with presence at the district, divisional and state levels. The state government is promoting development of several special economic zones (SEZ) across the state, such as IT and ITes, electronics hardware and software, handicrafts and agro-processing zones.

Agriculture is one of the largest industries in Uttar Pradesh. It is the largest producer of wheat and sugarcane in India. Mineral resources are also abundant in Uttar

Pradesh. There is huge scope for FDI investments in this sector. The following Table 3 shows the mineral resources and their location in the state.

Table 3: Mineral Reserves of Uttar Pradesh

Mineral	District	Reserves (thousand tonnes)	Industry usage
Bauxite	Chitrakoot	9,422	Alluminium, refractory
China clay	Sonbhadra	16,500	Ceramics, refractory
Coal	Sonbhadra	722,000	Thermal power, cement, ceramics
Diaspore	Jhansi, Mahoba, Lalitpur	50	Refractory
Pyrophyllite	Jhansi, Mahoba, Lalitpur	1,217	Refractory, ceramics, talc, insecticides
Feldspar	Jhansi	100	Ceramics
Silica sand	Allahabad, Chitrakoot	15,000	Glass and foundry
Granite	Jhansi, Mahoba, Lalitpur, Banda, Sonbhadra	48,492*	Polished slab and tiles
Dolominte	Sonbhadra	20,000	Iron and steel
Limestone	Sonbhadra	400,000	Cement and steel
Rock phosphate	Lalitpur	6,000	Fertiliser and elemental phosphorus
Sillimanite	Sonbhadra	3,200	Refractory

Source: Directorate of Geology and Mining, Uttar Pradesh

Assessed on of March 31, 2006

*Billion tonnes

Foreign Direct Investment (FDI) in Uttar Pradesh

The state has a robust industrial infrastructure, including 15 industrial areas, 12 specialised parks, three growth centres and four industrial infrastructure development centres (IIDC). The state has 17 notified special economic zones (SEZ), as of July 2010. These factors make Uttar Pradesh more viable for foreign direct investment. Up to March 2010, investments in the state amounted to US$ 85.2 billion. The power sector accounted for investments of over US$ 43.6 billion, which is more than 51 per cent of the total investments. The services and construction sectors attracted 26.3 per cent and 16.5 per cent of total investment respectively. As of March 2010, over US$ 23.8 billion was invested in infrastructure. Over 75 per cent of the total infrastructure-related investments are in power generation and distribution. Apart from power the railways, coal and lignite are other key infrastructure sectors for investment. U.P. has, however, failed to attract foreign investors to the desired extent, so far. According to Potential Index (World Investor Report), the state has favourable conditions for investments. But, small industries, which lie within the domain of domestic investors, are attracting more investment in the state. However, foreign direct investment in the state is very dismal. This is evident from the following. The FDI inflow in the state in 2010 stood at US$ 0.1 billion. FDI inflows between April 2000 and May 2010 were US$ 113 million. According to different economic parameters, U.P.'s FDI-PI Index at 0.37 is similar to that of Karnataka and West Bengal. But, U.P. has only 1.9 per cent FDI, whereas FDI in Karnataka and West Bengal accounts for 8.9 per cent and 2.9 per cent, respectively. This scenario is a cause for worry for the state.

FDI Attracting Sectors

FDI in the state is distributed in the following sectors.

Break up of Investments by Sector

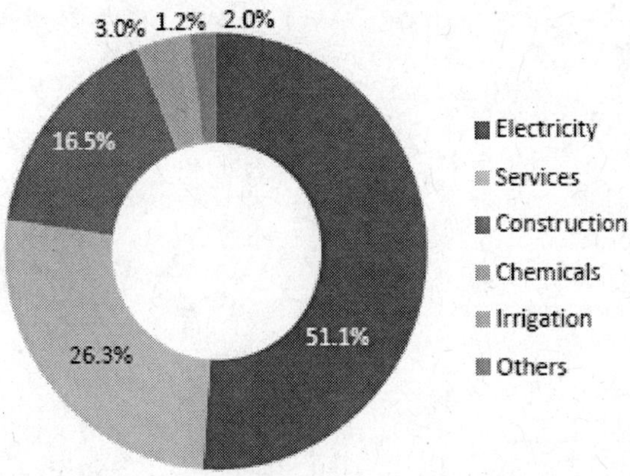

Source: CMIE

Others include food and beverages, textiles, non-metallic mineral products, metals and metal products and machinery.

Services other than financial.

Thus, power, services and construction account for the major proportion of the total investment. The following Table 4 from the Economic Survey shows the most attractive sectors for FDI in India.

The table gives us a brief picture that Uttar Pradesh simply does not have any advantage in the sectors which attract maximum FDI in other States. Other issues like the mismatch of infrastructural needs and capacities and installed power base are also important. Although U.P. has witnessed a lot of growth of infrastructure in the last 5 to 7 years, it still has a long way to go, if it wants to be at par with industrial giants like Gujarat, Maharashtra and Karnataka.

Table 4: Sectors Attracting Hightest FDI Flows

(Rs crore)

Sector	April-November			Growth (per cent) in 2009-10
	2007-08	2008-09	2009-10	
Services Sector	9,121	1,5919	16,566	4.06
Telecommunications	3,963	9,231	10,811	17.12
Housing & Real Estate	5,161	8,353	10,565	26.48
Construction	3,593	7,490	8,380	11.88
Agriculture Services	426	16	6,327	39,443.8
Power	208	3,420	5,994	75.26
Automobile Industry	1,191	3,401	4,499	32.28
Computer Software & Hardware	4,217	6,670	2,763	-58.58
Electrical Equipment	2,432	900	2,724	202.67
Hotel & Tourism	830	1,427	2,246	57.39
Information & Broadcasting (including Print Media)	747	1,711	2,015	17.77
Trading	2,108	2,427	1,982	-18.34
Metallurgical Industries	1,909	3,420	1,485	-56.58
Consultancy Services	606	825	1,341	62.55
Sea Transport	363	127	1,293	918.11
Petroleum & Natural Gas	234	947	1,084	14.47
Chemicals (other than Fertilizers)	731	1,991	1,000	-49.77
Grand Total of All FDI Flows				

Source: Department of Industrial Policy and Promotion.

Road Infrastructure

U.P. has a well connected road system that connects it to the nine neighbouring states and other parts of India through 42 national highways. The state's highways account for about 9.6 per cent of total the national highway (NH) network in India.

U.P. State Road Transport Corporation (UPSRTC) was established in 1972, to provide an economical, reliable and comfortable transport within the state, with connecting services to the adjoining states. The fleet has grown in size with 7,668 buses to generate US $ million per month revenue, and it provides services across the state in an extremely efficient manner. In September 2009, 29 projects of the National Highways Authority of India (NHAI) were in progress in the state.

Rail Network

Uttar Pradesh has the largest developed rail system in the country. The state is well-connected to other parts of the country by a railway network that spans over a distance of 8,890 km. Major sectors such as agriculture, cement, fertilisers, coal and manufacturing are serviced by the railways. Dry ports are also serviced by rail services. The intra-state rail network is well-developed, connecting the towns and district headquarters of U.P.

Power

The total installed capacity in the state increased from 8,181.7 MW in 2005–06 to 9,983.7 MW during 2009–2010. As of March 2010, the state's installed power capacity of 9,983.7 MW consisted of 4,621.2 MW of state share, 862.6 MW of private share and 4,499.9 MW of central share. Driven by the increased demand for power, the state is in the process of adding more capacity to its installed power capacity. Demand for power is driven by the agricultural and industrial sectors and rising households demand. Despite the rise in supply, the state suffers from an acute power shortage. All areas, especially villages, small cities and towns suffer from prolonged power cuts every day. This may be one of the reasons behind its failure to attract the requisite amounts of FDI.

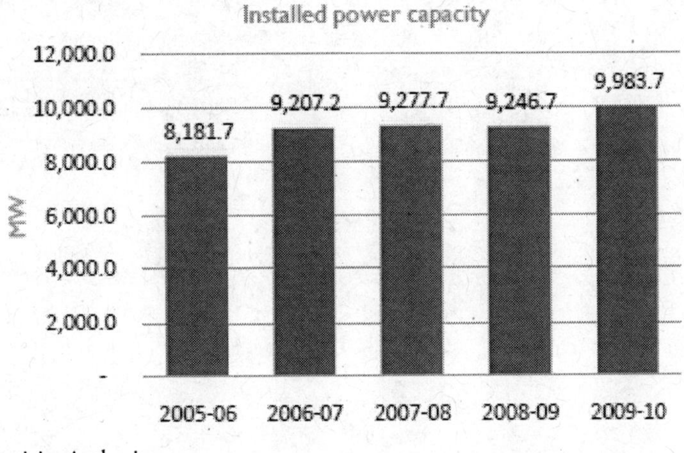

Source: Central Electricity Authority

FDI Promoting Measures

Some of the initiatives and steps taken by the Uttar Pradesh government to enhance FDI in the state are:

- Promotion of private participation in industrial development;
- Balanced development of tiny, small and heavy sectors;
- Promotion of exports;
- Promoting non-resident Indian (NRI) and FDI investments;

- Assured security of life and property. However, law and order continues to be a concern. This may be another factor that dissuades not only foreign but Indian investors also to seek investment opportunities elsewhere;
- Creation of a sensitive administrative body for industrial development;
- Recognition of the role of the service sector;
- Formulation of industry specific tailor-made packages;
- Review of tax structure. U.P. is among the most highly taxed states; and
- Revitalisation of existing investments to make them more productive.

There is huge scope for NRI investments in the state. Indians have achieved excellence by honing their entrepreneurial skills and abilities, which has led to remarkable achievements of Indians in every field of human activity in other countries. The state government has decided to improve the environmental conditions in order to attract more NRI investors for industrial development. Policies and systems are reviewed in order to create a conducive environment for foreign direct investment. Projects, entailing large scale investments such as power, roads, bridges etc., are in need of foreign investments. The state government has devised a plan to attract foreign investment in the state and aims at making U.P. one of the leading states of the Indian economy.

Comparative Analysis with Delhi, Karnataka and Gujarat

The states that are selected for comparison, are some of the highest FDI attracting states in India. A comparison will be helpful in identifying what gives these states an advantage over U.P. and areas in which U.P. falls short in attracting foreign direct investment.

Gujarat

Gujarat has an excellent infrastructure as compared to other states. There are 42 ports, 13 domestic airports and one international airport. The state also has an extensive road and rail network. Gujarat is one of the most industrially developed states. It contributes 34 per cent to petrochemicals and 27 per cent to the country's chemicals and pharmaceuticals business. It also contributes 21 per cent to India's exports and 13 per cent to its industrial production. It has good educational infrastructure with premier institutes in management, fashion, design, infrastructure planning and pharmaceuticals. There are industrial training institutes in each district for training manpower for the shop floor level jobs.

Gujarat is the only state in India, where the government has framed policies in almost all key sectors such as industry, power, ports, roads, IT, agriculture, minerals and tourism. Gujarat's Industrial Policy, 2009, offers attractive incentives and concessions. It has exploited its agro climatic conditions to emerge as the leading producer and exporter of BT cotton, and groundnut. Gujarat is the nursery of gems and jewellery, especially diamonds. These are also major exchange earners of the country.

Obviously, Gujarat is one of the premier FDI destinations in India, with a huge number of SEZs operating and providing incentives for industrial investment.

Key Industries in Gujarat

Key Industries with Policy Thrust and Factor Advantages

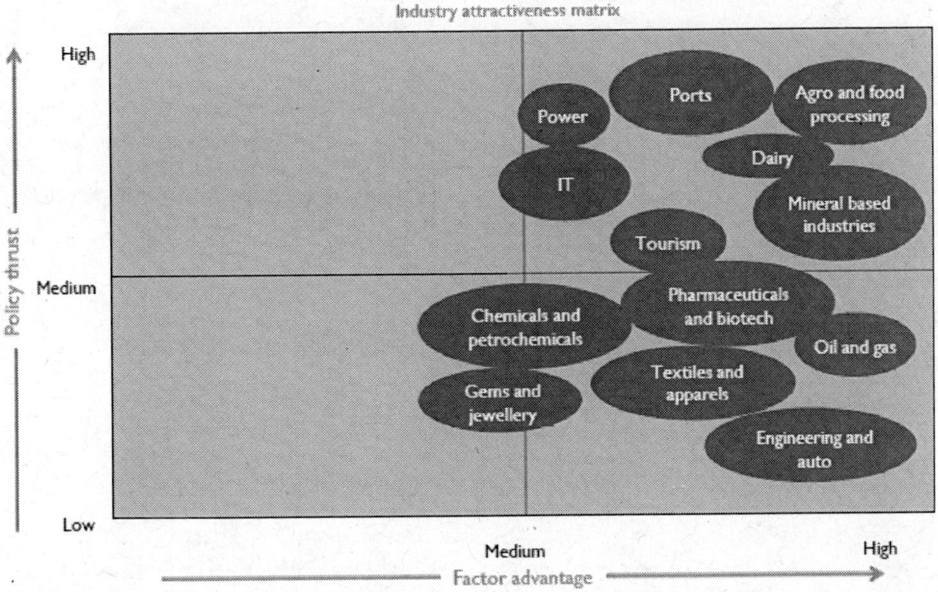

*Factor advantages include benefits due to geographical location and availability of factors such as talent pool, natural resources and capital.

This graph shows that there is a huge industrial advantage in terms of natural resources and policy thrust. Both of these offer an added incentive for investment in Gujarat.

Gujarat contributes 16 per cent of the industrial production of the country. There are 12 major industry groups that together account for 86 per cent of total factories,

96 per cent of total fixed capital investments, 94 per cent of output and 95 per cent of value-addition in the state's industrial products. Gujarat is a leader in several industrial sectors such as chemicals, petrochemicals, drugs and pharmaceuticals, dairy, cement and ceramics, gems and jewelry, textiles and engineering.

As of March 2009, the state had over 1,570 large units and more than 0.2 million micro, small and medium enterprises (MSMEs). Gujarat has the distinction of being the world's largest producer of processed diamonds and wall clocks. It also houses the world's largest gas-based, single-location sponge iron plant. It is the world's third largest producer of denim. It also has the world's third largest grass roots petroleum refinery (at Jamnagar).

Share of Industry Sectors in Gujarat

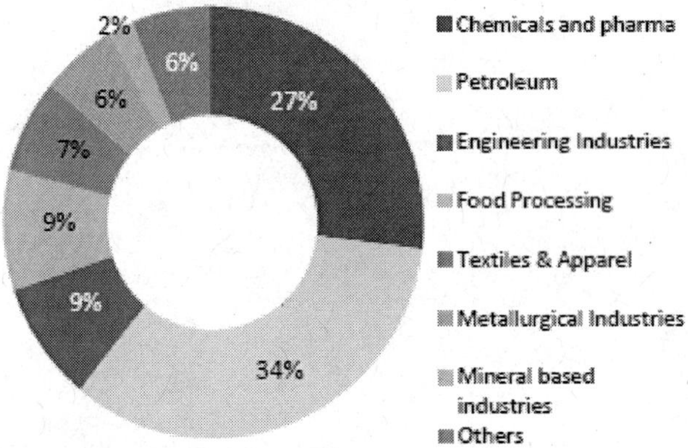

Source: "Socio-Economic Review Gujarat State 2009–2010". Directorate of Economics and Statistics.

As the chart indicates, the largest contributor to Gujarat's economy is petroleum, followed by chemicals and the pharmaceutical industry and engineering comes third. The state provides opportunities for investments and growth in other sectors also.

Agriculture also plays an important role in Gujarat's economy. Agricultural land covers more than 50 per cent of the state's total land area. The top-ten crops account for over 96 per cent of the total crop production of the state. In 2008–09, the total production of major crops of the state was over 40 million tonnes. Of these, sugarcane was the major crop. It was followed by cotton, wheat and potatoes.

FDI is hosted in Gujarat mainly by six sectors and their respective shares are shown in the following chart:

Breakup of Investments by Sector

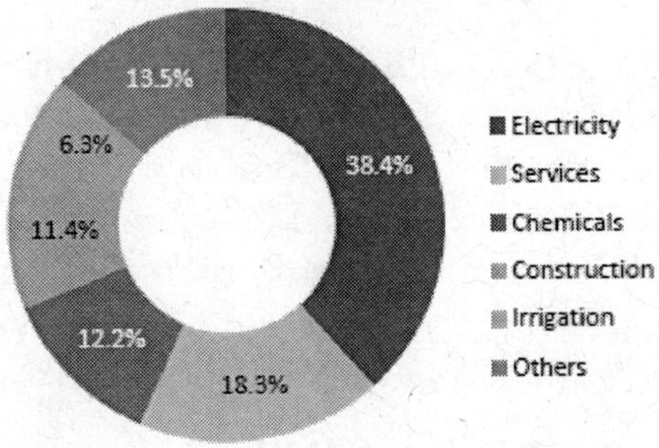

Source: CMIE.

Others include food and beverages, textiles, non-metallic mineral products, metals and metal products and machinery.

Investment in the state was US$ 257.3 billion in March 2010. The power sector accounted for over 38 per cent with investment worth US$ 98.7 billion, followed by services and chemicals. FDI between April 2000 and May 2010 was $6.6 billion.

SEZs

Gujarat had 47 formally approved SEZs in July 2010, 13 in-principle approvals and 30 notified SEZs. Gujarat with the geographical area of 27,125 hectares under SEZ, ranks first in India. Gujarat's three operational SEZs are: Kandla SEZ; SIR SEZ; Surat Apparel. It is the first state to formulate a SEZ policy, which includes flexible labour laws and exit options for investors. SEZs in Gujarat get a 10-year corporate tax holiday on export profits: 100 per cent for the initial five years and 50 per cent for the next five years.

Key Sector-wise break up of SEZs

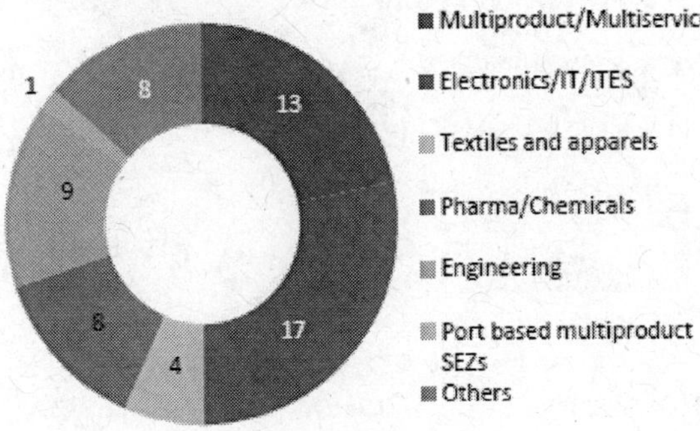

Source: Vibrant Gujarat 2009 summit.

Delhi

Delhi as the seat of the central government has an important position in the country's policies. It is also an important centre for trade and commerce with a number of key industry associations. The state hosts several trade conventions and fairs throughout the year. It is a key state with immense scope for development of the services industry such as banks and financial services institutions (BFSI), IT and ITes, consulting, etc. It is one of the most high profile agricultural centres of the country as well as a preferred tourist destination. Many of the global corporations have offices in the state.

Delhi has well developed physical and industrial infrastructure and virtual connectivity. It has an international airport and well developed rail and road infrastructure. There has been significant infrastructure and environmental development in Delhi in the last 20 years. Being the capital of the nation with myriad opportunities, Delhi attracts skilled and semi-skilled labourers from across the country. It has a large pool of skilled and semi-skilled labourers, especially in the 15 to 49 age group, who meet the manpower requirements of various industries. Having a stable single party rule for a number of years, Delhi is an attractive option for investment. The government has formulated forward looking policies to enhance and promote industrial development and investment.

Key Industries

Key industries with policy thrust and factor advantages

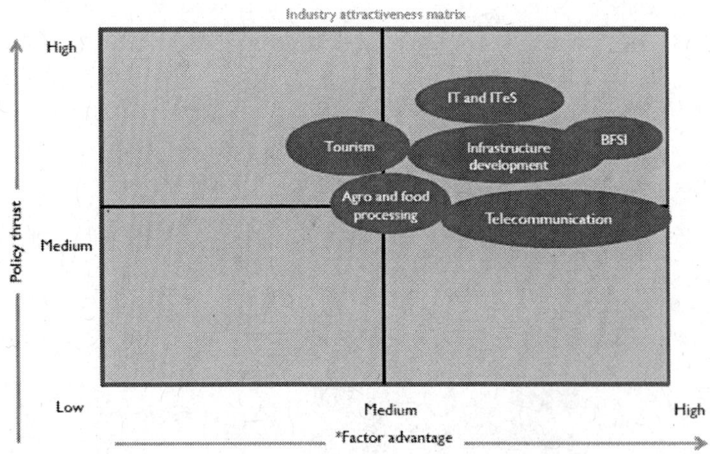

*Factor advantages include benefits due to geographical location and availability of factors like talent pool, natural resources and capital.

Source: www.ibef.rog

Delhi's economy is driven more by commerce and trade, manufacturing and agriculture. Delhi's economy is primarily dominated by the knowledge based service industry, such as information technology, consulting, etc.

In 2007–08, GSDP Delhi was US$ 28.3 billion, the tertiary sector contributed 79 per cent to the GSDP of Delhi at current prices, followed by the secondary sector, which contributed US$ 7.2 billion (20.3 per cent). The main emphasis in Delhi is given to financial institutions, ITes, food processing and tourism. The location advantage, policy incentives and infrastructure in the state support investment in sectors such as IT/ITes, banking and financial services industry (BFSI) and tourism. Sophisticated hi-tech industries are promoted with special emphasis on high value-added products. The plan emphasises industrial development without effluents, smoke and noise pollution. The government is also encouraging activities allied to industries, such as consultancy, information technology, training of skilled manpower through vocational training and entrepreneurial development programmes. Baprola for IT and ITes and gems and jewellery and IT Park, Shastri Park, DMRC are the SEZs in Delhi and in the Narela Industrial Complex, Bawana, Kirtinagar, Mongolpuri, Naraina and Okhla are the main industrial clusters.

Agriculture also has a special role in Delhi. Commonly grown foodstuffs are maize, wheat, rice, millet, fruits and vegetables. In 2008–09, 34,200 tonnes of potato and 23,500 tonnes of onion were produced. In 2007–08, the total production of rice and wheat in the state was around 98,000 tonnes. Delhi is also a growing export hub. In 2007–08, exports from Delhi's National Capital Region (NCR) increased by 10.2 per cent over the previous year. The annual growth rate was the highest in 2004–05. Some of the key products for exports include food products, electrical and engineering equipment, IT services, telecom equipment, oil and gas, steel products and other minerals and traded products.

Delhi as the capital of the nation is also a premier hub for FDI inflows. According to the Reserve Bank of India, FDI inflows into the state from April 2000 to May 2010 amounted to US$ 23.6 billion. Of the total outstanding investments of US$ 24.3 billion as of March 31, 2010, the services sector (excluding financial services) had the highest share in investment at 76.5 per cent. The chart shows the break-up of FDI sector wise.

Break up of Investments by Sectors

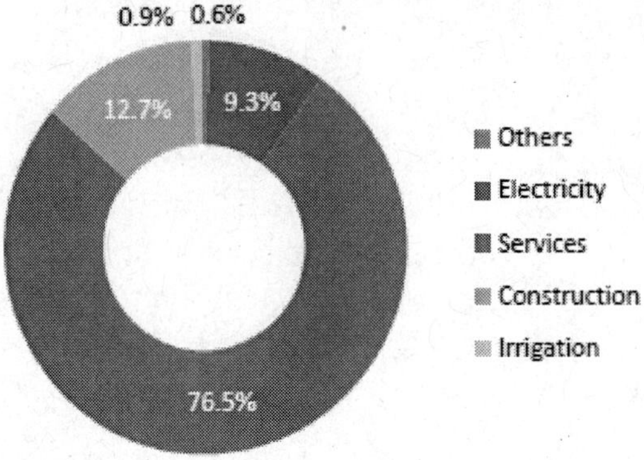

Services exclude financial services.
Electricity includes generation and distribution.
Others include food and beverages, non-metallic mineral products, machinery and chemicals.

Karnataka

Karnataka has emerged as a state with knowledge based industries such as IT, biotechnology and engineering. The state deals in IT and ITes export, which brought in about US$ 16.3 billion in 2008–09. It is commonly referred to the science capital of India with more than 100 research and development (R&D) centres and the preferred destination for multinational corporations. The state has a wide variety of policies drafted specifically for encouraging business opportunities and investments. The government works in cohesion with business to increase the productivity of the state. Additionally, the state has well drafted sector-specific policies for biotechnology, IT, business process outsourcing (BPO) and textiles.

Karnataka has successfully attracted skilled labour in the knowledge sector. Karnataka had been targeting nine per cent annual economic growth during the Eleventh Five Year Plan period (2007–12). Much of this growth is expected to come from the secondary sector; its growth rate is anticipated to increase from current rate of 6–7 per cent to 10 per cent. The tertiary sector also provides a huge percentage of revenue for the government. The state has an extremely well-developed physical and industrial infrastructure and virtual connectivity. It has good road, rail and air infrastructure, and a good supply and distribution of power, five airports and substantial port infrastructure.

Key Industries

The following chart shows the various industries that have received special attention during policy.

Key Industries with policy thrust and factor advantages

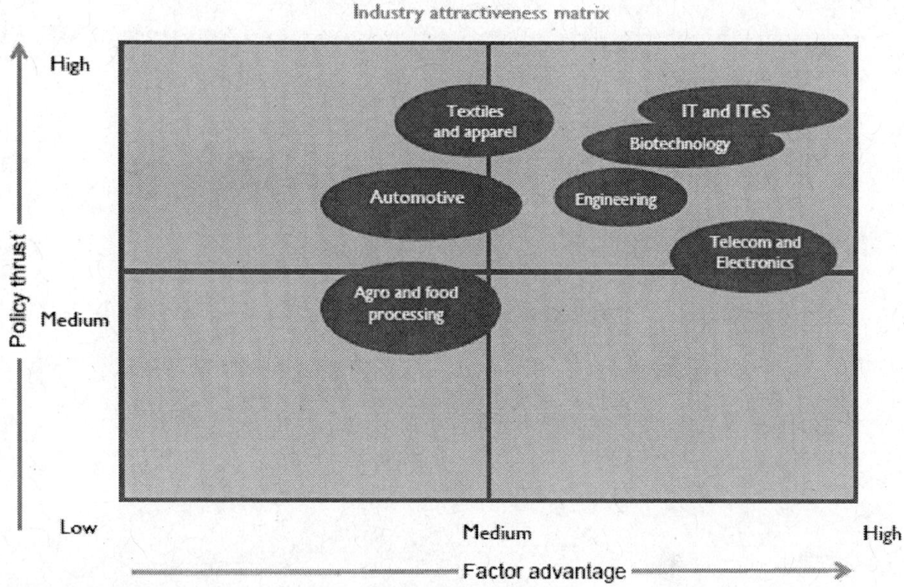

*Factor advanges include benefits due to geographical location and agailability of factgors like talent pool, natural resources and capital.

Source: www.ibef.org

The tertiary sector was the largest contributor of revenues. The tertiary sector's share in GSDP was 54.4 per cent in 2008–09, as compared to 45.3 per cent in 1999–2000. Community services and personal services, the largest sub-group of the sector, registered a growth of 17.8 per cent over the previous year. The secondary sector also registered the highest CAGR between 1999–2000 and 2008–09. The share of the secondary sector in GSDP was 29.1 per cent in 2008–09; its growth was driven by manufacturing, which recorded a growth of 14.0 per cent between 1999–2000 and 2008–09.

The key industries in Karnataka are ITes, biotechnology, mining, automotive, engineering, food and agro processing, textiles, electronics and telecom. During 2008–09, software exports from Karnataka were US$ 14.8 billion, registering a growth of 18 per cent over the previous year. During 2009–2010, software exports from the state increased to US$ 16.0 billion. BPO exports from the state during the same period were US$ 3.2 billion, registering a growth of over 95 per cent over the previous year.

Karnataka exported US$ 184 million worth of silk during 2008–09. Karnataka also receives huge amounts of FDI primarily in the minerals sector and biotechnology. R&D is also a significant attraction for foreign investments. In March 2010, investment in the state was US$ 149.9 billion. Of the total investment, the metal and metal products sector accounted for the maximum investment of 33.3 per cent, followed by electricity with 20.7 per cent. FDI inflows between April 2000 and May 2010 were US$ 7.2 billion.

The chart shows the break-up of the FDI sector wise.

Break up of Investments by Sector

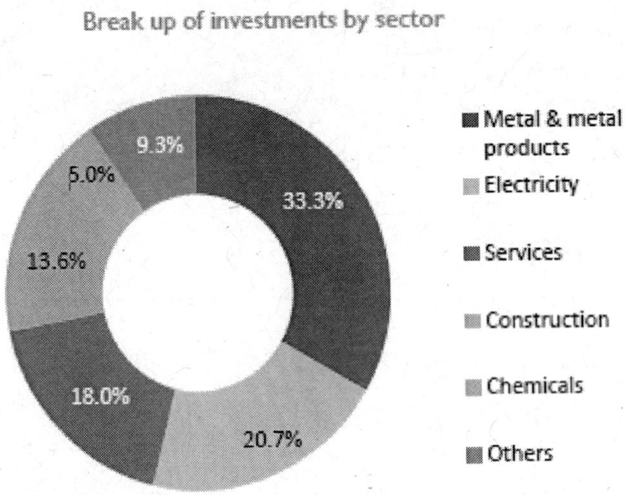

Soruce: CMIE.

Others include food and beverages, textiles, non-metallic mineral products, machinery, mining and irrigation.

Agriculture is another key industry in Karnataka. Sugarcane, foodgrains and horticulture are the main agricultural produce. In 2008–09, total production of major crops of the state was over 37.2 million tones Sugarcane. Sugarcane is followed by rice, onion and maize. In 2008–09, Karnataka was among the three largest producers of maize, sunflower seeds and onions in the country.

SEZs

There were 32 notified SEZs in Karnataka in July 2010. The Karnataka Industrial Areas Development Board developed 126 industrial areas across the 29 districts of Karnataka. The Karnataka State Industrial Investment Development Corporation has promoted over 135 start-up ventures in the state through equity participation, and has provided debt to core industries such as steel, cement, mining and textiles, as well as new sectors such as IT, aerospace and telecom.

Table 5: SEZs and Industrial Estates

Industry	Location	SEZs (No)
Pharmaceutical and biotech	Hassan, Bengaluru,	3
IT/ITeS	Mangalore, Bengaluru, (urban and rural) , Mysore, Dakshina Kannada, Shimoga	23
Engineering	Udupi, Shimoga	2
Food processing	Hassan	1
Electronics	Bengaluru	1
Textiles and apparel	Hassan	1
Petrochemicals	Mangalore	1

Source: www.sezindia.nic.in

A Comparison of U.P. with these States

The earlier discussion, though descriptive, furnishes the backdrop for a comparison of U.P. with these states.

The figures indicate that U.P. has the highest share in GSDP of all states in comparison to Gujarat, Delhi and Karnataka, though the growth rate of its average GSDP lags behind all other states. GSDP provides an easy-to-follow indicator of economic health of the state. The per capita GSDP is nearly half of the figure for all states, taken together. This is partly accounted for by the relatively large population size and its more rapid growth. This should be a serious concern for the state government, and adequate policy measures are needed to be taken.

With regard to physical infrastructure, though the installed power capacity is reasonably high, U.P. lags behind other states in GSM cellular subscribers and broadband subscribers. This again indicates that the state government needs to work and bring out policies for the development of the sector.

The social indicators show that, while the literacy rate in U.P. is below the national literacy rate, the birth rate per 1,000 persons is above the national average. These figures show that adequate measures need to be adopted. Policy measures by the U.P. Government are required to be undertaken to increase literacy rate and enhance the reach and effectiveness of family welfare programmes. High birth and population growth rates may partly be because of the by composition and age structures of the population. These measures would contribute to economic development, rise in standards of living, higher socio-economic status and better overall health of the

Table 6: Comparison of Key Parameters of U.P. with Gujarat, Delhi and Karnataka

Parameter	*U.P.*	*Gujarat*	*Delhi*	*Karnataka*	*All States*	*Source*
Economy						
GSDP as a %age of all states	8.7	7.8	3.6	6.0	100	CMIE, as of 2007–08 current prices
Average GSDP growth rate (%)	9.6	15.6	13.3	11.9	11.8	CMIE, 2000–01 to 2007–08, current prices
Per capita GSDP (US$)	453.7	1355.7	2136.0	1034.9	992.5	CMIE, as of 2007–08, current prices
Physical Infrastructure						
Installed power capacity (MW)	9983.7	13908.1	4114.7	10386.3	159398.5	Central Electricity authority, as of March 20101
GSM cellular subscribers (No.)	58,818,203*	26160079	18662646	27178061	456,586,162	Cellular Operators Association of India, as of June 2010
Broadband subscribers (No.)	238791	322656	588716	569,057	4,981,976	As of October 2008
National Highway length (km)	6774	3245	72	4396	70,548	Ministry of Road Transport & Highways, Annual Report 2008–09
Airports (No.)	6	14	2	5	133	Airport Authority of India
Social Indicators						
Literacy Rate (%)	56.3	69.1	81.7	66.7	64.8	Census of India, 2001
Birth rate (per 1000 population)	29.1	22.6	18.4	19.8	22.8	Ministry of Health and Family Welfare, RHS Bulletin, March 2008
Ease of doing Business						
FDI Inflows (US$ billion)	0.1*	6.6	23.6	7.2	120.2	Department of Industry Policy & Promotion, April 2000–May 2010
Outstanding investment (US$ billion)	85.2	257.3	24.3	149.9	1972.6	CMIE, as of March 2010
Industrial Infrastructure						
PPP projects (No.)	12	33	10	104	515	www.pppindiadatabase.com
SEZ (No.)	17	30	3	32	363	Notified as of July 2010, www.sezindia.nic.in

*includes Uttarakhand.

people. The states, which are more developed, have high literacy rates as compared to less developed states. It highlights the importance of literacy. Lower literacy rates mean that a greater proportion of the state's population is not capitalising on its skills, which could be utilised, if the population would have been literate. This could be a factor contributing to the low per capita GSDP.

The figures for FDI inflows and PPP in U.P. are negligible in comparison to Gujarat, Delhi and Karnataka. The state requires an urgent policy for attracting industrial investments. FDI would play a pivotal role in the development of the state. This can be instrumental in raising the levels of investments, employment generation, and improvement in export competitiveness and generation of revenue for the the government.

References

Aswathappa, K. (2009). *Essentials of Business Environment*, Himalaya Publishing House Pvt. Ltd., Chapter 4: Foreign Direct Investment, pp. 63–80.

Central Statistical Organisation (CSO) (various issues). India. Statistical Pocket Book, New Delhi.

Chakravarthy, M. Latha (2005). Foreign Direct Investment in India, ICFAI University Press CIA—The World Fact Book–India, Incomplete.

Datt, Ruddar and Sundharam, K.P.M. (2009). *Indian Economy*. New Delhi: S. Chand Group ISBN 978-81-219-0298-4.

E&Y 2010 Report-Doing Business in India 2010.

Fernando, A.C., *Business Environment*, Pearson Publishing, Chapter 38: Globalisation, MNCs and Foreign Capital in India, Page 479–496, ISBN 978-81-317-3158-1

FICCI Economic Outlook Survey, January 2011, New Delhi.

FICCI Foreign Direct Investment Survey 2010, Dec. 2010, New Delhi.

Government of India, Consolidated FDI Policy (2010), Department of Industrial Policy and Promotion, April.

Government of India, Fact Sheet on Foreign Direct Investment (2011), Department of Industrial Policy and Promotion, April.

http://commerce.nic.in

http://dipp.nic.in/English/default.aspx

http://finmin.nic.in

http://www.ficci.com

http://www.ibef.org

http://www.indiainbusiness.nic.in/investment/investment.htm

http://www.indiainbusiness.nic.in/know-india/states.htm

India Brand Equity Forum Report on Delhi November 2010.

India Brand Equity Forum Report on Gujarat November 2010.

India Brand Equity Forum Report on Karnataka November 2010.

India Brand Equity Forum Report on Uttar Pradesh November 2010.

India: Foreign Direct Investment, Policy and Procedures, Pricewaterhouse Coopers Pvt. Ltd., India, Ibef.

Lee, Byung-Hwa (2002). FDI from Developing Countries; A Vector for Trade and Development. Incomplete.

Ministry of Finance, Government of India, "Economic Survey 2009–10".

Mittal, V., *Business Environment Text and Cases*, Excel Books, Chapter 39: FDI in India, pp. 597–618, ISBN: 978-81-7446-975-5.

Neuhaus, Marco (2006). The Impact of FDI on Economic Growth, An Analysis for the Transition Countries of Central and Eastern Europe, Physica Verlag Heidelberg.

Reports on Investment Approval and FDI in India (2003). Academic foundation.

Reserve Bank of India (2006). Handbook of Statistics on the Indian Economy (http://www.rbi.org.in/scripts/AnnualPublications. Handbook of Statistics on Indian Economy).

The Global Competitiveness Report 2010–2011, World Economic Forum.

Theodore H. Moran, Edward M. Graham and Magnus Blomström (2005). Does Foreign Direct Investment Promote Development?

World Bank—India Country Overview.

CHAPTER 14

Fiscal Scenario of State's with Special Reference to Uttar Pradesh: Recent Trends

P.K. Bhargava

The study proceeds step wise and sequentially, to trace the item wise emerging trends in state's finances.

Revenue Surplus and Fiscal Deficit

After a gap of almost twenty years, the state governments for the first time in 2006–07 witnessed a surplus on revenue account. This was possible due to the state's improved fiscal discipline, which resulted from the adoption of rule-based fiscal policy, along with an increase in the buoyancy of state's own revenues and increased central transfers. Table 1 shows that, out of the 15 major state's, only Kerala, Punjab and West Bengal had a revenue deficit in 2007–08. However, this improvement in state finances could not be sustained, as the economy witnessed an overall macro-economic slowdown, and the state's also had to implement the recommendations of Sixth/State(s) Pay Commissions during 2008–09 and 2009–10. Consequently, in 2008–09, the number of state's with revenue surplus came down to only nine, as against twelve in 2007–08 (Table 1). In subsequent years, 2009–10 (revised) and 2010–11 (budget), only Andhra Pradesh, Bihar, Karnataka, Madhya Pradesh and Uttar Pradesh had a surplus on revenue account, which is clear from Table 1. It may also be noted that the quantum of revenue surplus in case of Uttar Pradesh decreased from ₹ 3,449 crore in 2007–08, to ₹ 1,862 crore in 2008–09 and further declined to ₹ 554 crore in 2010–11 (budget).

As against revenue surplus, the fiscal deficit of the state increased from ₹ 13,794 crore to ₹ 20,513 crore and further to ₹ 22,742 crore during these years. The gross fiscal deficit of the state, which averaged 3.5 per cent of the Gross State Domestic Product (GSDP) during 2005–08, increased to 5 per cent in 2008–09, and was estimated at 4.4 per cent

Table 1: Revenue Deficit/Surplus and Gross Fiscal Deficit/Surplus of the State Governments

(₹ crore)

	State	2007–08		2008–09		2009–10 (Revised)		2010–11 (Budget)	
		Revenue Surplus (–)/ Deficit (+)	*Fiscal Surplus (–)/ Deficit (+)*	*Revenue Surplus (–)/ Deficit (+)*	*Fiscal Surplus (–)/ Deficit (+)*	*Revenue Surplus (–)/ Deficit (+)*	*Fiscal Surplus (–)/ Deficit (+)*	*Revenue Surplus (–)/ Deficit (+)*	*Fiscal Surplus (–)/ Deficit (+)*
	1	2	3	4	5	6	7	8	9
1.	Andhra Pradesh	–159	8,787	–1,004	12,406	–2,942	14,282	–3,548	12,983
2.	Assam	–2,581	–790	–3,834	–1,407	5,331	10,088	5,960	9,315
3.	Bihar	–4,645	1,705	–4,469	2,507	–173	9,770	–6,557	4,594
4.	Gujarat	–2,150	4,771	66	10,438	4,357	12,629	4,502	15,143
5.	Haryana	–2,224	1,264	2,082	6,558	3,662	8,360	3,942	8,816
6.	Karnataka	–3,376	5,331	–1,631	8,732	–538	11,266	–500	9,708
7.	Kerala	3,785	6,100	3,712	6,346	4,082	6,698	3,630	8,543
8.	Madhya Pradesh	–5,088	2,784	–4,063	4,434	–5,308	6,593	–1,581	8,003
9.	Maharashtra	–14,803	–2,821	–5,577	13,999	12,730	30,904	7,655	24,294
10.	Orissa	–4,244	–1,323	–3,420	334	1,564	5,579	1,037	5,798
11.	Punjab	3,823	4,604	3,856	6,690	4,152	6,554	4,788	7,706
12.	Rajasthan	–1,653	3,408	827	6,973	3,993	9,900	1,098	8,461
13.	Tamil Nadu	–4,545	3,686	–1,452	8,548	5,020	12,860	3,396	16,222
14.	Uttar Pradesh	–3,449	13,794	–1,862	20,513	–1,988	23,870	–554	22,742
15.	West Bengal	8,147	[illegible],400	14,709	13,558	23,054	27,466	16,441	22,323

Source: 1. State Finances—A Study of Budgets of 2009–10, Reserve Bank of India, February 2010, pp. 149–51.
2. State Finances—A Study of Budgets of 2010–11, Reserve Bank of India, March 2011, pp. 125–27.

in 2010–11 (budget). With the decline in revenue surplus on the one hand, and increase in gross fiscal deficit on the other, a shift in the quality of the deficit is clearly visible. Thus, this runs counter to the objective of the NEP, and the earlier phase of economic reforms to keep fiscal deficit in check. It also runs counter to Dr. Manmohan Singh's idea that the current inflation in the country is accounted largely by the increased purchasing power in the hands of the poor on account of rising public expenditure on employment generation schemes. Does he mean that the government has been funding welfare schemes out of fiscal deficit? Fiscal deficit, or public expenditure on welfare schemes, especially employment generation for the poor led to an increase in the demand for of basic goods.

Rising Liabilities

The increasing gross fiscal deficit of the state has led to increased borrowings by it. In the process, the outstanding liabilities of the government of Uttar Pradesh have continued to increase.

Liabilities of Uttar Pradesh

Table 2 shows the total outstanding liabilities of 15 major state's, including that of Uttar Pradesh.

The table shows that the total outstanding liabilities of the Government of Uttar Pradesh as a per cent of Gross State Domestic Product (GSDP) increased from 32.8 per cent at the end of March 1991 to 45.8 per cent at the end of March 2001, and further to 55.6 per cent at the end of March, 2006. It may also be pointed out that in 1991, only four state's (Assam, Bihar, Orissa and Punjab), in 1996 only three state's (Bihar, Orissa and Punjab) and in 2001 only two state's (Bihar and Orissa) witnessed higher outstanding liabilities as a per cent of their GSDP than that of Uttar Pradesh. Further, from the year ending March 2007, the government of Uttar Pradesh continues to be at the top, in terms of total outstanding liabilities as a per cent of GSDP (Table 2). The increasing outstanding liabilities of the state government signify the fact that the government has resorted to increased borrowings to bridge the fiscal gap. It also necessitates an examination of the kind of assets that have been created, or financed out of increased borrowings. Further, whether the assets so created are contributing to the productive capacity of the economy, and strengthening the process of capital formation. The government of Uttar Pradesh must undertake to take stock of the situation, and see that the outstanding liabilities do not become a drag on the economy in the future and adversely affect the development process of the state. This is a significant challenge

Table 2: Total Outstanding Liabilities of State Governments—As Percentage of GSDP
(As on end-March)

(Per cent)

	State	*1991*	*1996*	*2001*	*2006*	*2007*	*2008*	*2009*	*2010 (Revised)*	*2011 (Budget)*
	1	*2*	*3*	*4*	*5*	*6*	*7*	*8*	*9*	*10*
1.	Andhra Pradesh	23.0	22.3	28.8	35.3	33.6	32.0	29.2	30.1	31.3
2.	Assam	39.7	32.6	27.8	31.8	30.6	28.7	28.8	28.0	27.8
3.	Bihar	38.1	42.3	52.3	59.4	50.0	46.0	39.1	39.7	39.5
4.	Gujarat	26.5	20.7	38.5	37.8	35.7	32.7	32.6	32.1	31.4
5.	Haryana	20.9	20.7	25.2	25.3	22.5	19.5	18.3	19.0	18.9
6.	Karnataka	23.6	19.7	23.3	26.6	28.9	25.9	24.1	24.3	25.1
7.	Kerala	30.2	27.7	36.1	38.5	36.7	36.0	35.3	34.3	33.4
8.	Madhya Pradesh	24.7	21.4	27.9	42.5	40.4	38.5	35.2	34.4	37.2
9.	Maharashtra	19.4	16.7	26.8	33.3	31.6	27.4	26.9	25.1	26.7
10.	Orissa	45.2	38.0	55.7	51.6	46.0	40.4	32.9	30.6	30.0
11.	Punjab	38.4	36.4	41.2	47.1	42.1	40.3	37.1	35.2	34.1
12.	Rajasthan	27.5	29.9	43.1	51.5	47.8	45.4	41.8	41.1	40.9
13.	Tamil Nadu	20.3	19.4	23.5	27.2	24.8	24.2	25.4	25.5	25.1
14.	Uttar Pradesh	32.8	34.3	45.8	55.6	54.2	52.2	46.8	43.5	45.8
15.	West Bengal	23.6	24.0	38.2	49.8	46.6	44.9	42.5	42.8	40.8
	All-states (Per cent of GDP)	22.5	20.9	28.3	31.0	29.0	26.8	26.3	25.0	23.1

Source: 1. State Finances—A Study of Budgets of 2009–10, Reserve Bank of India, February 2010, p. 181.
2. State Finances—A Study of Budgets of 2010–11, Reserve Bank of India, March 2011, p. 153.

to the public finances of the state of Uttar Pradesh, and it highlights the need for adopting a sound borrowing policy.

Revenues of Uttar Pradesh

An examination of the patterns of revenue receipts of Uttar Pradesh indicates that the state relatively raises an inadequate quantum of resources from its own sources—tax and non-tax. Table 3 shows that in 2007–08, the share of central taxes (42.7 per cent) and grants (12.5 per cent) constituted 55.2 per cent of the revenue receipts of the state. This percentage declined slightly in 2008–09, but was still as high as 54.5. In subsequent years 2009–10 (revised) and 2010–11 (budget), the corresponding percentage stood at 48.6 and 48.7, respectively. As against this, the percentage contributions of central transfers (share of central taxes and grants) for all-states taken together has been below 43 per cent throughout the period. However, an important aspect, that needs to be noted in the context of Uttar Pradesh, is that the state's own share in central transfers as also against all-states, taken together, the share of central taxes predominates, but does not compromise the fiscal independence of the state. This share accrues to the state as a matter of right.

If a comparison is made with all-states, taken together, as shown in Table 3, it is noticeable that the government of Uttar Pradesh raised relatively less from its own sources—both taxes (36.3 per cent) and non-tax (8.5 per cent) in 2007–08, as against the corresponding percentage of 45.9 and 12.4, respectively for all-states. Even when the situation improved in the years 2009–10 (revised) and 2010–11 (budget), the state was raising around 51 per cent from its own sources (tax and non-tax), as against the corresponding percentage of 57–58 for all-states taken together in these years.

Further, the state sales tax-VAT continues to contribute 50 per cent or more to state taxes for all-states as also for of Uttar Pradesh. Along with these state excise duties and stamps and registration fee accounted for over 88 per cent of revenues from state taxes in Uttar Pradesh during 2009–10 (revised) and 2010–11 (budget). This is much higher than the corresponding percentage of about 76 for all-states during these years. The heavy dependence of Uttar Pradesh on three taxes (sales tax-VAT, excise duties and stamps and registration fee) in its tax system, suggests that the state needs to explore and use other sources of raising the state's taxes which have the potential of generating additional revenue. Besides, in the area of non-tax revenue, such as user charges relating to irrigation, electricity schemes and similar other activities may be revised upwards or suitably modified so that, at least, the losses on these schemes are eliminated, or minimised. The burden of subsidy on the state exchequer needs to be done away with gradually. This is a difficult task, but there is hardly any choice in the matter, if the finances of the state are to be improved.

Table 3: Pattern of Revenue Receipts of Government of Uttar Pradesh and All-States

(₹ crore)

		2007–08		*2008–09*		*2009–10 (Revised)*		*2010–11 (Budget)*	
		U.P.	*All-States*	*U.P.*	*All-States*	*U.P.*	*All-States*	*U.P.*	*All-States*
		1	*2*	*3*	*4*	*5*	*6*	*7*	*8*
1.	Own Tax Revenue of which	24,959 (36.3)	2,86,546 (45.9)	28,659 (36.8)	3,21,930 (46.3)	35,255 (35.9)	3,65,527 (45.3)	42,306 (37.9)	4,26,681 (46.7)
	(a) State sales tax/VAT	12,464	1,53,007	14,126	1,78,715	20,287	1,91,350	24,893	2,24,821
	(b) State excise duties	3,948	34,127	4,720	40,990	5,695	47,729	6,763	55,478
	(c) Stamps and Registration	3,977	37,162	4,138	36,066	5,176	39,230	5,737	46,039
2.	Own Non-Tax Revenue	5,816 (8.5)	77,178 (12.4)	6,767 (8.7)	81,751 (11.8)	15,205 (15.5)	97,178 (12.0)	14,986 (13.4)	1,02,609 (11.2)
3.	Share in Central Taxes	29,288 (42.7)	1,51,402 (24.3)	30,906 (39.7)	1,61,052 (23.2)	31,712 (32.3)	1,65,477 (20.5)	35,517 (31.8)	2,00,466 (22.0)
4.	Grants from the Centre	8,609 (12.5)	1,08,622 (17.4)	11,499 (14.8)	1,29,924 (18.7)	15,952 (16.3)	1,79,206 (22.2)	18,812 (16.9)	1,83,282 (20.1)
5.	Total	68,672 (100.0)	6,23,748 (100.0)	77,831 (100.0)	6,94,657 (100.0)	98,124 (100.0)	8,07,388 (100.0)	1,11,621 (100.0)	9,13,038 (100.0)

Note: Figures in brackets show percentage to total.

Source: 1. State Finances—A Study of Budgets of 2009–10, Reserve Bank of India, February 2010, pp. 259–61.
2. State Finances—A Study of Budget of 2010–11, Reserve Bank of India, March 2011, pp. 225–28.

Table 4: Devolution and Transfer of Resources from the Centre

(₹ crore)

	State	2007–08		2008–09		2009–10 (Revised)		2010–11 (Budget)	
	1	2	3	4	5	6	7	8	9
1.	Andhra Pradesh	19,193	17,215	20,214	18,277	24,486	22,543	30,028	28,079
2.	Assam	9,770	9,630	11,700	11,424	17,339	16,821	18,712	18,202
3.	Bihar	23,066	21,997	25,804	24,730	30,161	29,153	36,789	35,678
4.	Gujarat	9,404	7,977	10,246	8,838	12,234	10,850	13,212	11,794
5.	Haryana	3,104	2,824	3,625	3,347	5,974	5,698	5,140	4,851
6.	Karnataka	12,613	11,418	13,082	11,863	15,299	14,089	15,733	14,380
7.	Kerala	6,645	5,960	7,731	7,003	8,476	7,788	9,468	8,318
8.	Madhya Pradesh	16,471	15,340	17,774	16,636	21,200	19,976	22,094	21,233
9.	Maharashtra	15,436	14,206	19,836	18,731	27,023	25,937	24,094	22,936
10.	Orissa	12,547	11,459	13,947	12,885	17,040	15,807	18,777	17,544
11.	Punjab	4,514	4,109	4,056	3,835	5,709	5,436	6,031	5,760
12.	Rajasthan	13,880	12,885	14,963	13,949	15,705	14,682	18,952	17,871
13.	Tamil Nadu	15,376	14,561	16,689	15,848	15,561	14,694	19,155	17,981
14.	Uttar Pradesh	38,266	35,360	42,826	39,968	48,945	46,144	55,610	52,773
15.	West Bengal	16,222	13,581	17,919	15,978	19,773	17,410	24,736	23,248
	All-states	2,67,276	2,47,299	2,97,981	2,79,124	3,57,466	3,38,185	3,99,193	3,79,833

Note: Gross Devolution and Transfers minus Repayments of Loans to Centre and Interest payments on Loans from Centre.

Source: 1. State Finances—A Study of Budgets of 2009–10, Reserve Bank of India, February 2010, p. 172.
2. State Finances—A Study of Budgets of 2010–11, Reserve Bank of India, March 2011, p. 148.

The contribution of Uttar Pradesh to the nation's resources needs to be augmented, as it is one of the most important state's of the country. The contribution of the economy of Uttar Pradesh in terms of its own taxes and non-tax sources in the all-state's kitty has been significantly inadequate. In 2007–08, the state's contribution in all-state's resources (tax and non-tax) was only 8.4 per cent, which increased to 8.8 per cent in 2008–09 and stood at 10.8 per cent in 2010–11 (budget). Keeping in view the size of the population of the state and accordingly its requirements, the fiscal situation of the state through rationalising the tax and non-tax system, suggests the urgency of raising additional resources.

As referred to earlier, the state of Uttar Pradesh is significantly dependent on the centre for its fiscal requirements. In fact, the state is a recipient of the largest quantum of resources, both in terms of gross and net devolution from the centre. This is clear from Table 4. The Table shows that the quantum of gross transfers, which stood at ₹ 38,266 crore in 2007–08, has continued to increase and stood at ₹ 56,610 crore in 2010–11 (budget). This amounts to slightly less than 50 per cent of the base year. Similarly, the net transfers increased from ₹ 35,360 crore to ₹ 52,773 crore during these years. While Uttar Pradesh ranks at the top amongst all-states in receiving gross/net transfers from the centre, the share of the state in all-states' transfers has been relatively inadequate. As per the Census 2011, the state of Uttar Pradesh has 16.49 per cent of the country's population, but central transfers (gross/net) in 2007–08 and 2008–09 were below 15 per cent of the total transfers. Similarly, in 2009–10 (revised) and 2010–11 (budget), central transfers constituted less than 14 per cent of gross/net transfers made to all-states. It only means that the state of Uttar Pradesh deserves a further increase in the quantum of resources from the centre. This claim is further reinforced by the fact that the proportion of the state's poor in the total poor of the country and the sprawling size (in area). The high proportion of SC/STs and Muslims who together account for a large share of the state's poor and low human development index, further strengthens this claim.

Public Expenditure

Public expenditure (development and non-development) is an important tool through which the state discharges its various functions for the development and welfare of its citizens. Total expenditure (revenue and capital account) of the 15 major state's has continued to increase as is clear from Table 5. Further, development expenditure constitutes a major part of the total expenditure, as the same is important and useful in a variety of ways. Table 5 shows that the share of development expenditure in all the state's was above 50 per cent in all the years, excepting for two years (2007–08 and

Table 5: Expenditure* Pattern of State Governments

(₹ crore)

	State	Development Expenditure				Total Expenditure				2 as %	3 as %	4 as %	5 as %
		2007–08	2008–09	2009–10 (Revised)	2010–11 (Budget)	2007–08	2008–09	2009–10 (Revised)	2010–11 (Budget)	of 6	of 7	of 8	of 9
	1	2	3	4	5	6	7	8	9	10	11	12	13
1.	Andhra Pradesh	51,153	56,466	70,180	75,155	69,430	75,322	92,635	1,03,588	73.7	75.0	75.8	72.6
2.	Assam	9,596	10,699	19,315	22,299	14,566	16,099	31,909	32,327	65.9	66.4	60.5	69.0
3.	Bihar	20,456	24,754	33,318	35,990	29,936	35,495	47,664	51,839	68.3	69.7	69.9	69.4
4.	Gujarat	26,887	35,645	39,550	44,624	40,622	49,148	56,601	64,730	66.2	72.5	69.9	68.9
5.	Haryana	15,420	18,820	23,444	24,285	20,902	25,153	31,506	33,524	73.8	74.8	74.4	72.4
6.	Karnataka	33,642	37,133	41,498	46,725	44,854	49,886	55,371	63,365	75.0	74.4	74.9	73.7
7.	Kerala	12,912	15,913	17,239	21,605	25,160	28,638	30,811	37,092	51.3	55.6	56.0	58.2
8.	Madhya Pradesh	22,597	26,027	35,008	34,057	32,025	36,314	47,587	48,405	70.6	71.7	73.6	70.4
9.	Maharashtra	52,064	67,311	84,704	82,370	76,571	94,604	1,18,591	1,20,989	68.0	71.2	71.4	68.1
10.	Orissa	13,174	17,571	22,185	24,565	20,648	24,788	33,261	37,072	63.8	70.9	66.7	66.3
11.	Punjab	11,879	12,929	16,484	17,855	24,931	27,172	32,714	35,330	47.6	47.6	50.4	50.5
12.	Rajasthan	24,048	27,705	31,801	33,691	35,955	40,510	47,215	51,024	66.9	67.9	67.4	66.0
13.	Tamil Nadu	32,443	42,705	44,971	49,899	48,869	61,545	65,834	74,641	66.4	69.4	68.3	75.8
14.	Uttar Pradesh	52,231	64,988	75,592	80,920	79,366	95,617	1,19,087	1,30,599	65.8	68.0	63.5	62.0
15.	West Bengal	22,698	34,730	34,699	42,133	41,633	55,651	63,580	69,458	54.5	62.4	54.6	60.7

*Comprise expenditure on Revenue and Capital Accounts and Loans and Advances extended by state's for non-development purposes.

Source: 1. State Finances—A Study of Budgets of 2009–10, Reserve Bank of India, February 2010, pp. 159–60.
2. State Finances—A Study of Budgets of 2010–11, Reserve Bank of India, March 2011, pp. 135–36.

Table 7: Select Committed Expenditure of State Governments—As Ratio to state's Own Revenue

	State	2007–08				2008–09				2009–10 (Revised)				2010–11 (Budget)			
		Interest Payments	Adminis-trative Services	Pension	Total (2+3+4)	Interest Payments	Adminis-trative Services	Pension	Total (6+7+8)	Interest Payments	Adminis-trative Services	Pension	Total (10+11+12)	Interest Payments	Adminis-trative Services	Pension	Total (14+15+16)
	1	2	3	4	5	6	7	8	9	10	11	12	13	14	15	16	17
1.	Andhra Pradesh	21.2	11.5	14.2	46.9	18.7	8.3	12.8	39.9	16.6	8.2	12.5	37.3	16.3	12.0	13.4	41.7
2.	Assam	27.5	29.7	24.4	81.6	24.8	29.3	22.4	76.5	29.5	48.2	32.3	110.0	31.0	51.6	32.5	115.2
3.	Bihar	66.1	38.4	49.7	154.2	51.2	33.3	47.5	132.0	45.8	43.2	51.9	140.9	38.1	31.4	49.6	119.1
4.	Gujarat	28.2	6.1	11.2	45.6	27.5	6.3	10.3	44.2	27.3	7.8	12.7	47.8	27.1	7.5	12.0	46.6
5.	Haryana	14.0	7.3	7.8	29.1	15.7	10.7	10.8	37.3	17.1	11.6	12.7	41.5	19.5	10.4	11.5	41.4
6.	Karnataka	15.4	7.9	11.0	34.3	14.7	8.8	13.4	36.8	16.5	11.2	11.0	38.7	16.2	10.5	11.5	38.2
7.	Kerala	29.1	9.9	33.1	72.1	26.6	9.4	26.7	62.6	27.1	10.4	24.1	61.7	24.9	8.6	23.4	57.0
8.	Madhya Pradesh	28.4	11.9	13.3	53.6	24.7	12.1	14.3	51.1	20.2	10.3	13.3	43.8	22.0	16.1	14.4	52.4
9.	Maharashtra	18.9	8.5	6.5	34.0	19.9	10.6	8.3	38.8	22.5	13.8	10.1	46.4	21.6	14.8	9.0	45.3
10.	Orissa	33.3	11.7	18.9	64.0	25.9	13.2	18.6	57.7	30.4	17.0	33.6	81.0	29.2	23.0	32.6	84.7
11.	Punjab	29.9	13.6	16.1	59.5	28.9	13.8	16.7	59.5	26.8	13.9	15.3	56.0	25.1	16.3	13.5	54.9
12.	Rajasthan	34.3	9.4	14.8	58.5	33.1	12.4	17.6	63.1	31.2	13.3	23.0	67.5	31.0	12.3	20.8	64.1
13.	Tamil Nadu	18.5	8.2	18.3	45.0	15.1	8.6	19.6	43.4	16.9	10.1	20.1	47.1	16.8	10.2	21.9	49.0
14.	Uttar Pradesh	35.2	15.2	19.9	70.3	32.1	17.2	19.6	68.9	24.4	20.1	22.7	67.3	23.6	17.8	22.4	63.8
15.	West Bengal	78.0	16.4	27.4	121.7	62.3	13.7	22.9	98.8	66.0	20.1	44.8	130.8	59.6	16.8	26.6	103.0

Source: 1. State Finances—A Study of Budgets of 2009–10, Reserve Bank of India, February 2010, p. 208.

2. State Finances—A Study of Budgets of 2010–11, Reserve Bank of India, March 2011, p. 180.

expenditure of 15 major state's as a ratio of the state's own revenue have been presented in Table 7. Uttar Pradesh spends a significant portion of its own revenues on committed items of expenditure. Table 7 shows that in 2007–08, the committed expenditure as a ratio of its own revenue receipts in Uttar Pradesh was as high as 70.3. This ratio witnessed a slight decline and stood at 68.9 in 2008–09. It declined marginally further to 67.3 and 63.8 in 2009–10 (revised) and 2010–11 (budget), respectively. It may, however, be noted that amongst the 15 major state's, Uttar Pradesh ranks quite high as far as committed expenditure as a ratio to state's own revenue is concerned. In 2007–08, Uttar Pradesh ranked fifth as only Bihar, West Bengal, Assam and Kerala had a higher ratio than Uttar Pradesh; in 2008–09, the state ranked fourth since only Bihar, West Bengal and Assam were ahead of Uttar Pradesh in this regard. During 2009–10, (revised) and 2010–11 (budget), the state ranked sixth as only five state's had a higher ratio amongst the 15 major state's listed in Table 7. As far as possible an attempt should be made to bring down the committed expenditure ratio to its own revenues of the State of Uttar Pradesh. If this ratio cannot be brought down, it should at least be contained at the present levels.

Conclusions

From this analysis, certain conclusions emerge which are as follows:

1. The Government of Uttar Pradesh must reorient its debt policy, whereby it should suitably reduce its outstanding liabilities. An agenda for borrowings should be prepared in advance so that, excepting emergency times, borrowed funds are used only for productive purposes and for capital formation in the state;
2. Potential sources of raising additional revenue from its own taxes should be identified and leakages, if any, should be contained. The state should also be ready with a road map, whereby it should be clear how the state's finances shall be augmented by the introduction of GST;
3. Non-tax sources, specially user charges must be modified and rationalised, so that the services provided by the state do not require a subsidy from the exchequer; rather the schemes/projects should ultimately become self-financed on a no-profit/ no-loss basis;
4. The state government must impress upon the central government for additional funds, as the state is not able to provide even the basic and essential services to all its citizens. The need for increasing expenditure on various social services should be clearly brought to the notice of the centre;
5. The state must make adequate investments in strengthening various infrastructural requirements, specially roads and electricity. Hence, the levels of development

expenditure both on revenue and capital account, must be accelerated, if the state has to be brought in the mainstream of development of the country;

6. Expenditure on committed items in terms, of its own revenues need to be reduced, if possible, without compromising efficiency. If the same cannot be brought down, every effort must be made to contain it at existing levels;
7. The revenue surpluses available to the state must be properly used. Together with a proper framework for additional resource mobilisation and expenditure management, the state should lay down a path for fiscal correction and consolidation, taking into account the various macro-economic factors that are likely to impact the state finances.

Author's Profile

H. Chaturvedi

Dr. H. Chaturvedi obtained his Master's Degree in commerce and doctorate in business management from Agra University, Agra. He has more than three decades of experience in teaching, research and administration. As a former Director of the All India Council for Technical Education, New Delhi, a statutory body under MHRD, Government of India, he was associated with the formulation of policies, planning, regulation and control of management education as well as other disciplines of technical education. While he worked with the National Board of Accreditation (NBA) and the Board of Studies in Management of AICTE, he contributed in the application of various quality concepts in management education.

Dr. Chaturvedi joined the Birla Institute of Management Technology, New Delhi as Director in 1999. Under his leadership, BIMTECH launched postgraduate programmes in insurance, retailing, entrepreneurship, international business and sustainable development. He forged linkages of BIMTECH with 20 B'Schools in the USA, Canada, the UK, France, Poland, Austria, Hungary and Tanzania. Because of the multifaceted growth, the institute has been consistently ranked among top 15 B'Schools in the country by reputed magazines like *Business Today, Outlook* and *The Telegraph*. Recently, BIMTECH has began setting up of a state private university under his leadership at Bhubaneswar, Orissa, India. The university is likely to start offering programmes from July, 2012.

Dr. Chaturvedi was Editor-in-Chief of four reputed refereed journals–*Business Perspectives, The Journal of Insurance and Risk Management, South Asian Business Review*, and the *Indian Retail Review*. He is also member of the governing bodies of several institutions of higher learning across the country.

In 2007, Dr. Chaturvedi was conferred the Honorary Professorship by the St. Stevan University of Hungary, which is a leading state-run university of that country. He is regularly invited by leading electronic channels and financial newspapers to present his views on contemporary issues.

In, 2005, he took the initiative to form "Education Promotion Society of India", a national platform of eminent educationists, education service providers and edu-entrepreneurs. Dr. Chaturvedi is the Alternate President of the Education Promotion Society for India (EPSI) and also the President of the Alumni Association of Agra University (AAAU).

Shri Prakash

Dr. Shri Prakash is currently Professor of Eminence at BIMTECH. He was Dean, Research at BIMTECH till recently. He has served in very reputed research institutions and universities in various capacities, including the UGC and NIEPA, now NUEPA. He headed the educational Planning Department at NIEPA and was associated with the formulation of education policy for the country as a part of the think-tank of NIEPA-MHRD. At NIEPA, he launched the four monthly journal-*Paripekhya-Socio-Economic Perspective of Education* in Hindi and edited it till 1997. A lot of literature on educational planning and administration was generated through his efforts. In recognition of his services, MHRD, Government of India nominated him for Gyanpeeth Award in 1996. He directed and conducted the one month training programme for I.A.S. officers in educational planning at NIEPA for three years. He was instrumental in the launching of vocationalisation of education at the first degree level at U.G.C.

He has authored nine books, including two edited books. His last book was on *Theory of Consumer Behaviour.* He has published nearly 200 research papers, more than 60 of which have been published abroad, 45 of his research papers are available on the Web-site of International Input Output Association. He has also been a consultant to UNESCO, UNICEF, World Bank, and State Planning Boards of Punjab and Nagaland.

He received the Government of India Bursary, and U.P. Government Merit Scholarship in B.A. He was awarded leverhulme Commonwealth Senior Visiting Fellowship, which is awarded once in three years for post-doctoral research at one of the designated British universities; his candidature was recommended by the Nobel Laureate Prof. Richard Stone, Cambridge University, who evaluated his research proposal. He was also Senior Visiting Fellow at U.G.C. Advanced Center of Research in Mathematical Economics at the Gokhale Institute of Politics and Economics, Pune.

He was President, U.P. Horakhand Economic Association in 2010, Vice President, Hill Geographers Society of India, Secretary General of the Input Output Research Association of India, Member Executive Committee of (i) International Input

Output Association, Vienna, (ii) Indian Economic Association, and is currently member of the Executive Committee of IORA.

He has edited *Business Perspectives,* the Bi-Annual Journal of BIMTECH for a decade. He is currently on the Editorial Advisory Boards of the *Bulletin of Political Economy,* Athens, and *VARTA*, a quarterly Journal of J.K. Mehta Foundation of Economic Research, Allahabad.

He has lectured at the University College of Wales, University of Bath, U.K., Budapest University of Economics, Hungary, Hungarian Academy of Sciences, Budapest, Institute of Statistics and Econometrics, University of Lodge, Poland, Tribhuvan University, Kathmandu, K.C. College, Kathmandu, Kerman University, Kerman, Iran, Taliba University, Tehran, Bangkok University Bangkok, and Berlin University.

He has been Visiting Professor at Jodhpur University, Dayanand Sarswati University, Ajmer, Rajasthan University, Jaipur, M.D. University, Rohtak, and Kurukshetra University, Kurukshetra, I.I.M. Shillong, Rani Durgawati University, Jabalpur, Rani Ahila Devi University , Indore, and Institute of Manpower Planning, New Delhi.

He a recognised research guide of Algappa University, NEHU, Shillong, Sagar University, Panjabi University, B.R. Ambedkar University, Agra, Mysore University, Mysore. AMU, Aligarh, and M.L. Sukhadia University Udaipur. He has successfully guided 14 Ph.D. scholars so far and 12 scholars are currently registered under his guidance. Besides, he has also guided 20 M.Phil scholars.

His research interests are consumer behaviour, educational and human resource planning, price theory, econometrics of (a) finance, (b) education and (c) time series, and productivity analysis, economics and management of growth, and financial econometrics.

His models of price theory, productivity analysis and human resource planning have been applied to Iraq, Porto Rico, Greece, the U.K. and India by foreign and Indian scholars. He is among the early pioneers of mathematical and econometric modeling of education, productivity and pricing.

M. Ramachandran

Dr. M. Ramachandran has had a distinguished career of 38 years in the IAS first in UP, later in Uttarakhand and at the centre. He has had long tenures as a District Magistrate and Divisional Commissioner in the state and was later Infrastructure Development Commissioner and Chief Secretary of Uttarakhand, before moving to the centre as Secretary, Ministry of Urban Development. He has specialised in infrastructure and project planning, and has done commendable work in facilitating infrastructural development. His outstanding contributions to the rejuvenation of India's urban sector through leadership of the national flagship programme of Jawaharlal Nehru National Urban Renewal Mission, and a large number of new policy initiatives taken for the sector distinguish him as a civil servant with a difference. He was also briefly Advisor, Infrastructure to the Government of UP in the rank of a minister.

Ajit Kumar Singh

Prof. Ajit Kumar Singh obtained his M.A. and Ph.D. degrees in economics from the University of Lucknow, Lucknow. He has taught at Lucknow University, Lucknow and Avadh University, Faizabad. He has been a member of various committees and working groups at the state and central level. He has written extensively on various aspects of economic and social development in UP. He has been President of U.P. and Uttarakhand Economic Association in 2007 and Vice President, Indian Society of Labour Economics in 2009. In 2010, he was given the Kautilya Award by U.P., and Uttarakhand Economic Association for his contribution to teaching and research in economics. Presently, he is Director of the Giri Institute of Development Studies, Lucknow.

Mohd. Muzammil

Prof. Mohd. Muzammil Currently vice chancellor, Ruhelkhand University Bareilly. He was Professor of Economics at Lucknow University (LU) till recently. He holds a Ph.D. in economics from LU. He conducted post doctoral research at the University of Oxford, UK, and has published six books on *Financing of Education, Political Economy of Education, Economics of Health, Human Development and Agricultural Economics*. He has published over 125 articles and has completed some 25 research projects (sponsored by the World Bank, DfID, UNDP, Government of UP, NUPEA, UGC, NUS (Singapore) and other agencies.

He is a recipient of the Saraswati Samman (2011), Shikhsak Shree Samman (2009), Govind Ballabh Pant Economics Award (2000) and Career Award for Young Social Scientist (1989).

P.K. Bhargava

Professor P.K. Bhargava is a former Emeritus Fellow, UGC, Dean, Faculty of Social Sciences, B.H.U., Director, IRD Centre and Head, Department of Economics, Banaras Hindu University.

Professor Bhargava has published eleven books and contributed chapters to 14 books. In addition, he has published over 100 papers in various national and international journals.

Professor Bhargava has teaching experience of over 40 years to graduate and postgraduate students, in addition to guiding research leading to the award of Ph.D. degrees to 20 students at Banaras Hindu University.

Tabassum Khatoon

Dr. Tabassum Khatoon holds Ph.D., in Economics from the University of Lucknow, Master's Degree in economics from the University of Lucknow, when she topped the examination in 2001. The University of Lucknow conferred on her the D.N. Gurtu Memorial Gold Medal, S.S. Shukla Gold Medal and Wilhelmina Buck Gold Medal for her distinctions in the M.A. examination of the university. She qualified the first State Level Education Test (SLET) of Uttar Pradesh in 2003. She has presented papers in seminars and conferences and published articles in reputed journals and edited books.

G.N. Patel

Dr. G.N. Patel, is Professor at the Birla Institute of Management Technology, Greater Noida, India in the area of decision science. He obtained his Ph.D. from Sambalpur University in operations research and also did his Master of Philosophy in applied mathematics from the Indian School of Mines, Dhanbad and master's degree in the same subject from REC (presently NIT), Rourkela. He is also an alumnus of IIM, Ahmedabad. His interests are in mathematical programming, efficiency measurement and productivity and e-governance. He has published more than 70 papers in both national and international journals and guided seven candidates for their Ph.D. successfully so far.

M.L. Pandit

Dr. M.L. Pandit is presently Professor and Area Head in Economics at the Birla Institute of Management Technology. He had been on the faculty of the Department of Humanities and Social Sciences at the National Institute of Technology, Srinagar, Kashmir, before taking up his current assignment. His publications include over two dozen research papers and a book titled *Industrial Development of Punjab and Haryana*. Professor Pandit holds a Ph.D. degree from the Jawaharlal Nehru University, New Delhi.

A. Bose

Prof. A. Bose is engaged as an Associate Professor in the decision sciences unit in Bimtech. He teaches courses in quantitative techniques. An M.Tech and a M. Stat. from the Indian Statistical Institute, Professor Bose's interests lie in multivariate analytic techniques, artificial intelligence—neural networks, genetic algorithms, data envelopment analysis and mathematical modelling.

Prof. Bose has extensive consulting experience in IT, having worked with several IT majors before his current engagement with BIMTECH.

Shalni Sharma

Dr. Shalni Sharma is a Professor at the Sharda University, Greater Noida. She obtained Ph.D. in economics from Aligarh Muslim University, and is among an extremely limited number of young scholars, who have researched in such frontier areas of knowledge as theory of flex prices and determining values of product and company brands, and contribution of insurance and banking industries to the growth of the Indian economy. Her contribution has been extensively referred in the Review of Research on Impact of NEP on Indian Economy (ICSSR). She has already published 32 research papers in reputed Indian and foreign professional journals so far. Six of her research papers are available on Web-site of International Input Output Association. She has extended and modified the Mahalanobis Model of Growth by incorporating inventory investment as an endogenous variable of the model and estimated theoretically, mathematically and empirically growth reducing impact of inventory investment.

Managerial economics, research methodology, entrepreneurial development, consumer behaviour and price theory are her areas of special interest. She has worked on several research projects, including those sponsored by UNESCO and the World Bank.

Pooja Misra

Prof. Pooja Misra is an Assistant Professor and has spent 12+ years in the industry with such organisations as the American Express, Standard Chartered Bank and Lazard Credit capital. She shifted to academics in 2008 and is currently pursuing her Ph.D. at Gautam Buddha University in the area of: compensation components and their effect on employee engagement and turnover intent.

Her research interests include current trends in business environment, corporate strategies, compensation, employee engagement and corporate ethics. She has published six research papers and articles in national journals and presented papers in various national and international conferences.

Jaya Gupta

Prof. Jaya Gupta, is an Assistant Professor in organisational behaviour and human resource management at BIMTECH. She has completed her PGDBM from the Birla Institute of Management Technology, New Delhi. After completing her M.A in sociology, she cleared UGC-NET examination. She is pursuing her doctoral research in the area of positive psychology.

She has over twelve years of teaching experience at the post graduate level.

She has attended and presented papers at many international and national conferences. Her case study on gender inclusivity @ corporate culture, in case study competition organised by IIM, Ahmedabad, 2009 was appreciated and recognised.

Amit Sharma

Dr. Amit Sharma holds a Ph.D. Degree in management from the University of Mysore, Mysore. He also holds M.A. and M.Phil degrees in economics from NEHU, Shilong, and a B.A. honours degree in economics of Delhi University, Delhi. He has 13 years of industry experience and about 10 years teaching, training and research experience. He has worked in senior positions in private and public sector companies (i.e. Director of J B Group Co), and has taught in Indian and International Business Management Institutes (i.e. Head at GIMT and Asst. Dean at MAII). He has worked as a research associate in a project on perspective land use policy for India in the Northeastern Region. The project was sponsored by the Ministry of Agriculture, Govt. of India. He has published ten papers, in reputed journals such as the Scandinavian Journal of Development Alternatives, Geneva, The Indian Journal of Economics, Business Perspectives and Manpower Journal. One of his research papers is forthcoming in the IIM Shillong's Journal of Management Science. He teaches managerial economics, micro-economics, banking and money, HRM and strategic management to MBAs.

Nimisha Singh

Prof. Nimisha Singh is an Assistant Professor in information technology at BIMTECH. She has a Bachelor of Applied Sciences degree from Delhi University and M.C.A. from S.N.D.T. University, Mumbai. She has worked with the Tata Consultancy Services in Mumbai as a software programmer. After moving to the U.S., she worked as a web developer, designing HTML and CSS based websites. She subsequently specialised in .net technology. After spending 10 years in the U.S. she joined BIMTECH in 2008 as lecturer in Information Technology.

Her core competency area is software project management, e-business and cross cultural communication. She is also coordinator of faculty and student exchange programme and she and her team works on building collaboration with foreign institutions as a means to provide international exposure to students and faculty of BIMTECH.

Gautam Negi

Mr. Gautam Negi, MBA, is an Asst. Professor at Manav Rachna International University, Faridabad. He has 15 years of corporate experience in the banking industry, and his last assignment was with the HDFC bank as Asst Vice President for the bank's cross sell division. He has teaching experience of three years. His areas of interest is corporate finance an security analysis and portfolio management. He is currently pursuing his Ph.D. from MLSU, Udaipur in the area of finance at BIMTECH.

Gunjan Bhatnagar

Ms Gunjan Bhatnagar received her PGDBA from Jaipuria Institute of Management. She has worked with corporates for six years, and is in the teaching profession for the last seven and half years. Presently, she is working as assistant professor in the at Sharda group of institutions. She is pursuing her Ph.D. in management, her focus is on quality of education. She has presented one research paper at UPUEA's seventh conference at BIMTECH; and per paper at a conference at IIT, Delhi, the paper has been submitted for publication to an International Journal of Economics and Management, Malaysia.

Anshu Goel

Ms. Anshu Goel is Asst. Professor of marketing in the Management Department of The Raj Kumar Goel Institute of Technology, Ghaziabad. She is an M.Sc, PGDBM, DEM, and is pursuing her Ph.D. from the University of Mysore under the aegis of BIMTECH Greater Noida. She has 12 years of management experience, including one year of an executive level position with a corporate. Her areas of interest in research and teaching include consumer behaviour, supply chain management, and retail management.

Ajeet Singh Rauthan

Mr. Ajeet Singh Rauthan is Assistant Manager of the Centre for Research Studies, Birla Institute of Management Technology, Greater Noida. He holds an M.A. Degree in economics from Dr. Hari Singh Gaur University, Sagar, formerly known as Sagar University. He also has a B.Com degree from Delhi University, and has attended the ICSSR sponsored Workshop on "Writing Research Paper", organised jointly by BIMTECH and UPUEA. He assisted and guided the participants of the conference in the application of EXCEL Software to estimate the statistical parameters of various statistical/econometric models to data. His specialisation is application of statistical methods and econometric models with the help of computer software. He helps and guides research scholars at BIMTECH in the use of software for application to data base.

Tom George

Tom George is a student of PGDM-international business at Birla Institute of Management Technology, Greater Noida. A management graduate in marketing from Christ University, Bangalore. He is a voracious reader and has interests in the fields of advertising and media.